John Muir

and

the Ice That Started a Fire

ALSO BY KIM HEACOX

Memoir:
The Only Kayak

Biography:
Shackleton's Challenge

Essays & Photography:
Alaska Light
Alaska's Inside Passage
In Denali
Iditarod Spirit

Natural History & Conservation:
Visions of a Wild America
Antarctica: The Last Continent

History & Conservation:
An American Idea: The Making of the National Parks

Fiction:
Caribou Crossing

JOHN MUIR
AND
THE ICE THAT STARTED A FIRE

How a Visionary and the Glaciers of Alaska
Changed America

KIM HEACOX

LYONS PRESS
Guilford, Connecticut
An imprint of Globe Pequot Press

Lyons Press is an imprint of Globe Pequot Press.

Project editor: Meredith Dias
Layout: Melissa Evarts

Library of Congress Cataloging-in-Publication Data

Heacox, Kim.
John Muir and the ice that started a fire : how a visionary and the
glaciers of Alaska changed America / Kim Heacox.
      pages cm
   ISBN 978-0-7627-9242-9 (hardback)
   1. Nature conservation—Alaska. 2. Glaciers—Alaska. 3. Muir, John,
1838-1914. 4. Climatic changes—Alaska. I. Title.
   QH76.5.A4H43 2014
   333.7209798—dc23

                                        2013050235

Printed in the United States of America

10 9 8 7 6 5 4 3 2

for William E. (Bill) Brown,
Historian (ret.), US National Park Service

The Master Builder chose for a tool not the earthquake nor lightning to rend and split asunder, not the stormy torrent nor eroding rain, but the tender snowflowers, noiselessly falling through unnumbered seasons.

—JOHN MUIR

I learned from Muir the gentle art of sleeping on a rock, curled like a squirrel around a boulder.

—S. HALL YOUNG

AUTHOR'S NOTE

For the sake of simplicity and to avoid confusion, John Muir is referred to in this book as a naturalist and a casual glaciologist, while during his time (and still today) he would more accurately have been regarded by friendly scientists as a glacial geologist, one who studies the impacts of glaciers on the landscape, as opposed to a glaciologist, who studies the physics and chemistry of glacial ice, its composition, and dynamics. As for the word *Tlingit,* John Muir and S. Hall Young used different spellings. This book quotes them as they spelled the word in various forms.

Steeped in western thought, Muir and Young often wrote about Tlingit "chiefs," whereas Tlingit hierarchy was more complex, honorary, and highly evolved. Today most Tlingits prefer the titles "house master," "clan leader," and "headman." The term Hoonah refers to the Tlingit village on the north shore of Chichagof Island; the term Huna refers to the Tlingit people who lived there. Muir and Young used different spellings here as well.

I refer to John Muir's father, Daniel, as a Calvinist, a member of the Church of England, as he was raised. While he remained faithful to Calvinism's basic tenets, in adulthood a disillusioned Daniel Muir joined the Secessionist Church and later the "Campbellites," also known as the "Disciples of Christ," before taking his family to America as a "preaching elder." Because the term Calvinist broadly frames the core of his upbringing and lifelong values, and is more commonly known and understood, I chose it over Campbellite. Last, I refer to S. Hall Young as Reverend Young (as opposed to Minister Young, etc.), as that's how John Muir addressed him in their correspondence.

John Muir at about the time he first went to Alaska

CONTENTS

PROLOGUE

the gospel of glaciers

WAS IT MADNESS?

A death wish of some kind?

The five Tlingit Indians said little as they glanced at the quiet missionary sitting among them and stabbed the sea with each stroke, paddling their cedar canoe northwest into iceberg-filled waters where no man dared to go this time of year. No man, unless he was a seal hunter. No man, until this other man came along, their second passenger, the one up front who scribbled notes and nibbled on dry crusts of bread. No hunter at all. More of an observer, charismatic in his own way, a good listener, a real talker, this scrappy, bearded Muir, his blue-gray eyes drinking up the country. Half wise elder, half wondrous child, he seemed interested in *everything*.

Shouldn't somebody say something? Insist on turning around? They could all die, be overturned and drowned by *Kushtaka,* the trickster land otter man of Tlingit legend. Or, if they continued on, they might receive mercy from *Gunakadeit,* a benevolent sea monster.

Onward, Muir compelled them. Onward to the glaciers, he would say. Never mind the wind or rain or ice or cold.

———

A DOUR SKY pressed down. Rain occasionally lashed them. Pieces of floating ice, calved from tidewater glaciers up ahead, tapped an ancient, forgotten language against the canoe. Ice everywhere, and little sign of life in a land that was once rich in salmon, berries, forests, and firewood. Most of that is gone now, the land's richness and bounty having been destroyed by an advancing glacier that evicted the Tlingits and entombed the bay for many generations, in some places swallowing entire mountains. Only recently had the glacier begun a dramatic retreat, unveiling a vast, raw, woodless, ice-chafed land in somber shades of gray. A foreboding place.

Summer was over. It was *yeis,* autumn time, the month Americans called October. Soon it would snow, and the cold, carved moon would turn brittle in the tangle of winter stars. The glaciers would grow still under deep blankets of snow, and darkness would strike all moisture from the air; stillness would pound the land silent, and stretch all the way to the Arctic.

John Muir was forty-one that autumn, engaged to be married the next spring to the only daughter of a prosperous California fruit merchant. With her reluctant blessing—"do not be vexed with me," she wrote him—he had come to Alaska to see glaciers firsthand, to find out how they worked and shaped the land, how they carved rock and moved mountains. All to help buttress his theory that glaciers, not catastrophic down-faulting, had shaped his beloved Yosemite Valley and much of the Sierra Nevada, the mountains Muir called "the Range of Light."

While Muir often rode in the front of the canoe, the other white man, S. Hall Young, a Presbyterian missionary, rode farther back. If anybody were to argue for turning around and getting them out of there, it would not be Young. In Muir's company he was a follower. Young had met the effervescent California naturalist more than three months before, in early July, in Fort Wrangell, some two hundred miles by water to the south; he saw in Muir a man to be admired, not questioned. It would be up to Toyatte, the Tlingit chief and captain of the thirty-five-foot canoe, to bring this adventure to an end. But Toyatte might have seen in Muir the same thing Young saw.

They pushed on.

Camped that night on the west side of what we know today as Glacier Bay, near Charpentier Inlet, with Muir off somewhere climbing a mountain by himself, the Tlingits huddled around a wet, smoky campfire and confided in Reverend Young: This Muir must be a witch of some kind, a *nakws'aati,* to be so crazy happy in this lean, hard country. Why does he climb mountains in such miserable weather?

"To seek knowledge," Young told them.

THE YEAR was 1879.

Across the continent, and in western Europe, industrious men went about the exciting business of progress. For ten years, a railroad had spanned the young United States from Boston to San Francisco, and every year more tracks spidered their way over mountains, deserts, and plains, "obliterating great distances," said one historian, to make the land safe for commerce and cows. No task was too great, no vision too absurd. Thomas Edison invented the incandescent lightbulb to make cities shine at night; Andrew Carnegie introduced the open-hearth blast furnace to mass-produce American steel. The first canned fruits and meats would soon appear, along with the world's first electrostatic generator. Out west, camps became forts, forts became towns, towns became cities, and cities grew. Custer and his men had been massacred only three years earlier, and quickly avenged.

America must be harnessed and put to work, people said. Natural "capital" must be turned into consumable products. Materialist expansion must sweep away misery and social inequality and put us on the road to universal abundance. It was the right thing to do, our destiny, written in books, newspapers, the Bible, and the stars. To argue against such improvements was a fool's errand.

Yet the great American novelist and Muir contemporary Mark Twain was beginning to do just that. An eloquent gadfly on the sticky paper of progress, he would be Muir's soul brother in more ways than one, noting that Shakespeare created King Lear's fool for a reason: to express a wisdom others did not.

Twain and Muir, only three years apart in age, would both live three-fourths of a century. In that time, from their births in the 1830s until their deaths in the second decade of the 1900s, America would transform itself from an agrarian democracy into an industrial oligarchy that brought with it feasts of conspicuous consumption—an era that Twain called the "Gilded Age." He further used a term not unfamiliar to Muir: "citified," an epithet, Twain noted, "which suggests the absence of all spirituality, and the presence of all kinds of paltry materialisms, and mean ideals, and mean vanities and silly cynicisms."

Alaska would be to John Muir what the Mississippi River was to Mark Twain, or the mountains of Assisi, in central Italy, had been to Saint Francis. It would be his wildest dream, a place of healing distances and deep silence and blessed meditation. While California was Muir's home, Alaska would be his hope, his escape, incomprehensible in its beauty, vastness, and unforgiving ruggedness.

Just the way he liked it.

Over the next twenty years, until the eve of the twentieth century, Muir would make seven journeys to Alaska. In that time he would evolve from a self-taught naturalist, glaciologist, and ecologist into a best-selling author and unapologetic preservationist, America's preeminent fang in the fight against irresponsible industry and runaway development.

"Nothing dollarable is safe," he would say. Alaska inspired him to battle the universal conceit that nature was here for us to use as we please.

TRAVELING by canoe into the icy wildness of Glacier Bay in October 1879 was not madness, as the Tlingits might have thought. For John Muir, it was a joy, a revelation.

Madness was out there, all right, but not in the temples of wild nature. Any student of natural history could see that nature was beautiful and brutal. Witness how the swallow skims the river and catches bugs on the wing, how the cougar takes down the deer, how the eagle snaps the duck. It's a lethal, bloody affair. But none of these animals create a machine to magnify their killing. None invent an economy that can never be satiated. None create corporations that at all costs—the loss of dignity or even human life—must keep growing.

It was a simple matter of how you saw the world, and your place in it.

Where others found gold, John Muir found glaciers; where they saw timber, he saw trees. Where they sought profit, he sought a prophet, an expression of God's greatest creation, nature, the wisest of all teachers, not to be chopped up and sold, but left as it was, held in deep regard.

Never mind utility. Wild nature had value in and of itself, what he called "mountain nourishment."

Clearly, glaciers had shaped Alaska, and were shaping it still. How then did Alaska shape Muir? And how did he reshape us?

To Muir, glaciers had character, power, and grace. They were alive and deserving of our deepest understanding and respect. In their presence, he became a Druid, of sorts, a Celtic priest. More accurately, he was the Johann Wolfgang von Goethe of his day, a holistic thinker who challenged the modern scientific revolution to find a balance between the rational, quantitative mind, and the intuitive, qualitative mind. Muir could have done this with wolves or bears, or with flowers, as Goethe had. But he did it with glaciers, cold rivers of ice that appeared static but in fact moved dynamically over the land and shaped everything around them. They would become the perfect piece of symbolism in the twenty-first century's warming world.

"THE ONLY THING that counts is that which can be counted," said Galileo three hundred years before Muir. Together with René Descartes, Isaac Newton, and others, Galileo gave us our modern scientific revolution, our Age of Reason, the triumph of the rational mind. And while he and his brilliant contemporaries carried us forward, they also crushed things in our path. They separated us from nature, rather than making us participants in nature. They made us clever and powerful, but not wise.

Muir was a revolutionary of another kind; he said there's much more to good science—and right livelihood—than connecting data and dissecting frogs. There's a deeper meaning than conventional analytical reason. Experiment is not enough. Good science also requires *experience,* a deep knowing and sense of wonder that comes from being out there, barefoot in the meadow, alone on the ice, naked in the storm. "When we try to pick out anything by itself," Muir would write, "we find it hitched to everything else in the universe."

Galileo and Descartes had rational knowledge acquired from books and experimentation; Muir had intuitive wisdom acquired from the smallest flower and the largest glacier. He didn't merely learn *about* the natural world, he learned *from* it and *in* it. He went out there and slowed down and listened until his intuitive mind could dance with his rational mind. By doing so, he could "feel" the qualities of things around him. This enabled him to widen his circle of compassion. And with this wisdom and compassion, with this deep sense of the sacred, he would begin to write about the natural world. While the rest of America hypnotized itself with a thousand clever devices that consumed nature wholesale, Muir would honor Nature and campaign for its defense.

THERE WAS NOBODY quite like him. John Muir popularized geology, especially its young subset science, glaciology. He gave America a new vision of Alaska, and a new and brighter vision of itself. He suggested a reordering of our priorities, and contributed to a new scientific revolution picked up a generation later by Aldo Leopold and Rachel Carson, and championed today by E. O. Wilson, Carl Safina, Stephan Harding, and others. He was a gentle rebel, a talkative hermit, an enthusiastic wanderer, a distant son of the Scottish Enlightenment, inspired by ice.

YOU CANNOT STARE into the eyes of a glacier. It's not a wolf. But you can stare into its face, its tidewater terminus, a stunning, imposing ice wall rising from the sea, two hundred feet high, deeply weathered, a threshold where the glacier ends and everything else begins, where blue seracs collapse into the ocean and primal thunder booms down rock-ribbed inlets. In rare cases the glaciers might advance. Most often, though, in today's changing world, they retreat; they shrink back and die. Sometimes they hold steady, as a few do in Glacier Bay. John Muir found inspiration in these blue ice faces, as if the glaciers, like wise elders, had stories to tell and warnings to give.

To this day he continues to challenge us to see what he saw and do what he did, and more.

He became our patron saint of flowers and birds, glaciers and bears, wilderness and wolves. By far the most vocal nature preservationist in a young nation hell-bent on making money, Muir became our corrective lens, our better conscience. He spoke for the wild places and gave them credible value. He showed us an Alaska as a New World's new world, a place to reimagine what remained of America, and our destiny in it.

THE GLACIERS Muir found in Alaska were larger and more dynamic and robust than anything he had ever seen or imagined. They were his abacus, his new ruler and measuring stick that made all remaining wild lands down south seem small and vulnerable. They were his metaphor, flowing through the land, yes, but also through his open heart and mind, and through time and events and all things until he transcended the mentality of separateness and reductionism.

Muir would then experience man and nature as one, the wholeness outside continuous with a healthy inside.

These great ice rivers, tumbling down mountains and into the sea, birthed icebergs and blended as a single essence with the snow, which in turn, blended with what Muir called "the invisible breath of the sky." They inspired him to preach his "gospel of glaciers," an awareness and red-hot activism that would burn on and carry him through the rest of his days, even consuming him in his later years. By sheer force of their power and beauty, the glaciers of Alaska would help give birth to the modern American conservation movement.

They were the ice that started a fire.

PART ONE

1879–1880

CHAPTER ONE

the heaven right here

HE TRUNDLED down the gangplank in Fort Wrangell, Alaska, fresh off the steamship *California*, different from other men. Standing apart in his long shabby gray coat and Scotch cap, Muir watched, bemused, as a young missionary, Samuel Hall Young, greeted a gaggle of distinguished Presbyterians (and their dutiful wives) who had sailed with Muir. They had not taken well to him, as he had not to them. "That wild Muir," they called him. The men represented the Board of Native Missions. Foremost among them was Dr. Sheldon Jackson, Young's supervisor and head of the mission.

Fort Wrangell was a rough-and-tumble Indian village on the edge of a bog, and the missionaries had come to Alaska, as they went everywhere, to Christianize the natives—clean them up, teach them English and scripture, save their souls, ban their language and customs and dress. It no doubt made Muir uncomfortable. Raised by a strict Calvinist father, he was prejudiced against proselytizing, unless it was the doctrine of Nature, the teachings of wild things. Unless it was the writings of Louis Agassiz, the Swiss naturalist and pioneering glaciologist, or Charles Lyell, the father of the modern science of geology, or William Wordsworth, the English Romantic poet and cultural contrarian, or the wisest—and only American—among them, the author of the illuminating essay "Nature," Ralph Waldo Emerson, whom Muir had met in Yosemite eight years earlier, in 1871.

Reverend Young extricated himself from his stuffy clerical guests and approached the "lean, sinewy man" in the long shabby coat, who was introduced as "Professor Muir, the naturalist." A hearty grip of the hand,

Fort Wrangell (also spelled Fort Wrangel) in the late 1800s
PHOTO COURTESY OF THE ALASKA STATE LIBRARY

Young would later recall, "and we seemed to coalesce at once in a friend-ship which, to me at least, has been one of the very best things I have known in a life full of blessings."

"From cluster to cluster of flowers he ran," Young described Muir in Fort Wrangell that July, "falling on his hands and knees, babbling in unknown tongues, prattling a curious mixture of scientific lingo and baby talk, worshiping his little blue-and-pink goddesses." Muir loved flowers and, at this point, considered himself first and foremost a botanist. But after this watershed trip to Alaska, what he would come to love most, what he would worship more than anything else in the natural world, were rivers of ice. *Glaciers.*

Before embarking on their great canoe journey north, Muir joined Young on the river steamer *Cassiar* to make forays into Tlingit country around the Stickeen River (today's Stikine River). One morning, with the steamer docked, the two men set off on an all-day climb of nearby Gle-nora Peak. Though Muir was already forty-one, more than nine and a half years older than Young, he could easily out-hike him. As they approached the summit, they reached a narrow chasm that Muir scrambled up. Young attempted to follow, lost his footing, fell, and yelled. Muir climbed back down and found the missionary on the edge of an abyss, feet hanging over midair, his chin dug into the treacherous shale slope, hands over his head, useless, both shoulders dislocated, his entire body slipping inch by inch as he held his breath. "Hold fast," Muir told him, "I'm going to get you out of this . . . keep cool."

Muir disappeared, whistling "The Blue Bells of Scotland" and chattering to himself as his voice receded. And suddenly he was back, below Young this time, having somehow reached the other side. He told the missionary to lower himself slowly. While using his own hands to hold on to the cliff, Muir caught the missionary by his shirt collar, using his teeth, and pulled him to a ledge. "How he did it, I know not," Young would later write.

> *The miracle grows as I ponder it. The wall was almost perpendicular and smooth. My weight on his jaws dragged him outwards. And yet, holding me by his teeth as a panther would her cub and clinging like a squirrel to a tree, he climbed with me straight up ten or twelve feet, with only the help of my iron-shod feet scrambling on the rock. It was utterly impossible, yet he did it.*

The sun had gone down. Muir pulled Young to safety, set one shoulder, and aided him down the mountain, at times carrying him on his back. Young later wrote:

> *All that night this man of steel and lightning worked, never resting a minute, doing the work of three men, helping me along the slopes, easing me down the rocks, pulling me up cliffs, dashing water on me when I grew faint with the pain; and always cheery, full of talk and anecdote, cracking jokes with me, infusing me with his own indomitable spirit.*

On the return trip on the *Cassiar*, while Young convalesced on board, Muir once again set off up the same mountain. This time, fleet-footed and with no one to slow him down, he reached the top.

John Muir on the steamer *Cassiar* shortly before his first epic canoe
journey in the fall of 1879

THE HEAVEN RIGHT HERE

BY EARLY OCTOBER, they were ready to leave Fort Wrangell on their epic journey, but problems arose. The wife of Chief Toyatte, owner and captain of the canoe, said a sea monster might get them, or a storm, or hostile tribes. To paddle a canoe far north into cold, dangerous country was a death wish. For all their artistry, grace, and generosity, all the bounty of foods that surrounded and sustained them on land and in the sea, the Tlingit could be a fierce and revengeful people. They occasionally warred between clans, took slaves, and staked captives on tide flats to let them drown.

The mother of Kadashan, who would serve as interpreter, told Reverend Young that if anything happened to her son on this crazy journey, she would steal Young's next newborn child.

Reading letters from his fiancée back in California, Muir found her pining for him:

> *O Friend Beloved, if ever the dear Lord leads you out from the depths of those blue glacier caves, and will let me once more look upon your face, that I may know you are not become only a white wraith of the northland—there will be no happier woman than I in all the world . . . fate seems to have willed only punishment for me because I was not patient . . . I shiver with every thought of the dark cruel winter drifting down, down—and never a beam of sunshine on that wide land of mists . . .*

She wanted him home for Thanksgiving, probably never wanted him gone in the first place. Proposing marriage as he did, as if it were a requirement, then fleeing north, Muir might have found her domestic desires tedious and confining. She made her desperations too obvious, as did the Tlingit women now in Fort Wrangell, upset by the imminent departure of the men they loved. Muir's fiancée had more in common with these dark-faced women than would meet the eye. As Muir biographer Linnie Marsh Wolfe wrote, they were "sisters under the skin."

"Surely you would not have me away from this work," Muir wrote back before leaving, *dawdling in a weak-willed way on your lounge, dozing and drying like a castaway ship on the beach.*

On the day of the departure from Fort Wrangell, as the Tlingit women wept and waved good-bye to their husbands and sons, Muir wrote to his fiancée, "Leave for the north in a few minutes. Indians waiting. Farewell."

HER NAME was Louie Wanda Strentzel. Raven-haired and gray-eyed, she had attended Miss Atkins' Young Ladies Seminary (later Mills College in Oakland) and learned to play the piano so well she could have become a concert performer and basked in what she called "the world's prizes." She chose the country life instead, living with her parents on their large orchard in Martinez, a pastoral existence, almost Mediterranean, near where the Sacramento River flowed like honey into San Francisco Bay. "Round-faced and plain," wrote biographer Stephen Fox, "she disliked facing the camera. A few extant photographs show her to bad advantage, unsmiling and uncomfortable."

Louie dabbled in astronomy and followed politics and current events. She loved going about town in her horse-drawn buggy, yet she seldom visited the big city of San Francisco thirty-five miles away. Yosemite was a foreign land to her until she met John Muir, and even then she had no desire to go. Alaska must have seemed as cold and far away as Siberia. In 1879, Louie Strentzel was thirty-two (nine years younger than Muir), bordering on spinsterhood, and not happy about it. Her father, an exile from Poland who'd come west in the 1849 Gold Rush, was astute and hardworking, one of the first scientific horticulturalists in California. From him, Louie learned gardening, botany, and a keen sense of business, as she came to oversee the hiring and payment of many work hands. Each year, the Strentzel family ranch produced and shipped hundreds of tons of fruit.

It was a smooth life, sweet and soft, like the domesticated fruit it orbited around. A universe of peaches, cherries, and apricots, far removed from the rough-cut granites and glacial ice that Muir loved. He would have to get used to it . . . when he got back home.

But not yet, not here, not in wild Alaska.

Once the canoe was out of sight and earshot from the wailing women back on shore, leaving behind what Muir called "the doleful, domestic dumps" of civilization, the men whooped "like a lot of truant boys on a lark." They were feral and free, as if playing a part in Mark Twain's new novel, *The Adventures of Tom Sawyer*, a band of roustabouts making mischief and breaking out of church. God wasn't *in there*, he was *out here*.

"So truly blind is lord man;" Muir wrote, "so pathetically employed in his little jobs of town-building, church-building, bread-getting, the study of the spirits and heaven, etc., that he can see nothing of the heaven he is in."

EARLIER THAT SUMMER, while traveling up the Alaska coast en route from Puget Sound to Fort Wrangell, Muir had described "new scenes . . . brought to view with magical rapidity." His eye, "called away into far-reaching vistas, bounded on either side by headlands in charming array, one dipping gracefully beyond another and growing fainter and more ethereal in the distance." He called it his "high altar." The islands, rivers, mountains, and clouds folded together in wild perfection, water everywhere, as if the land itself were made of water, all painfully beautiful, untouched, undefiled, like a garden, an Eden. *Could it always stay so?*

"Not a leaf stirring;" Muir wrote one windless morning, "one bird, a thrush, singing sweetly, lancing the silence . . . the whole blessed scene coming into one's heart as to a home prepared for it. We seem to have known it always."

The thrushes were gone now, having migrated south. It was October, the rainiest month of the year, and getting cold. Muir and his canoe mates no doubt accepted the conditions without much complaint. Standing in the stern at the end of each day, cedar paddle in his hand, old Toyatte, an imposing figure, would survey the shore to find the best campsites, as often as possible moving the canoe with the weather, not against it. Kadashan, the son of a Chilkat chief, would offer his counsel, chosen as he was for his keen knowledge of Indian lore and powers of oratory, and his expertise in Tlingit etiquette. Kadashan was "chief of protocol for the party," in the words of writer/photographer Dave Bohn.

Steady at the other paddles were Sitka Charley, who as a boy had hunted seals up north where they were headed, in a mythical place John Muir called "the big ice-mountain bay," and Stickeen John, who acted as a second interpreter. All four Tlingits belonged to a race of people who had lived in this liquid rain forest world for a long time. Tough, resourceful, and weather-wise, they were extensions of the sea. They knew canoes and ocean currents like the Sioux knew horses and the wind. Early white explorers into this country had all reported the same thing: The Tlingits hunted and fished with great skill, and moved like poetry on water, as if they'd been born with canoe paddles in their hands. They learned by storytelling, and told about their history and myths—as they did now with John Muir and Reverend Young—how Raven created the world, how everything they ever needed to know could be learned from the animals and their spirits, the wisdom in the woods.

Muir listened with interest and acknowledged their deep regard for the natural world. He told a few stories of his own about his early childhood in Scotland and Wisconsin. He'd been an inventor in his youth, he said, coming up with all kinds of clever mechanical devices. After two years at the University of Wisconsin–Madison he found work in an Indianapolis carriage factory. One night, while working late to unlace a belt joining, a metal file flew from his hands and pierced the cornea of his right eye. Stunned, he held his hand under the socket as the aqueous humor flowed out and left the eye sightless. Soon the other eye went blind in sympathetic nervous shock. For three days he could not eat or drink. For a month he could not see. He lay still in a dark room and hardly moved, waiting, hoping, praying for his sight to return.

He made a vow. If his sight did return, he would not squander it; he would dedicate the rest of his life to God's creation. Not Christianity. Not a religion. Not a church. Those were all inventions of men. He would dedicate his life to the beauty of nature, the wild earth, the original church, the one God made.

"God has to nearly kill us sometimes," Muir noted, "to teach us lessons."

Nature was what made him joyful. Slowly his sight returned, first in one eye, then the other, and he set off. Never mind the workaday world.

"All drawbacks overcome," he wrote, "joyful and free ... I chose to become a tramp."

His rationale was simple. If he walked through his life joyful, walked until he found his new home, not Wisconsin or Indiana or any other overfarmed patch of America, but something wild, then he'd do his best work and be his best self; he'd find his new home and make people around him more joyful. Was this not the greatest task before us, to find a passion and live it with great deliberation, and make the world a better place?

He returned to Wisconsin to help with the harvest at the Muir home on Hickory Hill, and to say good-bye to his family. With the harvest in, according to biographer Gretel Ehrlich, "He appeared at his brother David's store in Portage, Wisconsin, shoeless, wild-haired, dressed in ragged clothes. David, now a successful merchant and embarrassed by his brother's appearance, tried to find him a pair of shoes ..."

Here was his older brother, John, twenty-nine, delinquent yet also wise in some ineluctable way, once a promising inventor, always smart and good with his hands, like their father, now a scarecrow bum. John spoke as if he wouldn't come back for a long time, if ever. Their father, Daniel, demanded that John pay for his room and board for the weeks he'd lived at home during the harvest. "Dutifully but resentfully," wrote Ehrlich, "John paid."

He was nearly penniless and uncertain where to go. He'd read about Alexander von Humboldt in South America, and Charles Darwin on the *Beagle*. He'd read about the granite cathedrals of a place called Yosemite, in California. He didn't know how to get there, other than by "the wildest, leafiest, least trodden way." On the inside cover of his journal, he wrote, "John Muir, Earth-planet, Universe."

His pilgrimage had begun.

That same season, in the fall of 1867, as young John Muir set off on his thousand-mile walk to find a new life, Secretary of State William H. Seward, a strident abolitionist and expansionist who had served President Lincoln and retained his job under President Andrew Johnson (after Lincoln's assassination), completed the purchase of Alaska from Russia for $7.2 million, roughly two cents an acre. An obvious good deal today, in the wake of a devastating Civil War, it seemed absurdly expensive. Faced with the huge task of rebuilding itself, how could the traumatized United States of America squander that kind of money on a frozen wasteland? "Seward's Folly," the press called it. "Seward's Icebox." The Russians had taken all the sea otter pelts. What more could Alaska have of any value?

It would be an idealistic tramp, a lover of glaciers, a student of all things wild, who would show America another side of Alaska, and of America itself, one that found value in beauty without utility.

NORTHBOUND from Fort Wrangell, the six men found their canoe ran true, and in a few days they were in Icy Strait, off the northeast coast of Chichagof Island. At Pleasant Island they stopped to collect firewood. Muir carried with him a copy of an eighty-five-year-old chart made by Lieutenant Joseph Whidbey of His Majesty's Royal Navy, when he served under Captain George Vancouver on board HMS *Discovery* in 1794. The lieutenant had commanded three longboats (dispatched from the ship, the men at the oars, sometimes with small sails aloft) through tricky currents and the iceberg-filled waters of Icy Strait, while the sickly Vancouver remained back on *Discovery*, anchored safely at Port Althorp, near present-day Elfin Cove. Whidbey's chart showed a bay about five miles from head to back, emptying into Icy Strait from the north, blocked at its head by "compact solid mountains of ice," according to Vancouver, who wrote the expedition log so he could take full credit with the Admiralty back in London.

In simpler terms, a massive tidewater glacier stood at the head of the bay.

Given the geography then and now, the terminus—or tidewater face—of the glacier must have been an astounding sight: eight miles across and nearly three hundred feet high. All that ice, a single glacier filling the entire bay, backdropped by what Vancouver said were "stupendous" mountains. He called the ice wall a "barrier," underscoring his desire, the desire of every British mariner since Frobisher, Hudson, and Cook, to find the fabled Northwest Passage, a commercially viable sailing route over the top of North America that would unite the Atlantic and

Pacific Oceans. Such a route would make the British Empire's dominion over the world's oceans even greater.

Vancouver, like the men who served under him, probably assumed that the massive ice sheet, being so large, must extend hundreds if not thousands of miles from the north, all the way from the Arctic perhaps, and the North Pole.

It did not.

It was an alpine glacier roughly one hundred miles long, fed by heavy snowfall in some of the highest coastal mountains in the world, the Fairweather Range and the St. Elias Mountains, peaks climbing to twelve, fifteen, and eighteen thousand feet above sea level. Layer upon layer the snow would accumulate and re-crystallize into dense ice, and begin to flow as glaciers that coalesced into one great glacier that moved with such vigor it advanced forward and buried an entire bay.

From a few miles south of the tidewater face of the glacier (about where Rush Point is today), Whidbey and his men had no idea what they were seeing or talking about. No Englishman did when it came to glaciers. They were an island people who hailed from green, flat, rainy terrain. They had never been exposed to a deep history of intense mountain geography and glaciation; they knew little if anything about what glaciers were, how they worked, how they eroded and deposited and shaped entire landscapes, how they advanced and retreated, and why. It was the French and Swiss and other mainland Europeans, living in and near the Alps, who first explored the anatomy and behavior of glaciers, and explained them with just those kinds of terms—"anatomy" and "behavior"—as if the blue ice rivers were alive. It was a language John Muir loved. The French nouns remain with us to this day: *glacier, arête, moulin, serac, crevasse.*

Whidbey's chart, accurate in 1794, was no longer so in 1879. The "compact solid mountains of ice" were gone. The glacier had retreated, and in its place was a newborn bay roughly eight miles wide, framed by tall mountains, running north, shaking off its icy tomb, a fine temptation. Muir could hardly stand it. He saw floating ice all around, pieces shaped like castles and birds.

Onward, he beckoned his companions. Onward. To the glaciers.

They made camp that first night near the mouth of the bay, on what Muir called, "a desolate, snow-covered beach in stormy sleet and darkness." He continued:

At daybreak I looked eagerly in every direction to learn what kind of place we were in; but gloomy rain-clouds covered the mountains, and I could see nothing that would give me a clue, while Vancouver's chart, hitherto a faithful guide, failed us altogether.

It failed them because they were in waters that didn't exist in Vancouver's time, waters filling in a geography that until recently was occupied by a glacier.

Tensions mounted. Sitka Charley, brought along as a guide because he had spent time here as a boy, was lost. The land looked nothing like he remembered it from many years ago. Everything had changed. Everything was changing.

What kind of place was this?

Early that morning they saw smoke. The group approached a camp and were greeted by the very thing Toyatte's wife had feared: gunshots fired over their heads.

A band of Huna Tlingits stood on shore, one man with a rifle, his face painted black. No doubt alarmed by the approach of strangers in a canoe, the black-faced man shouted, "Who are you?"

"Friends," Stickeen John shouted back, "and the Fort Wrangell missionary."

For a tense moment, nobody spoke.

CHAPTER TWO

a skookum-house of ice

THEY PADDLED in close, heads low. Again, Stickeen John identified himself and his party, and Kadashan, the son of a Chilkat chief, boldly rebuked the black-faced man for greeting a missionary with a loaded gun.

The Huna Tlingits said they meant no harm; they invited the Fort Wrangell men ashore.

Inside a nearby shelter (Muir called it a "bark hut"), relations eased. He wrote, "It seemed very small and was jammed full of oily boxes and bundles . . . and heavy, meaty smells . . . a circle of black eyes peering at us through a fog of reek and smoke." Their hosts were "seal-hunters laying in their winter stores of meat and skins."

Stickeen John said the two white men had good hearts; that Muir, the blue-eyed friend of the missionary, was the one who came to this country seeking ice mountains (glaciers).

The Huna Tlingit had heard of the missionary, and couldn't imagine why he was here so late in the season. Did he intend to preach to the seals and gulls?

Kadashan offered the Huna Tlingits rice, tea, and tobacco, after which, Muir wrote, "they began to gain confidence and to speak freely. They told us . . . that there were many large ice-mountains in the bay, but no gold mines; and the ice-mountain they knew the best was at the head of the bay, where more of the seals were found."

Muir was eager to push on, but Sitka Charley, their guide, was uneasy in the much-changed land. So many new islands had been born, so much ice had vanished. He wanted a Huna Tlingit seal hunter to accompany them.

After much discussion, one of them consented to go. His wife pre-pared dried salmon, strips of seal meat, a blanket, and a piece of cedar matting for him to sleep on. She accompanied them down to the shore and said with a pretty smile as they pushed off, "It is my husband you are taking away. See that you bring him back."

If this plea stirred in Muir any misgivings or guilt or desires to return to the woman who loved him back in California, he kept them to himself.

At midday they passed their first large ice-mountain, to the west. Muir wrote, "Its lofty blue cliffs, looming through the draggled skirts of the clouds, gave a tremendous impression of savage power." He named the glacier after the Scottish geologist James Geikie.

Two hours later, farther up the bay to the northwest, they made camp. The minister wished to stay back the next day, since it was Sunday, and the Indians did because of the weather. Muir set off on his own to see what he could see.

"Wet, weary and glad" is how he described himself when he returned to camp at dusk. He had climbed some fifteen hundred feet up a ridge into swirling clouds and a cold rain, conditions that would dispirit most men. At one point the clouds had opened to where he could see "the imposing fronts of five huge glaciers" flowing into "the berg-filled expanse of the bay." Such a grand adventure—his first real view of Glacier Bay. He was thrilled. Yet the Tlingits shared none of his enthusiasm. In his absence, they had grown mutinous. If Muir kept up this crazy ice-mountain chas-ing, they would all die.

Young told Muir that the Tlingits had been asking all day about why he climbed mountains when storms were blowing. When Young had explained that Muir was seeking knowledge, Toyatte announced, "Muir must be a witch to seek knowledge in such a place as this, and in such miserable weather." It was time, he said, to turn around and go home.

Muir poured himself some coffee and joined the Tlingits at their campfire. The Tlingits, according to Muir,

[B]ecame still more doleful, and talked in tones that accorded well with the wind and waters and growling torrents about us, telling sad old stories of crushed canoes, drowned Indians, and hunters frozen in

snow-storms. Even brave old Toyatte, dreading the treeless, forlorn appearance of the region, said that his heart was not strong, and that he feared his canoe, on the safety of which our lives depended, might be entering a skookum-house (jail) of ice, from which there might be no escape; while the Hoona guide said bluntly that if I was so fond of danger, and meant to go close up to the noses of the ice-mountains, he would not consent to go any farther.

The affable Muir said he understood their concerns, but they had nothing to fear. He had wandered among mountains and storms for ten years and more. Good luck always followed him.

WE can only guess the specifics of Muir's campfire oratory, but it must have been compelling. Did he tell of his accident in the Indianapolis Carriage Factory, when he lost his eyesight for a month? Of his thousand-mile walk from Kentucky to Florida? Inspired by Humboldt and Darwin, "in the vine tangles, cactus thickets, sunflower swamps, and along the shore among the breakers," Muir had hoped to sail to South America. He got as far as Cuba, and from there by fast schooner to New York City, where he felt "completely lost in the vast throngs of people, the noise of the streets, and the immense size of the buildings." Then south again, by steerage to Panama, and across the isthmus by train, and north by ship to California, a twist of fate that would forever change the maps of wild America.

Did he tell of landing in San Francisco that momentous March of 1868, one month before he turned thirty? The vibrant city went about its business, growing and growing, and Muir, charmed by none of it, stopped on Market Street to ask a local carpenter the quickest way out of the city.

"But where do you want to go?" the carpenter replied.

"Anywhere that is wild."

Did he tell of his walk across California's Central Valley when it was knee-high wildflowers as far as he could see? One vast "bee-garden," he called it. And his first sighting of the Sierra? And Yosemite Valley? Since his arrival in the Sierra, he had climbed many mountains in storms, and to the tops of great conifers as they swayed in the wild wind. He'd gone for days on little food, and frozen his foot on Mount Shasta, and stranded himself on cliffs. Every time he survived, and more—he thrived. He'd been more alive in those moments than at any other time. They defined him. They enriched him. We are not here to exist; we are here to live, to face death and stare it down. We are here to trust in God and to embrace this world in all its quiet and violent beauty, to break down the walls of our own prejudices and believe in something greater than ourselves. We are here to paddle into our worst fears and come out the other side to discover glaciers, to meet them face-to-face, and to celebrate a sense of wonder and God's plan that we find only in Nature.

We don't know what Muir said to the Tlingit. But whatever it was, it worked.

When Muir finished, Kadashan acknowledged that he liked sailing with "good luck people." Toyatte stood and said his heart was strong again. Muir was a "great ice chief," and Toyatte would take him where he needed to go. If the canoe became crushed in the ice, then Toyatte would have a good companion to wrap his arms around and travel with into the next world.

REVEREND YOUNG could see that Muir was more than fearless; he was passionate yet serene, an inspiration to others. He would have made a brilliant preacher, a successful capitalist, or a great salesman, getting people to buy all sorts of things they didn't need. But money didn't interest him.

The day after lecturing at a conference in Yosemite Valley earlier that year, where Muir had shared the stage with Young's Presbyterian supervisor, Sheldon Jackson, it was Muir, not Jackson, who had one hundred people follow him on a hike—he called it a "saunter"—up Eagle Point Trail. Jackson had spoken on the heaven *up there* while Muir had rhapsodized on the heaven *right here*, the earth at our feet. And it was Muir, the charismatic naturalist, who won the most disciples.

Young also saw in Muir a wild child who despite his talents as a perfect instrument of God would suffocate inside a church. "Muir was a devout theist," he wrote:

*The Fatherhood of God and the Unity of God, the immanence of God
in nature and his management of all the affairs of the universe, was
his constantly reiterated belief. He saw design in many things which
the ordinary naturalist overlooks, such as the symmetry of an island,
the balancing branches of a tree, the harmony of colors in a group of
flowers, the completion of a fully rounded landscape.*

John Muir knew his scripture. His father, Daniel, had pounded the
Bible into him and his seven brothers and sisters, sparing none. A so-
called "preaching elder," Daniel was a stern and imposing disciple of a
religious sect that railed against the professional clergy of Wisconsin,
those "reverend dandies," he called them. Arriving at a schoolhouse in
his black suit and chimney pot hat, children in tow, he would lead families in Sunday service, singing hymns and delivering his sermon and
praying for forty-five minutes straight, his head up and eyes closed as if
in a trance.

"The Muirs all sacrificed much to the cause of making money to carry
on the Lord's work," wrote biographer Linnie Marsh Wolfe, referring to
life on the family farm, "but beyond question the children paid the greatest price. John as the eldest son bore the brunt of the toil." He had barely
turned twelve, in 1850, when his father put him to work behind a plow.
"Tis dogged as does it," John would say, using the Scottish folk adage to
help him get through the backbreaking day, his sweaty head barely rising
above the plow handles.

When the hired men complimented him on his straight furrows, his
efficiency and speed, John savored their praise, something he never got
from his father. Four years later, when Daniel bought a half-section (320
acres) to build their new home at Hickory Hill, and make good money
raising wheat for the Crimean War, John protested. War profiteering was
wrong, he said. Men should occupy small tracts of land to make a living,
not large tracts to make a killing.

Daniel would hear none of it. The money would help build orphan
asylums, hospitals, and schools, and fund missionary work. While he
studied his Bible in the parlor downstairs, preparing like Abraham to
sacrifice his own son if need be, Daniel's three skinny boys, John, David,

and Dan Junior, would rise each winter morning, slip their cold feet into frozen boots, and go to work all day in the frigid Wisconsin air. Years later, David would write to his older brother:

John, do you remember our bedroom at Hickory Hill, on the north side—never smelt fire or sun, window none too tight, three in a bed, Dan in the middle, and quilts frozen about our faces in the morning, and how awful cold it was to get up . . . and dress and go down to the kitchen barefooted. Oo-oo-oo, it makes me shiver to think of it, and going to Portage with loads of corn, running behind the wagon to keep warm and having to eat frozen bread for lunch.

John recalled, "No pains were taken to diminish or in any way soften the natural hardships of this pioneer life."

When it came time to dig a well, Father refused to use the new explosive called dynamite, and instead put his children to work digging by hand. As the hole deepened, John found himself in the shaft using a chisel against hard sandstone. At one point, eighty feet down, he grew faint and called out in a weak voice. Father yelled from above to get into the bucket. By the time they hauled him up, John was unconscious.

"Old Man Muir works his children like cattle," the neighbors said.

A few days later John was back down in the dark shaft. He dug ten more feet and struck good water.

—◦—

A PRISONER of his own convictions, Daniel Muir believed that struggle and misery unlocked the door to everlasting salvation. Paradise was not an earthly kingdom; it awaited us in heaven, but only if we suffered down *here* doing daily obedience to God's commandments. Whenever he headed down a Wisconsin road to save a soul or rebuke a sinner, his children, free of his long shadow, would launch into mischief. John was the most spirited; he would dance about, his limber body fluid and strong, his mind quick to make up a ballad, or to pretend to play the bagpipes and do a jig while his sisters giggled, and his mother, Ann, smiled as she knit by the stove.

Once Father returned, dour-faced and pious, the house became solemn again.

They had no fireplaces, only the single wood cookstove in what John called "a barren empty shell" of a home. Despite its severity, this is where he first discovered his inventiveness in things mechanical, and more important, in ways of thinking, seeing, and being. "His inventive genius was in conflict with his spiritual longings," wrote Gretel Ehrlich:

He was pulled by passions he had just begun to define, yet he had to make his way in the world. How could he find a profession that did not harbor this conflict—the factory versus the wilderness, spirituality versus practicality? He wanted to make a contribution to society somehow, but it had to be on his own terms—that is, outside the conventions of a civilization that he felt showed no real concern for the happiness and well-being of living things and no regard for the world's beauty.

He loved the freedom of the outdoors and often referred to local ravens, chickadees, and geese as "Wisconsin bird-people." When Father overworked a favorite family horse, Old Nob, to death, John was devastated. "Too often," he wrote, "the mean, blinding, loveless doctrine is taught that animals have neither mind nor soul, have no rights that we are bound to respect, and were made only for man, to be petted, spoiled, slaughtered, or enslaved."

This break from Genesis, the first book of the Old Testament that proclaimed man as master of all living things, would in a few years send John down his own long road away from the Muir family farm, not to save others as his father did, but to save himself.

———

THE SEVEN MEN—five Tlingit Indians, John Muir, and S. Hall Young—made their way farther up the bay, their canoe winnowing through fingers of brash ice, closer and closer to the mighty glacier that stood as a looking glass into another time. Muir found the glacial face,

broken into an imposing array of jagged spires and pyramids, and
flat-topped towers and battlements, and many shades of blue, from
pale, shimmering limpid tones in the crevasses and hollows, to the most
startling, chilling, almost shrieking vitriol blue on the plain mural
spaces from which bergs had just been discharged.

He could see that the glacier, while supported on its flanks by the bedrock walls of the bay, was undercut at its tidewater face by the encroach-
ing sea, making it unstable as it calved off pieces of itself. Higher up, the
glacier extended far back into the mountains as a blue ice river fed by
bountiful snowfall deep in the Fairweather Range.

So much was beginning to make sense, how glaciers advanced and
retreated over long periods of time—tens of thousands of years, probably millions of years—and shaped whole geographies, entire continents.
Earthquakes shattered landscapes and made mountains rise; water and
ice cut them down. Islands came and went. Shorelines shifted. Take
any natural process, however slow it might appear, and give it enough
time—unfathomable amounts of time—and it would add up to profound
change, as Charles Lyell had proposed in his book *Principles of Geology*,
published in 1830. Earth is immeasurably old, he said.

A decade later, in 1840, when John Muir was just a two-year-old
boy living in Scotland, Louis Agassiz built a hut on a glacier in the Swiss
Alps to study how it moved. He concluded that ice once covered most of
mainland Europe (in fact, it had covered Europe many times). In North
America, glaciers had shaped northern Wisconsin, excavated the Great
Lakes, pushed the Ohio River south to its present position, sculpted
Puget Sound, and dropped Plymouth Rock at Cape Cod Bay. The cape
itself was a terminal moraine deposited by a glacier. Every large aquifer in
the American West was supercharged by ten-thousand-year-old glacial
meltwater. Pioneering geologists such as Agassiz, Joseph LeConte, James
Geikie, and Hugh Miller—all of whom Muir studied on his own time—
had over the past few decades proposed something remarkable: glaciers
once ruled the Earth.

They called it the Ice Age.

And now here was this bay, chilling, exciting, not unlike Puget Sound of long ago, emerging from its own little ice age, a land of resilience rising yet again, shaking off its long winter coat.

— ❧ —

THE CANOEISTS came ashore and made camp on a rocky beach near the tidewater face of what is today the Grand Pacific Glacier. While the others went about their chores, Muir set off up a mountain. The rain ceased, and before he was a thousand feet up he watched the clouds "lifting their white skirts" to reveal enticing views.

> *Climbing higher for a still broader outlook, I made notes and sketched, improving the precious time while sunshine streamed through the luminous fringes of the clouds and fell on the green waters of the fiord, the glittering bergs, the crystal bluffs of the vast glacier, the intensely white, far-spreading fields of ice, and the ineffably chaste and spiritual heights of the Fairweather Range, which were now hidden, now partly revealed, the whole making a picture of icy wildness unspeakably pure and sublime.*

— ❧ —

WILLIAM WORDSWORTH would have appreciated Muir's choice of words. The English Romanticist had been dead for nearly thirty years in 1879, but his poetry was still alive. In nineteenth-century America and Europe, a time before television, telephones, and the Internet, people read real books. They drank literature like water. The literacy rate was not high in some places, but in southern Scotland, along the Firth of Forth, from Dunbar to Edinburgh, where Muir spent his first eleven years, it was higher than 80 percent.

Among those who could read, books were prized possessions. Words on paper were powerful magic, seductive as music, sharp as a knife at times, or gentle as a kiss. Friendships and love affairs blossomed as men and women read to each other in summer meadows and winter kitchens. Pages were ambrosia in their hands. A new novel or collection of poems was something everybody talked about. Wordsworth, Coleridge, Shakespeare,

Bronte, Austen, Dickens, Keats, Emerson, Cooper, Thoreau, Hawthorne, and Twain. To read these authors was to go on a grand adventure and see things as you never had before, see yourself as you never had before.

In 1798, the year George Vancouver died and Ludwig van Beethoven wrote his first symphony, William Wordsworth revisited Tintern Abbey on the River Wye, in Wales, on a beautiful July day. He was twenty-eight, the same age as Beethoven. Calmed by the balm of nature, far removed from the coal dust and city industry that seemed to disenchant European life more every year, the young poet penned "Lines composed a few miles above Tintern Abbey on revisiting the banks of the Wye during a tour, 13 July 1798." He wrote of his "boyish days," and lamented, "I cannot paint/ What then I was."

Five years had passed since he was last at the old abbey. In that time, he had split with his French lover and their illegitimate daughter, a heartbreaking good-bye. Napoleon was rampaging through Egypt, and England would soon declare war. The most carefree days of his youth were gone, and with them his youthfulness, a playful way of seeing and being filled with enchantment, wonder, and joy. The grinding complications of adulthood seemed to bleed all innocence from his soul. Deeper into the poem, Wordsworth described a "tranquil restoration" found by the whispering, singing river, a divine inspiration, something "sublime," how it touched him with a "spirit" that "rolls through things." Until then this guarded word, *sublime,* had been reserved for the clergy to describe God's gifts and wrath through formal doctrine and religious structure.

Wordsworth debunked all that; more than in stuffy little churches or grand cathedrals, he argued, *God was in nature.* On the banks of a river embroidered with flowers and birdsong, near a stone abbey abandoned for more than 250 years, a young poet, a "worshipper of Nature," implied that he felt "a far deeper zeal/Of holier love" than he ever had inside stone or wooden walls. We all can, if we slow down and set aside our frantic ambitions, egos, and money-getting.

It was a daring thing to write, heretical to some, but once published there was no going back. It appeared in *Lyrical Ballads,* a poetry collaborative with Wordsworth's dear friend Samuel Taylor Coleridge. Others followed, Romantics and radicals who dared question the prevailing order. Wordsworth permitted them to extol the virtues gained through an intimacy with wild nature, and to question the dark side of industry and progress. He influenced Emerson, who influenced Muir, who one day would influence President Teddy Roosevelt, who in turn would influence his distant cousin, FDR, who would influence President Jimmy Carter, who, in 1980, a century after John Muir made his first two trips to Glacier Bay, would sign a congressional bill creating more than one hundred million acres of new national parks, preserves, monuments, wildlife refuges, and wild and scenic rivers in Alaska.

In his book, *Alaska Days with John Muir*, Reverend Young, himself a theist, thanks in no small part to his growing friendship with Muir, would note that Muir was fond of quoting Wordsworth:

> One impulse from a vernal wood
> will teach you more of man,
> Of moral evil and of good
> Than all the sages can.

SOUTHBOUND, the canoeists sailed down the bay's eastern shore and sighted a massive tidewater glacier descending from the north. If it was in a stage of dramatic retreat, like the others, it would soon open up an entire new upper inlet of the bay, fed as it was by snowfall not in the Fairweather Range, but the Takhinsha Mountains, peaks of lower elevation. Muir was tempted to explore the glacier that would one day carry his name, but winter was on them. Pan ice covered the upper inlets. Soon much of the bay would freeze over.

At the Huna Indian seal camp, men, women, and children swarmed to greet the canoeists as they dropped off their local guide—his wife happy to see him again. On the evening of the next day, the last of October, after five days in the bay of great glaciers, they arrived at Pleasant Island, in Icy Strait, and made camp. Muir accurately summarized:

> *Glacier Bay is undoubtedly young as yet. Vancouver's chart, made only a century ago, shows no trace of it, though found admirably faithful in*

general. It seems probable therefore, that even then the entire bay was occupied by a glacier of which all those described above, great though they are, were only tributaries . . . That this whole system of fiords and channels was added to the domain of the sea by glacial action is to my mind certain.

Instead of turning south down Chatham Strait for Fort Wrangell, they turned north up Lynn Canal, bound for Chilkat Country, urged on by Reverend Young, who wrote this would be, "The climax of the trip, so far as the missionary interests were concerned." For here lived "the most northern tribes of the Alexander Archipelago," a fierce people who answered to

the proudest and worst old savage of Alaska, Chief Sathitch. His wealth was very great in Indian treasures, and he was reputed to have cached away in different places several houses full of blankets, guns, boxes of beads, ancient carved pipes, spears, knives and other valuable heirlooms. He was said to have stored away more than one hundred of the elegant Chilcat blankets woven by hand from the hair of the mountain goat. His tribe was rich and unscrupulous.

And his tribe had little or no idea that nearly two thousand years ago Jesus Christ had died for them on the cross.

That would change. Sheldon Jackson had assigned Young the task of building a mission among the Chilkats, "the most quarrelsome and warlike of the tribes of Alaska," their villages, according to Young, "full of slaves procured by forays upon the coasts of Vancouver Island, Puget Sound and as far south as the mouth of the Columbia River."

He meant to Christianize them—a dangerous affair, coming into other people's homes and telling them how they should live, what they should believe. Consider the apostles. As best we know, most had been martyred—Peter, Andrew, and Philip crucified, James the Greater and Thaddeus cut down by sword, James the Lesser beaten to death as he prayed for his assailants, Bartholomew flayed alive, Thomas and Matthew speared, Matthias stoned to death, and Simon either crucified or sawed in half. Only John died peaceably.

So it was that Reverend Young had with him his own John, a secret weapon, not a traditional Christian in any sense of the word, but an apostle in his own right, a disciple of Nature, a gifted storyteller.

A SHORT DISTANCE from the Chilkat village, they stopped to clean up and make themselves presentable. Muir noted that Toyatte and the other Stickeen Tlingits "sat on boulders and cut each other's hair, carefully washed and perfumed themselves and made a complete change in their clothing, even to white shirts, new boots, new hats, and bright neckties." The Huna Tlingits had said that rumors of hostilities among the Chilkats were false, but still, anything could happen. Whenever Muir and Young mentioned other Tlingits they had met on this journey, men from powerful tribes and clans, how interesting they were, Toyatte and his crew had said, "Oh yes, these are pretty good Indians, but wait until you have seen the Chilcats."

When Joseph Whidbey and his homesick, sallow-faced men had encountered a band of aggressive Auke Tlingits off Point Retreat, at the northern tip of Admiralty Island, they rowed for their lives while the Aukes gave pursuit in their wooden helmets and war canoes, daggers at the ready. The Aukes were ferocious, and yet they too, according to Toyatte, feared the Chilkats.

"Mr. Young also made some changes in his clothing," Muir observed, upon returning to camp after sketching glaciers, "while I, having nothing dressy in my bag, adorned my cap with an eagle's feather I found on the moraine, and thus arrayed we set forth to meet the noble Thlinkits."

They raised an American flag, "as was our custom," wrote Young, and paddled north. Several miles from the village, they were spotted as they moved into the mouth of a mighty, silt-laden river. A messenger on shore shouted, "Who are you? What are your names? What do you want? What have you come for?"

Muir described his voice as "heavy and far-reaching."

Stickeen John shouted back, "A great preacher-chief and a great ice-chief have come to bring you a good message."

The Chilkat caller relayed to another, and him to another, each a quarter mile from the next in succession up the river to where the Chilkat chief sat in camp at his fireside. This was not the first contact between whites and Indians in this area, but for a moment it must have seemed to Muir more than a little pre-Columbian, as if from the fifteenth century, save for the rifles, white shirts, and cold November air. Years later, in his seventies and dying of a broken heart due to a dam that was scheduled to be built on another river, one in his beloved Yosemite National Park, Muir would describe the Chilkat communication system as a "living telephone," men shouting up and down a river to carry important news, members of a mighty canoe culture thousands of years old that would soon vanish, like so much else.

For the second time in little more than a week, Muir and company were greeted by a salutation of gunfire, what Young called "too warm a reception—a shower of bullets falling unpleasantly around us." The two white men immediately stopped paddling, but Toyatte and his crew did not.

"*Ut-ha, ut-ha,*" Toyatte commanded. "Pull, pull."

And the canoe moved up the river.

CHAPTER THREE

it is not a sin to go home

THE MOMENT the canoe touched shore, everything happened. A dignified young man welcomed them, saying he represented Chief Don-na-wuk, Old Silver Eye. Villagers swarmed about while forty to fifty men—Young called them warriors, Muir called them slaves—charged forward with war cries.

It was "as if," Young said, "they were going to take us prisoners. Dashing into the water they arranged themselves along each side of the canoe; then lifting up our canoe with us still in it they rushed with excited cries up the bank to the chief's house and set us down at his door."

This was a Tlingit way of bestowing honor on their new guests.

Muir noticed how the village children played in a nearby meadow, running races, shooting arrows, and wading in the icy river, "without showing any knowledge of our presence except quick stolen glances."

Old Silver Eye was apparently called such because he wore a calico shirt, a blanket, and a large pair of silver-bowed eyeglasses he'd gotten from a Russian naval officer. As Muir and the others entered his large cedar plank house, he shook their hands but kept his head down, making no eye contact. In the center of the house, on a square of gravel, a fire burned, the smoke rising through a hole in the ceiling. For a good fifteen minutes, Old Silver Eye stared into it, saying nothing. Finally he offered food: a feast of dried salmon, deer back strap, small Russian potatoes, rose hips, and seal-grease sauce. The food was filling, and the house so warm after days of cold traveling that Muir and the others became drowsy with sleep. They struggled to stay awake as Old Silver Eye, suddenly loquacious, had many questions. *Why did the water rise and fall twice a day? What caused an eclipse? Why did white men want gold? What made whiskey?*

After some time, Chief Sathitch ("Hard to Kill") entered the house dressed in a regal chinchilla blanket. Slowly he turned, and Muir and Young were astonished to see printed on the blanket: "To Chief Sathitch, from his friend, William H. Seward."

Of course. Ten years ago, in 1869, just two years after concluding the purchase of Alaska from Russia, Seward, then seventy-one and retired from politics, had visited Sitka and the Chilkat Country with his son, Frederick, and the famous scientist-surveyor George Davidson. A total solar eclipse was predicted for early August of that year, and Davidson had selected the Chilkat Country, with its hostile reputation, as the best place to watch it and impress the natives. It worked.

Sathitch told Seward that before the eclipse, the United States had proved itself a superior force, "able to purchase the interests of the Russians and drive away King George's Men whom we know to be strong." The eclipse confirmed that power. The United States was indeed mighty; it could make the sun disappear in the middle of the day. Sathitch had responded with a show of his own strength and wealth, and William H. Seward, one of America's foremost abolitionists, found himself trading gifts with one of the last slaveholders left in the New World, a regal Tlingit Indian chief.

Now here were more white men, this preacher-chief and ice-chief, highly regarded by Toyatte and his crew, having paddled and sailed all the way from Fort Wrangell. They deserved an audience.

Word spread upriver and down, from one valley to the next, and soon Chilkat and Chilkoot Tlingits—members of two feisty tribes often at odds with each other—began to arrive from all over to hear the two men speak, especially the charismatic ice-chief, Muir, his words translated by Stickeen John. Tlingits filled the clan house and packed themselves outside the door, and they climbed onto the roof to listen through the smoke hole. According to author and frontier rhetorician Dan Henry:

> The famed naturalist's tempest-tossed exploration of Glacier Bay confirmed his geologic theories. But in the following week, Muir

was forced to re-examine his understanding of humanity, wild or civilized, as he witnessed the fortitude of an unconquered people. For four nights Muir delivered the only sermon of his life to a thousand or more Chilkat and Chilkoot Tlingits.

Warriors told him they were preparing to travel south to collect blankets as blood money for a Chilkat woman who had died drinking whiskey supplied by Hootsenoo Tlingits on Admiralty Island. It might get nasty, and turn to killing. They asked Young and Muir to pray for them.

Muir gave five talks altogether, but he didn't speak on Christ and salvation as Young did. For his entire adult life, Muir would keep his views on formal religion largely to himself. He spoke instead on brotherhood and respect and getting along, on the brutality of war and the terrible cost of slavery that had befallen the United States, and on the strengths and weaknesses of all men, the importance of finding common good in the gifts of Nature and the wild earth.

When Muir finished the last of his talks, an old Tlingit shaman stood and said that for many years he'd heard white men speak as if on another side of a loud river from the Tlingits; white men always wanting gold, furs, the best deal for the least amount of money, seeking only their own good—until now. For the first time, with Muir and Young, the shaman said, "the Indian and the white man are on the same side of the river, eye to eye, heart to heart."

As more men spoke, Muir watched an attractive slave girl bring Chief Sathitch food and light his pipe. The next morning, as Muir and the others prepared to travel south, Stickeen John overheard Sathitch tell the slave girl that after hearing the sermons of Muir and Young, he intended to send her to school and dress her well and raise her in every way like a daughter.

—◆—

REVEREND YOUNG may have intrigued the Tlingits, but John Muir charmed and dazzled them; he was the better speaker, by far. They wanted to keep the ice-chief, to have him live among them so they might know God and all his gifts, how better to live and die. If Muir stayed, the

Chilkats told him they would always obey him; they would build him a church and a school, pick up stones from his paths to make them smooth for his feet, and give him as many wives as he desired.

Muir and company considered paddling upriver to visit the fierce Tlingits of Klukwan, where the whiskey was flowing and the guns loaded for a warm welcome. But due to a perceived insult to a Chilkat chief a few months earlier, Toyatte was not welcome there. Muir decided to head south. "Just as we were leaving," he wrote, "the chief who had entertained us so handsomely requested a written document to show that he had not killed us, so in case we were lost on the way home he could not be held accountable in any way for our death."

They left on a Saturday morning and made good time all that day, while the next day, being Sunday, they stayed in camp, "though the wind was fair and it is not a sin to go home," wrote a frustrated Muir. The next day Reverend Young wished to stop and preach to the Auke Tlingits, but Toyatte feared the Aukes, called them a "bad lot." They were the same tribe that had given chase to Lieutenant Whidbey and his men in 1794.

Muir wanted to inspect every glacier, as if each were a book like the others, similar in general characteristics yet distinctive in its specifics. Some were a deep, compelling blue, others pale and white. Some were heavy with overburden, others clean and gleaming. Some were steep and twisted and tortured by crevasses as they spilled down tight mountain valleys; others ran straight and on a gentle gradient that enabled them to wear few wrinkles, as if they'd had an easier life.

———

ANY MAN with imagination could see that glaciers had sculpted coastal Alaska and been much larger once, in the past, maybe many times in the past; they had shaped everything from mountain summits to the shore. The Alaska John Muir found in 1879 was a mountainous geography punctuated by ice, while in the past it must have been an icy geography punctuated by mountains. All of Lynn Canal, Stephens Passage, and Chatham Strait—the primary waterways of northern Southeast Alaska—were filled by rivers of ice thousands of years ago, thousands

Early field sketches by John Muir show a keen interest in glaciers and glacial topography. His sketches from California (in the early and mid-1870s) reveal pocket glaciers hidden high in the mountains, while those from Alaska (shown here) reveal large glaciers that run for tens of miles and dominate entire valleys.

of feet thick. More recently, only hundreds of years ago, ice had filled all of Glacier Bay. The scale might change, but the processes remained the same. Ice had been shaping this land for a long time, and—on a smaller scale—was shaping it still.

Muir found kame terraces on the mountainsides and recessional moraines along the shore, telltale signatures of glaciers. In the forest he found erratics—boulders carried by glaciers from high in the mountains and deposited at lower elevations. He'd found them years before at Olmsted Point and elsewhere in the Sierra Nevada, his "Range of Light"; he surmised, as Louis Agassiz had in the Alps, that the entire region owed its morphology to glaciers.

Rubbish, said Josiah Whitney, chief geologist for the state of California. What does this Muir know, this man with no academic or scientific credentials, this "mere sheepherder," an "ignoramus." Muir at the time, in the early 1870s, was living a handyman existence in Yosemite Valley, taking whatever work he could find. Whitney insisted that the valley had been created by catastrophic down-faulting. Not glaciers.

How did Muir respond? *Go see for yourself,* he told Whitney. With two good legs and two good lungs you too can hike high into the mountains and find their secrets. You'll see striations everywhere, the grooves in granite bedrock where rocks embedded in the flanks of the glaciers were dragged along by glacial action, scouring parallel lines that still showed the direction of ice flow, as readable as fox prints in fresh snow.

Agassiz had found striations and erratics all over Europe, from Switzerland to Scotland, and later, after he became a professor at Harvard, in the United States. The name erratic comes from the Latin *errare,* to wander, which to Muir made perfect sense.

As they flow downslope and undercut mountain flanks, glaciers collect boulders and rocks that roll onto them and go for a ride, sometimes for hundreds of miles, until the glaciers encounter warmer conditions at lower elevations, melt away, and drop the wanderers.

Though a wanderer himself, John Muir didn't ride a glacier to Yosemite or Alaska. But in a metaphorical way he did. Raised in northern geographies that harbored the ghosts of glaciers—Scotland and Wisconsin—he became a keen observer. He developed ice age eyes. Even as a boy, he listened to the land in ways others did not. He regarded the long view, the wisdom of rocks. He matured and left behind the factory for the wilderness, the trappings of secure employment for adventure, the seduction of money for freedom. He followed his passion and went looking for that which shaped the places that shaped him—glaciers; in so doing, he made his life extraordinary.

"Man, man, you ought to have been with me" he once said to Reverend Young upon returning to camp after a big adventure on a glacier,

> *You'll never make up what you lost today, I've been wandering through a thousand rooms of God's crystal temple. I've been a thousand feet down in the crevasses, with matchless domes and sculpted figures and carved ice-work all about me. Solomon's marble and ivory palaces were nothing to it. Such purity, such color, such delicate beauty! I was tempted to stay there and feast my soul, and softly freeze, until I would become part of the glacier. What a great death that would be.*

YES, WELL, the others in the canoe were not ready to die. Not on this day or any other. It was a sometimes difficult and perilous trip back to Fort Wrangell, beset with strong November winds and cold temperatures. Muir often exhorted the others into "the beyond," to visit out-of-the-way glaciers, and many times Toyatte had to say no. More than once they nearly fetched up on rocks and lost their canoe.

Around the campfire one night, old Toyatte, his patience growing thin, told of similar adventures in his youth, when his canoe smashed into rocks and he had to swim to shore with a gun in his teeth. Turning to Muir, he asked if the ice-chief could today manage to swim ashore in these cold waters, and if so, could he make a fire without matches? And find his way to Fort Wrangell without food or a canoe?

The next day, as if he'd heard none of Toyatte's caveat, Muir again beckoned the party into icy waters toward a magnificent tidewater glacier that thundered with icefalls, its tall seracs collapsing into the sea. Toyatte again, concerned for the safety of his canoe and crew, said it would be foolish to take such a risk so close to the end of their journey.

"Oh never fear, Toyatte," Muir replied. "You know we are always lucky—the weather is good. I only want to see the Thunder Glacier for a few minutes, and should the bergs be packed dangerously close, I promise to turn back and wait until next summer."

Muir was already planning his return. Never mind his impending marriage to Louie Strentzel in California, whose patience was tested daily.

They got to within two miles of the glacial face, "a blue, jagged ice-wall," according to Muir, "one of the most imposing of the first-class glaciers I had as yet seen." Today it's named after Muir's geologist friend Joseph LeConte, who supported his theories on glacial history in Yosemite Valley.

To navigate back out, with ice hemming them in on all sides, Toyatte put Kadashan in the bow to point the way. Later, off the mouth of the Stikine River, with everybody exhausted, they ran aground several times on the muddy bottom. Finally, Wrangell Island hove into view, and on November 22 they arrived back. (They had left Fort Wrangell on October 14.) When Reverend Young said he was anxious for news, Muir quipped, "there could be no news of importance about a town."

As for his Indian companions on this remarkable canoe journey of eight hundred to nine hundred miles in forty days, Muir said "they all behaved well . . . under tedious hardships without flinching for days or weeks at a time; never seemed in the least nonplussed; were prompt to act in every exigency; good as servants, fellow travelers, and even friends."

The mail steamer had departed eight days before. Muir would have to wait another month for passage south to Portland. He declined an invitation to live with Reverend Young and his family, choosing instead to live alone as he compiled his notes and finished sketches from his epic journey. As winter deepened and the mercury dropped, everything grew still, and Muir basked in his Alaska monastery. He seemed in no great hurry to return to a world busy with its buying and selling, worn down by the feet of too many people.

"YOU MUST BE SOCIAL, JOHN, you must make friends . . . lest your highest pleasures, taken selfishly, become impure."

More than a few scholars have marveled over the influence Jeanne Carr had on young John Muir while he was a university student in Madison, and later, in California, as he explored the Sierra Nevada and began to blossom into a nationally acclaimed writer, thinker, and environmental activist. Her letters to him were often flattering and encouraging; some were puritanical. She was the one who had matched him with Louie Strentzel, writing Louie, "I want you to meet my John Muir."

"Write as often as you can," Jeanne once told John as he set off on another adventure. "Your letters keep up my faith that I shall lead just such a life myself one day." She never did. Photos show Jeanne Carr as a woman of her time, strong-willed but risk-averse, a conformist despite her curiosity and keen intellect, her hair in a tight bun, her dress Victorian and countenance severe, a chicken in a coop. While everything about Muir—his hair, beard, dress, and eyes—appears feral, playful, a contrarian. A fox on the run.

She once lamented to him that she was "a woman whose life seems always to be used up in little trifling things, never labeled 'done,' and laid away as a man's may be. Then as a woman I have often to consider not the lilies only, in their perfection, but the humble honest wayside grasses and weeds, sturdily filling their places through such repeated discouragements."

They found a smooth compatibility, Jeanne and John, and seemed to prosper greatly from each other. They shared a deep love of learning and natural history, and a dedication to personal development. According to biographer Stephen Fox:

> What she brought Muir was his first prolonged contact with a mind of substantial range and ambition. She told him what to read, introduced him to important people, and extended his horizons in a dozen directions. She reinforced his dawning sense that God was best appreciated in nature. "It is only from our Great Mother," she proclaimed, "that we really learn the lessons of our Father's love for us."

Jeanne's husband, Professor Ezra Slocum Carr, John's geology and chemistry teacher at the University of Wisconsin, proved himself a difficult man and got fired. He later found a teaching post at the University of California at Berkeley, where again he'd get fired, but where his wife could continue to shape her favorite project: the genius of John Muir.

She loved it that John loved botany but was horrified by his later infatuation with glaciers, those icy rivers that could turn him distant and cold. John's father, Daniel, had also condemned geology, saying the young science was blasphemous and contradicted the Bible.

IN 1650, Irish Archbishop James Ussher had divined from scripture that the Earth was close to 6,000 years old, and was in fact fully formed on an October night in the year 4004 BC. Legions of biblical scholars, clerics, and preachers had lined up to teach Ussher's interpretation. In 1830, with the publication of *Principles of Geology*, Charles Lyell announced that it was time to wake up and "free the science from Moses." In 1859, when John Muir was an impressionable twenty-one years old, Charles Darwin's *The Origin of Species* turned the world upside down (or right-side up, depending on one's sensibilities). It was such a radical idea—evolution by natural selection—that Louis Agassiz, the most famous natural historian in America in the 1860s, never did buy into it. Even Lyell proclaimed, "Darwin goes too far."

But Jeanne Carr wrote, "Darwin has left us no escape, from the necessity of finding our titles to respect in our own characters and not those of our forefathers."

People who knew her well—she was a seventh-generation New England Puritan raised with values that honored equality—said she played with black children and invited servants to her wedding. She always wanted to do something remarkable. In John Muir she found her chance.

"You have sent me all my best friends," Muir once wrote to her. She wanted the world to know him, and him to know the world, not just the beauties of nature but the minds of its best thinkers, that he might shape them as they shaped him. Were it not for Jeanne Carr, Muir never would have met Ralph Waldo Emerson, the "Great Man from the East," who in 1871, at age sixty-eight, visited Yosemite with a gaggle of Boston literati. John at the time was thirty-three. Reserved at first, Muir stood back as others surrounded Emerson, eager to hear what he had to say. As the days went by, Muir built up his courage, knowing that Emerson had been told about him. When finally they met, they talked at length and savored every minute. Muir showed Emerson his books, field notes, and sketches, and his humble lodgings in a cracker-box room above a lumberyard.

Emerson no doubt understood the value of a young man paying tribute to—and learning from—an older man. He'd done it himself, in 1825, when he journeyed to Braintree to visit John Adams, second president of the United States; Emerson wanted to glean whatever wisdom he could just before the old man died. Now it was time to pass the torch. He spoke to Muir about his famous disciple, Henry David Thoreau (who'd died nine years before, in 1862, at age forty-four) and transcendentalism. Muir had yet to read Thoreau's *Walden,* but he'd read Emerson's essays, filling their margins with dissenting arguments. For Muir, Emerson and Thoreau were insufficiently wild; they thought from the head down, not the feet up.

When it came time for Emerson to leave the mountains and travel by horseback down to a world of noisy hotels, Muir begged him to stay and sleep on the ground, in the grove of big trees. "You are yourself a Sequoia," he told the old man. "Stop and get acquainted with your brethren . . . It will do you good." But Emerson's acolytes, always worried about the old man's health, prevailed; Emerson rode away. He later added John Muir to his list of the most inspiring people he'd ever met, the list he called "My Men."

NOT UNTIL late December did Muir leave Fort Wrangell, telling S. Hall Young to be ready for next summer, with a good canoe and a crew. He'd be back. There were more glaciers to explore.

Louie Strentzel, his fiancée, had hoped he'd be home by Thanksgiving, then Christmas, then New Year's. "O John, John," she had written, "do not stay too long. Surely you can go again next year with the new summer . . ." And she added, "Ah me, what a blessed Thanksgiving."

But it was a sad Thanksgiving. She received no letters, and knew of John's whereabouts only through articles he sent to the *San Francisco*

Bulletin. "For his lonely fiancée," wrote Stephen Fox, "it was a distressing, even humiliating situation. Lost in his glaciers he was—even if unintentionally—hurting her grievously. The reaction of his future in-laws may be imagined. Six years had passed since Jeanne Carr first suggested the match."

In early January he broke a three-month silence with a dispassionate letter from Portland saying he'd be home soon, after exploring the Columbia River Gorge and giving lectures to satisfy last-minute requests. While her letters to him brimmed with love, his were cool, distant, matter-of-fact. The reluctant suitor, he arrived in San Francisco and kept to himself and close friends for several weeks, and finally showed up at the Strentzel house in mid-February. Despite his heel-dragging, it was, by all accounts, a happy reunion, and things thereafter went well.

John and Louie were married on April 14, 1880, one week before he turned forty-two. She was thirty-two. For the occasion, John cut his hair and borrowed a nice coat and a white shirt, and even considered hiring a second preacher, in case the first failed to show. Many of his friends, upon learning later of the marriage, were astonished by the news, as if a glacier had been corralled.

The next day John went to work in the fruit orchards, a changed man.

CHAPTER FOUR

we must risk our lives in order to save them

THE MONTHLY MAILBOAT, *California*, pulled into Fort Wrangell in early August 1880, and S. Hall Young stood on the wharf with everybody else. Waving eagerly from the boat rail was a familiar figure in a long, gray Ulster and Scotch cap. Young waved back. The *California* tied up, and John Muir bounded down the gangway, youthful and fleet-footed as ever. He embraced Young and said, "When can you be ready?"

Young, a bit befuddled, inquired about Muir's wife; he knew the exuberant naturalist had gotten married in April.

"Man," Muir said, "have you forgotten? Don't you know we lost a glacier last fall?"

Yes, they had left many glaciers unexplored, Young recalled. Muir would not be satisfied until he crawled into the blue sapphire heart of each one and touched its soul, learned its secrets. To Muir, glaciers were living beings, winter's children, the offspring of tall mountains and deep snow.

Muir explained, "My wife could not come . . . Get your canoe and crew and let us be off."

Muir was, in fact, concerned about his wife. He had left Louie pregnant and bedridden, her morning sickness lasting all day during the hottest time of the year. Yet she had insisted he go north. It would be good for him after nearly one hundred days of wearisome toil in the fruit fields.

As he sailed up the British Columbia coast, deeper and deeper into wild country, Muir's letters to her were more loving than a year earlier. "I shall make haste to you and reach you ere you have time to grieve and worry . . . I have been alone, as far as the isolation that distance makes, so much of my lifetime that separation seems more natural than absolute contact, which seems too good and indulgent to be true."

Hurry home, she told him, so together they could wait for their baby, what she called, "our own Precious Hope."

Once Muir arrived in Alaska, however, his letters to Louie stopped. He belonged again to the glaciers.

Reverend Young had sad news. In early January, Chief Toyatte, a man of peace, the man Muir had called "the noblest old Roman of them all," was shot and killed trying to mediate a dispute between two drunken bands of Tlingits. Toyatte had offered all his blankets to assuage the angered parties, asking them to put away their guns and go home. Young had stood with his hand on Toyatte's shoulder when the shooting began, and the great man fell with a bullet through his heart.

Years later, Young would recall "the darkest day of my life," when Toyatte, "one of the simplest and grandest souls I ever knew, fell dead at my feet, and the tribe was tumbled back into barbarism; and the white man, who had taught the Indians the art of making rum, and the white man's government, which had afforded no safety guard against such scenes, were responsible."

Muir was stunned and saddened to lose such a friend who, "never under any circumstances did I ever see him do anything, or make a single gesture, that was not dignified, or hear him say a word that might not be uttered anywhere."

Young introduced Muir to a Tlingit named Lot Tyeen, who was ready with a swift canoe, twenty-five feet long (ten feet shorter than Toyatte's), five feet at the beam, with two small sails to be manned by the able crew: Lot Tyeen's son-in-law, Hunter Joe, and a half-breed, Smart Billy.

They took off in mid-August, eager for adventure. The Indians, in Muir's words, welcomed "the work before them, dipping their oars in the exact time with hearty good will as we glided past island after island . . ."

—✦—

RIDING ALONG WAS a sixth member of the party, an indifferent little dog named Stickeen, a silky mutt—more terrier than anything, white and black, with tan on the face, almost smug in his standoffish manner.

He contributed nothing to the expedition that Muir could see. Muir had never been a champion of domestic animals, preferring instead their wild cousins that lived free of men's harsh and frivolous dominion. Self-contained and aloof, Stickeen didn't amuse others by fetching a stick or frisking about. He never sought to win favor, be petted, or share a blanket. He never obeyed an order.

Young's wife had received him as a wedding present, the missionary told Muir. Insisting that the little dog could swim like a seal and climb like a bear, Young made out a list of attributes so long that it implied the little dog would be, according to Muir, "the most interesting member of the party."

Muir agreed to bring him, a profound decision that would affect the rest of his life. The dog would give Muir his best adventure story ever, and one day Stickeen would help him settle into his own aging and growing domesticity.

Stickeen often rode in the canoe with his head on the bowsprit, detached yet circumspect, wise in his own quiet way, keenly aware of everything that was about to happen. Whenever the canoe approached land, he would jump into the cold water and scamper ashore and into the forest to investigate things, disappearing for hours. When it came time to leave, the others would call for him and finally set off, assuming he was lost, only to see him swimming out to meet them from a distant point, far from where they had landed.

After a few days, Muir stopped comparing Stickeen to other dogs he'd known.

———

THEY EXPLORED the glaciers of Sumdum Bay, Taku Inlet, and Stephens Passage. So many, all alike yet each different in detail, all shapers of the land but also shaped by the land, hand and glove with the topography. All glaciers moved, Muir knew, and as they did they exerted tremendous forces on the land. He sketched and made notes based on his careful observations, how glaciers advanced and retreated, eroded and deposited. Every inlet, he could see, was a flooded Yosemite Valley, where the ocean had reclaimed topography previously occupied by ice. His canoe party was floating through a mountain range, the Coast Range of Alaska, where everything was in flux and changing into something else.

In a huge way Alaska confirmed Muir's theory that glaciers—not catastrophic down-faulting (as championed by Josiah Whitney)—had shaped the Sierra Nevada and its centerpiece, Yosemite Valley. Tectonics did raise mountains over many millions of years, but glaciers added the finishing touches; they were the chisel, the sandpaper, the lathe. As Muir saw it, you had to be open-minded, unblinded by rigid doctrine. Science and faith were inseparable. The best science wasn't just quantitative, built on numbers; it was also qualitative, built on intuition. It demanded head knowledge, to be sure, but also heart and—most important—imagination. Alaska provided the natural laboratory and wild church of John Muir's dreams, the place that held the answers to questions he'd not yet considered.

Furthermore, he immediately recognized that indigenous hunter-gatherer cultures had a deep spiritual bond with the natural world, how they saw themselves as citizens—not masters—of the earth. This was part of his attraction to the Tlingits of southeast Alaska. They possessed great humility, courage, wisdom, and wit. They were authentic, grounded, tough, and deeply wise in the outdoors; they gave him his chance to be a true explorer, a Catlin, Bartram, or Audubon, those early artists and natural historians who saw the original America before it was subjugated and tamed. By 1849, when Daniel Muir brought his family to Wisconsin from Scotland, and John was just eleven years old, Audubon's America was already gone.

THE SCHISM between one way of thinking and another—a reverence for nature versus its subjugation—was easy to trace in Muir's time (and still is today). On November 10, 1619, René Descartes, a French mathematician, had a revelation. Then only twenty-three, he was lying on the banks of the Danube River when he saw himself rise above the earth, a disembodied intellect, separate, supreme, while everything else below— all physical and biological processes, all organisms other than himself and his fellow man—worked according to precise mechanical laws. Nothing else had conscious thought.

Man alone, Descartes convinced himself, was above nature; he was its master. Everything else was a vast treasure of inanimate resources we can—and should—exploit. Nature should be subdued; feelings suppressed. Years later, as a professor, Descartes would instruct his students to dissect live animals and pay no attention when the animals screamed. After all, they were just machines breaking down.

In 1644 Descartes published *Principia Philosophicae* and cemented his stature as a premier thinker, declaring men as "lords and possessors of nature." Four hundred years earlier, Thomas Aquinas had said man could kill animals "without any injustice," and Francis Bacon, only one generation before Descartes, said, "the world is made for man, not man for the world."

These bookish men were products of their time; they saw nature as a beastly impediment to humankind's improvement. Standing as they did with one foot still in the dark ages, they knew nothing about genetics, geology, ecology, or evolution, how the world worked, had evolved, was evolving. They had no way to know, and little reason to ponder, how everything in nature was interconnected. Man's footprint on the earth back then was small, a tiny fraction of what it is today. The world was big and dangerous; people were small and vulnerable. Life was short and often rife with hardship. The flower was beautiful, the forest frightening. Best to cut it down.

This was the slow-to-change culture in which John Muir found himself in his own time, trapped, a hopeless bleeding heart in a civilization enamored with money and machines.

Muir knew Descartes was wrong. But to convince others, so proud of their progress, would be an uphill battle he'd fight for the rest of his life—a fight still being fought.

MUIR had already proved himself capable of standing up to cruel authority. He had walked away from his father to find his own path and a better definition of goodness and success, one where nature could be his salve, not his slave, where the woods would preach to him a gentle sermon—not of dominion, but of harmony.

A century before, philosopher David Hume, a member of the Scottish Enlightenment, had said sympathy was fundamental to one's humanity, and a "feeling for the other" was central to one's ethics and moral grounding. Planting seeds of insurrection, Hume added that one must distinguish between "what is" and "what ought to be." Jean-Jacques Rousseau said the same thing: "Man is born free and everywhere he is in chains."

Then came Darwin, announcing, "There is grandeur in this view of life, with its several powers, having been originally breathed by the Creator into a few forms or into one; and that, whilst this planet has gone cycling on according to the fixed law of gravity, from so simple a beginning endless forms most beautiful and most wondrous have been, and are being, evolved."

Like Copernicus and Galileo, Darwin broke the castle mirror; he took us out of the ivory tower and put us in the forest. Any crackpot could easily find a previous crackpot whose philosophical mutterings confirmed what he already thought to be true. By going deep into the mountains of California, and later Alaska, John Muir sidestepped the mutterings of men and forced upon himself the harsh realities of what it meant to be free of civilization's chains and society's mirrors, where philosophy meant little, and a man could go back to the original text: the wind, rain, and weather of a beautiful yet unforgiving place, the wildness we all came from.

Years earlier, while hiking in Canada, he had dropped to his knees and cried upon discovering the perfection of a single flower, a calypso orchid; he'd grown still with admiration watching a water ouzel work the streams of the Sierra Nevada. But coastal rain forest Alaska, with its brown bears and blue ice, was something else entirely. Muir's brightest benediction would be to find good company in the cold glaciers other men bypassed en route to the goldfields and timber mills. If America were to find—or invent—another vision of itself, it would have to be here, and now, on the far side of the continent. Muir could wait for a revolution, or he could be the revolution.

When he walked away from Wisconsin and his overbearing father, young John walked away from everything: religion, society, culture, the rules of progress, the rules of the game. Just as a society handed down its rules to any individual, parents handed down rules to their children, and the children accepted them—even if the rules didn't feel right or make any sense at all.

Children are not critical thinkers; they cannot bear to identify the all-powerful parent as the source of their confusion and pain. They assume the problem is within them, and if damaged, they grow up wounded, losing faith in themselves and others around them.

It's not easy for children to reject their parents, just as it's not easy for each new generation to reject its civilization.

The more we are removed from nature, the more we are denied our birthright to play in forests, climb mountains, follow streams, and fall in love with meadows, to become creative, self-actualized, deeply intuitive. We come to rely on civilization to tell us what's good and bad, what's right, wrong, and essential to our success. The march of progress is a great thing, we are told; it's the best thing, our destiny. *Get on board. Go for a ride. Invest now.*

Railroads and steam engines, stock markets and canned foods, feathered hats and fur farms. Everything was possible in the promised future of 1880, the year John Muir paddled into the ice age with four men and a little dog.

One day we'll civilize all of North America, the boomers kept saying. It's our manifest destiny. We'll invent machines to provide us with everything. We'll achieve a grand technological utopia, a material paradise and a universal wealth cleverly extracted from the inexhaustible forces of nature around us. We'll live forever, above it all, and find eternal abundance and happiness. One day, any day, real soon.

AGAIN AND AGAIN, the canoeists paddled late into the night, passing good campsites, beckoned on by Muir and his unquenchable desire to see glaciers. This voyage, beginning in mid-August, was two months earlier than the previous year's epic, and Muir reveled in the fine summer weather. He and Young sat forward and paddled, while Lot Tyeen commanded from behind, sitting high in the stern. In the middle, Joe and Billy pulled on oars, Joe their cook and hunter, an excellent oarsman; Billy, only seventeen, their interpreter and Joe's assistant. They put in long days and covered many miles, "against the protest of our Indians," observed Reverend Young, "whose life of infinite leisure was not accustomed to such rude interruption. They could not understand Muir at all, nor in the least comprehend his object in visiting icy bays where there was no chance of finding gold and nothing to hunt."

Muir was tireless, relentless, rapturous, the ice-chief once again.

"What a plucky little giant," he effused, upon finding a tidewater glacier in Sumdum Bay, its icy features a marvelous deep blue, compressed by sheer granite walls on both sides, nothing like the broad-faced white giant glaciers of Glacier Bay. He went on: "To think of his shouldering his way through the mountain range like this! Samson, pushing down the pillars of the temple at Gaza, was nothing to this fellow. Hear him roar and laugh."

Muir named the glacier Young Glacier, for which Young, years later, wrote:

> [R]ight proud was I to see that name on the charts for the next ten years or more . . . but later maps have a different name. Some ambitious young ensign on a surveying vessel, perhaps, stole my glacier, and later charts gave it the name of Dawes. I have not found in the Alaskan statute books any penalty attached to the crime of stealing a glacier, but certainly it ought to be ranked as a felony of the first magnitude, the grandest of grand larcenies.

According to Young, they spent days of "unmixed pleasure" among the glaciers. Muir loved it, scampering about like a mountain goat with little Stickeen at his heels, "unfussy as a tree." Not for another ten years would Muir once again be among the glaciers of Alaska, as the next decade would find him dedicated to his new life as a father, fruit farmer, and businessman.

Northbound, the canoe party visited Taku Inlet and proceeded up Stephens Passage. Camped on the east side of Douglas Island, on Gastineau Channel, Muir found a streambed that promised gold, something he'd report to authorities in Sitka at the end of this canoe trip.

S. Hall Young as he appeared as a young missionary in Alaska
PHOTO COURTESY OF HOLT-ATHERTON SPECIAL COLLECTIONS, UNIVERSITY OF
THE PACIFIC

Two prospectors, Joe Juneau and Richard Harris, would soon confirm
Muir's suspicions when, under the guidance of a Tlingit (who cajoled
them upslope into today's Silver Bowl Basin), they made a huge discovery. Thirty years later, the towns of Juneau and Douglas, facing each other
across Gastineau Channel, would be home to the richest gold mines in
the world, and Juneau would be the bustling new capital city of the territory of Alaska.

WEST OF DOUGLAS ISLAND, the canoeists entered Icy Strait and visited Pleasant Island, where again Stickeen ran wild. Only after the canoe party pushed off did the dog come swimming after them, otter-like. Muir ordered them to turn around to pick him up. Hauled into the canoe, soaking wet, the little dog passed by everybody until he was between Muir's knees, then shook himself dry. Muir pretended to give him a disapproving kick.

They camped that night in a driving rain in Taylor Bay, near Cross Sound and the open Gulf of Alaska. To the north, Brady Glacier ascended into the wintry heart of the Fairweather Range, one of the highest coastal mountain ranges in the world. Immediately above the glacier, rising more than ten thousand feet above sea level, Mount La Perouse gathered snow in the storm. The French explorer Jean-Francois de Galaup, comte de La Pérouse had visited this region in 1786, and despite warnings from the local Tlingits to avoid certain treacherous areas, he lost two longboats in the vicious tide rips of Lituya Bay. Beneath a stone marker, the grieving Frenchman left a note, "At the entrance of this harbour perished twenty-one brave seamen. Reader, whoever thou art, mingle thy tears with ours."

Muir was about to discover what La Pérouse had learned ninety-four years earlier, and what the Tlingit Indians had known for centuries: The north country, while beautiful, can be dangerous. It swallows people. The ice inspires, and the sea provides, but neither shows mercy.

The next morning, August 30, while the others slept, Muir rose early and left camp. The weather remained dour, with steady wind and rain, yet Muir pushed on, tempting fate. He had a glacier to explore. Suddenly at his heels was little Stickeen.

"Go back," Muir commanded. But the dog, imperturbable, would not obey. "Small and worthless," Muir had said of him earlier. "This trip is not likely to be good for toy-dogs." But Stickeen was not a toy or a pet. It was hard to say what he was.

Man and dog climbed the east flank of the mighty glacier, a vast plateau of ice broken into a bewitching maze of crevasses. They worked their way north. Muir kept telling the dog to be careful, but Stickeen, according to Muir, "showed neither caution nor curiosity, wonder nor fear, but bravely trotted on as if glaciers were playgrounds. His stout muffled body seemed all one skipping muscle."

Man and dog gained confidence from the other, and soon they were deep into the glacial maze, beyond the point of an easy return. In every direction was an ocean of ice. The sky darkened with heavy clouds and gave only an occasional hint of the position of the sun, a signpost back to camp. The rain turned to wet, blinding snow. The temperature fell, and Stickeen trotted on with his usual aplomb.

Muir made guesswork of which way to go. For hours they jumped many smaller crevasses and winnowed their way through obstacles. But then they came upon a crevasse so deep and wide they were forced to move a mile to the left, then a mile to the right, each time without success. The only route home, Muir knew, was over a long sliver of ice, like a suspension cable, that bridged the chasm. It began ten feet below the brink and ran seventy feet across to the other side, ending again ten feet below the brink. A sobering prospect, rife with peril.

Wet and shivering and smart enough to know the fix they were in, Stickeen whimpered while Muir used his ice axe to cut steps down to the ice bridge, then across it, careful not to look down as his "other self" took over: "At such times one's whole body is eye, and common skill and fortitude are replaced by power beyond our call or knowledge." Muir notched steps on the other side and hauled himself up.

Stickeen ran back and forth on the opposite side, howling with despair. He stopped and stared at the task before him, the impossibility of it, and cried more. The day was ending, the light fading. It was now or never. Down on his knees, Muir encouraged Stickeen from the other side. Again, the dog howled with despair. Then slowly he took one step down where Muir had cut a notch, and another, easing his trembling body one step at a time, doing his best, suspended above a sudden frozen death.

"Hush your fears, my boy," Muir said. "We will get across safe, though it is not going to be easy. No right way is easy in this rough world. We must risk our lives to save them."

PART TWO

1888–1898

CHAPTER FIVE

old friends, new friends

IN THE SPRING of 1888, more than seven years after he'd last been among the glaciers of Alaska, John Muir was busy in the fruit fields of his California orchard, picking and boxing cherries, when an old friend came calling. Muir had always been good with his hands, building, improvising. He planted, picked, and shipped fruit and oversaw those he employed. With Scottish shrewdness, he bartered uncompromisingly with agents and buyers, checked his ledgers, and made his own deposits, driving his horse-drawn buggy into town, his right leg dangling out the side, carrying cash in a big white bag marked "laundry." Biographer Linnie Marsh Wolfe wrote, "In the ten years he gave to more or less intensive ranching, it is said he laid away in that local bank a savings account of $50,000 which he never touched in his lifetime."

For all his aversions to the humdrum workaday world, Muir was a keen businessman. He knew how to play the game and knew it was *a game,* a folly of sorts. "Through want of enterprise and faith," Thoreau had written, "men are where they are, buying and selling and spending their lives like serfs."

This was no way to live, but neither was it a bad way to make a living.

He had a stable, loving marriage, and he adored his daughters, Wanda, born in 1881, reserved like her mother, and little Helen, just a wisp, born in 1886, frail yet animated like him, or like he used to be. It was all so long ago, his life in Yosemite and the California high country, tramping from peak to peak, making field sketches and notes, sating his curiosity about everything, sailing north to Alaska, eating hardtack (dried biscuits made of water, flour, and salt) and dried salmon in a cedar canoe, befriending Tlingit Indians

Summer tourists ferry ashore off the *City of Topeka* steamship in Glacier Bay.
PHOTO COURTESY OF THE ALASKA STATE LIBRARY-HISTORICAL COLLECTIONS

and hearing their stories about Trickster Raven, telling a few of his own; getting lost and found on glaciers, and lost again, and found.

Not anymore.

He was a farmer now, a businessman.

On this particular May day, a voice called, and Muir looked up from picking cherries to see S. Hall Young approaching. He dropped everything to greet the Alaska missionary. "Ah! My friend . . .," he exclaimed. "You have come to take me on a canoe trip . . . have you not?"

They retired for cool drinks and for hours reminisced deep into the night about canoe journeys and Chilkat Tlingits; the little bighearted dog Stickeen, and the steamships *Idaho, Queen, Spokane,* and *City of Topeka* now visiting Glacier Bay every summer, carrying tourists keen on seeing tidewater glaciers. All because of Muir's stories in newspapers and national magazines, which had also gained him a following.

Since the appearance of his first published article in 1871 in the *New-York Tribune*—wherein he compared Yosemite's glaciers to an old book (weathered and worn but still easy to read)—his writing had given voice to the voiceless and touched thousands of readers. Even his letters were lyrical. To his sister Sarah he'd written in 1873 about a hike into the High Sierra with friends who ate their packed lunches of beef and bread while John sat alone and munched on a dry crust: "To dine with a glacier on a sunny day is a glorious thing and makes common feasts of meat and wine ridiculous. A glacier eats hills and drinks sunbeams."

He hadn't been to Alaska since 1881 (his third of what would be seven trips total) when he voyaged on the Revenue Marine vessel *Thomas Corwin* all the way to the Bering Sea, Chukchi Peninsula, and Arctic Ocean, leaving home only two months after Wanda's birth in 1881. Asa Gray, the famed Harvard botanist, had written to Muir, "Pray find a new genus, or at least a new species, that I may have the satisfaction of embalming your name, not in glacier ice, but in spicy wild perfume."

On the Arctic shore of Alaska, near Cape Thompson, Muir found an aster now called *Erigeron muirii.* It was a bright footnote, given the purpose of the *Corwin's* voyage: to rescue the men of the scientific expeditionary steamer *Jeanette,* two years gone and presumed lost in the Arctic ice. While the rescue mission was unsuccessful, and there were, eventually, a few survivors, Muir's writings for the *San Francisco Evening Bulletin* were some of his best.

But now his muse was gone. He'd written nothing of significance in years. Reading, yes. He read voraciously every night until he fell asleep, tired from his days in the fields. So while busy and productive, and up every morning at six sharp, being an attentive businessman, husband, and father, he didn't look or feel well.

"This is a good place to be housed in during stormy weather . . .," he once told a friend of his house in Martinez, "but it is not my home."

The high country was his home. Yosemite. The Sierra Nevada.

"I am degenerating into a machine for making money," Muir told Young as he motioned toward his cherries. "Condemned to penal servitude with these miserable little bald-heads! Boxing them up, putting them in prison! And for money."

To Young, John Muir was a shell of who he'd once been. The man he'd met nearly nine years ago in Fort Wrangell, happy and childlike among flowers, strong in the mountains, at home among rough-cut granite and shimmering glaciers, was gone.

Anybody who knew him well could see that Muir needed to *move*, to climb, ramble, and scramble again.

As Goethe had advised: "Keep not standing, fixed and rooted. Briskly venture, briskly roam."

———

HOW ANIMATED Muir became, his voice rising, Scottish brogue in full swing, when he recounted for Young his "big glacier adventure" with little Stickeen, the dog inching his way across the icy sliver of a bridge, using the steps Muir cut, encouraged by his you-can-do-it persuasions. The frisky terrier perched over the yawning crevasse, facing the last icy pitch, seeming to memorize the steps before him. Then in a sudden rush he bounded up to safety and ran in crazy circles, so happy to be alive.

Muir would later write:

He flashed and darted hither and thither as if fairly demented, scream-ing and shouting, swirling round and round in giddy loops and circles

like a leaf in a whirlwind, lying down, and rolling over and over,
sideways and heels over head . . . and launched himself at my face,
almost knocking me down, all the time screeching and screaming and
shouting as if saying, "Saved! Saved! Saved!"

For the rest of the 1880 canoe journey, Stickeen was Muir's faithful
shadow.

S. Hall Young had a story as well. While Muir and his new dog friend
were out on the Brady Glacier, working their way back to camp over
crevasses, through the dying light of day's end, Young was asked to visit
a Huna Tlingit subchief in his summer fishing camp near the terminus
of the glacier. Surrounded by his salmon weirs and many wives, the chief,
using his best oratorical skills, compared Young to "the many great things
of the universe," saying he was not only the father to all the Hunas, "he
was the sun, the stars, the moon . . ."

Young stopped him and asked what it was he wanted.

"I wish you to pray to your God," the chief replied.

"For what do you want me to pray?"

Wrapped in a Chilkat blanket, the old man rose to his feet and
motioned his arm toward the nearby advancing glacier: "Do you see that
great ice mountain? Once I had the finest salmon stream upon the coast
. . . to spear them or net them was very easy; they were the fattest and
best salmon among all these islands. My household had abundance of
meat for the winter's need. But the cruel spirit of that glacier grew angry
with me. I know not why, and drove the ice mountain towards the sea
and spoiled my salmon stream. A year or two more and it will be blotted
out entirely. I have done my best. Have prayed to my gods. Last spring I
sacrificed two of my slaves—members of my household, my best slaves,
a strong man and his wife—to the spirit of that glacier to make the ice
mountain stop; but it comes on; and now I want you to pray to your God,
the God of the white man, to see if he will make the ice mountain stop."

Young was displeased to hear about the sacrificed slaves. He abhorred
slavery and shamanism. He felt it his duty to end both among the Tlingits, to bring them into the fold of Christianity, teach them English, the
King James Bible; show them a loving God, put them on a righteous path

to eternal salvation. His boyhood hero had been Abraham Lincoln, who preserved the union and abolished slavery.

This was Young's calling, a focus second to none: ending slavery, saving souls. There was no greater work.

And it was not unprecedented.

—~—

WHEN COLUMBUS and other explorers reported the presence of savages in the New World, European clerics were intrigued. This New World, this so-called America, did it have wheat for bread and grapes for wine? Did it—could it—produce the body and blood of Christ? This was important. If it did, or could, then the savages who lived there were children of God, and they must be saved. If it did not, the savages were heathens and could be slaughtered. This question vexed the Catholic Church well into the sixteenth century, through the trial of Martin Luther and into the Great Schism, the Protestant Reformation. Many sallow-faced monks spent their lives on wooden benches within cold monastic stone walls, folded over thin soup and well-worn Bibles, making arguments for and against.

With the Age of Enlightenment, scientific truths began to challenge those of the church, and Voltaire clucked, "If God did not exist, it would be necessary to invent him."

If anybody knew the Bible, Muir did. His father had pounded it into him. But like so many others, young John interpreted scripture to fit his own ideals. Once while in a sequoia grove in his beloved Sierra, he noted birds and flowers, the musical sounds of water and wind all around him, and wrote "Everything busy, as if hearing the command 'Increase and multiply and replenish the earth.'" In so writing, Muir turned Genesis on its head, according to biographer Stephen Fox, "for in the Bible it ordered man to multiply and then 'subdue' the world to his own purposes, to establish 'dominion . . . over every living thing that moveth upon the earth.'" In Muir's version, all natural organisms were to reproduce for their own purposes, not to serve man alone.

"In his pantheism," Fox wrote, Muir "sensed a corresponding affinity with their [Tlingit] religious ideas. Freed of Christianity's human

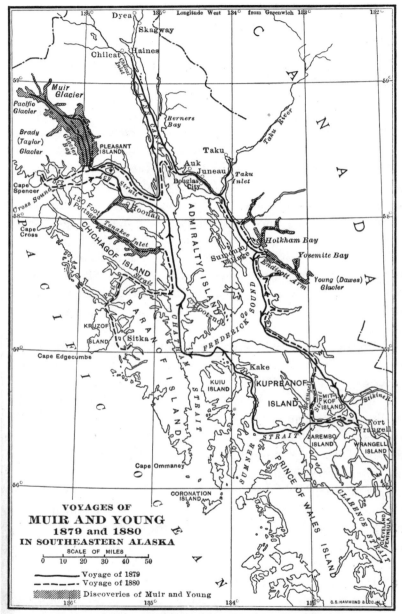

VOYAGES OF
MUIR AND YOUNG
1879 and 1880
IN SOUTHEASTERN ALASKA

SCALE OF MILES

0   10   20   30   40   50

———————— Voyage of 1879
- - - - - - - - Voyage of 1880
▨▨▨▨▨▨▨ Discoveries of Muir and Young

conceits, they prayed to nature gods and allowed nonhuman creatures—like Stickeen—into their heaven. 'Indian dogs,' he noted with approval, 'go to the Happy Hunting Grounds with their master—are not shut out.'"

After their time on the Brady Glacier, the canoeists paddled into Glacier Bay and spent the first few days of September on shore next to the massive tidewater face of the glacier that in a few years would be Muir's namesake.

John scrambled over it long and far and found it a great prairie of ice, magical, complex, alive like other glaciers in Glacier Bay, shrinking back to unveil a new, ice-chafed land.

From Glacier Bay they paddled south across Icy Strait to the village of Hoonah, and down to Port Frederick, where they portaged through to Tenakee Inlet, then through Peril Strait and down Olga Strait to Sitka, where Muir said good-bye. He caught a steamer home while the others, including Stickeen, traveled on by canoe to Fort Wrangell. Three years later, in the summer of 1883, the little dog was stolen off the docks by a tourist and never seen in Alaska again.

———— ◆◆◆ ————

THESE WERE the stories they told in 1888, John Muir and S. Hall Young, a Druid priest and a Presbyterian missionary who had found friendship in Alaska, and rekindled it in California, guarding their differences while sharing common ground. How good it felt. Young's visit was just the medicine Muir needed, the spark to light his fire. It was time to get into the mountains again, get back north, be among the glaciers of Alaska, get off the farm. His beloved wife, Louie, knew it. She in fact encouraged it. The wilderness wasn't her place—they had made one trip together to Yosemite, in 1884, and it didn't go well.

But the wilderness was his place, no question; that's where he needed to go. She wanted him to write again. She had fallen in love with him because he was such a good writer, so passionate about how things are and ought to be. Not that writing came easy to him; it didn't. But she had come to almost despise the ranch for how it had tamed and dispirited him. She wanted him to sink his teeth again into words, paragraphs, polemics, the fertile ground of language and lyrical persuasion. He had a legacy to create, a world to defend. Timbermen were felling the forests of California as if noble trees were blades of grass. It had to stop, and her John could stop them.

"The Alaska book and the Yosemite book, dear John, must be written, and you need to be your own self, well and strong, to make them worthy of you. There is nothing that has the right to be considered beside this except the welfare of our children."

THROUGHOUT the 1880s, while Muir was busy picking and shipping fruit, Robert Underwood Johnson, the editor of *Century* magazine in New York City, had contacted him and asked for article ideas. Muir always demurred. No more. Soon after Young's visit, John and Louie began to sell off pieces of the farm. And when Johnson visited San Francisco, Muir went calling.

"Johnson, Johnson," he shouted in the maze of hotel corridors, looking for the distinguished editor in his room. John of the Mountains, who never got lost in the wilderness, always got lost in the city. Friends said he had a hell of a time finding Golden Gate Park.

"Muir is of my height," Johnson would write,

> slender, thin in the leg, a farmer-looking man, black, curly hair, full long brown beard, graying near the ears where it is more closely kept. A keen gray eye, deep-set, a nose of graceful and delicate profile and with sensitive lines in the high forehead and about the eyes. His temples are rather hollow. He has quite a Scotch air in a fatigue suit of blue with a black slouch hat, and his movements are rather meditative, but show enthusiasm on occasion.

Well-connected and possessing a high eastern degree, Johnson was accustomed to fine company. Muir stunned him with his authenticity and knowledge, his effervescence and wit. The lean Scotsman had attended only two years of university, in Madison, but he was the real deal; he'd learned to go alone into the wilderness, as Thoreau had, to slow down, look, and listen, become a keen observer, a critical thinker. Muir saw himself as a scientist more intuitive than reductive. Breaking knowledge and nature into smaller and smaller pieces didn't interest him. His specialization was generalization: rocks, flowers, trees, glaciers, the grand interconnectedness he found everywhere and in everything. He wanted to celebrate them unabashedly. He made no apologies.

Relationships interested him as much as names, processes as much snapshots in time. He was an ecologist decades before the science of ecology even existed. Despite all he'd learned from nature and books and well-educated company, he made no pretense about being intellectual. In the blistering debate over Darwin's theory of evolution by natural selection, he at first landed in the pro-Darwin camp, as did most field naturalists, championed by Harvard botanist Asa Gray, as opposed to the anti-Darwin camp championed by Louis Agassiz (who'd died in 1873).

The anti-Darwin arguments reminded Muir of his father's narrow-minded condemnations of the new science of geology some thirty years earlier. As the Darwin debate would move into the next century, however, and be picked up by Thomas Henry Huxley and Ernst Haeckel with agnostic overtones, Muir would find himself prizing Darwin as a scientist but not a philosopher. In a book by Alfred Russel Wallace, a Darwin contemporary and fellow evolutionist, Muir would scribble in the margin, "Every cell, every particle of matter in the world requires a Captain to steer it into its place."

Where Darwin saw grim competition, Muir saw harmony. "Evolution—a wonderful, mouth filling word, isn't it?" he would write. But before evolution, Muir said, there had to be "an Intelligence that laid out the plan, and evolution is the process, not the origin, of the harmony."

FOR ALL HIS granite-hard Scotch convictions, Muir had an open mind. He could change. Through the influence of friends and books he could see things and digest ideas as he hadn't before. When he first read John Ruskin during his Yosemite years, in the 1870s, he found the English art historian colored by "conceit and lofty importance." But after receiving a copy of Ruskin's collected works some ten years later, during his contemplative Martinez years, Muir found himself admiring the Englishman's plea to turn away from cities and technology. In *Time and Tide*, Ruskin awakened Muir to the radical notion that the destruction of nature was the result of not just greed—which was obvious—but a greed allowed to thrive due to systemic flaws in capitalism itself.

In 1889 Muir and Johnson struck a deal. They would go to Yosemite and visit the place that inspired the first chapter of Muir's literary career, hoping it would inspire a second. Once there, after breezing up trails and skipping from rock to rock in the middle of a stream, John wrote to Louie, "I fancy I could take up the study of these mountain glories with fresh enthusiasm . . ."

Writer and editor had a grand but sobering time; in the high country they witnessed illegal lumbering and overgrazing by sheep (what Muir called "hoofed locusts"), and in Yosemite Valley the crass commercialization of tourist sites. One local entrepreneur had diverted part of Nevada Fall into a side cascade to improve the view, please visitors, and make more money. Muir wrote:

> *Tinkering the Yosemite waterworks would seem about the last branch of industry that even Yankee ingenuity would be likely to undertake. Perhaps we may yet hear of an appropriation to whitewash the face of El Capitan or correct the curves of the Domes.*

He was not beyond sarcasm or insurrection, or, for that matter, revolution.

That night by a campfire, Muir and Johnson talked. Johnson was moved by Muir's love of beauty and his heartbreak at seeing such destruction; he described Muir as having "tears in his voice." They began to hatch an ambitious plan. Yosemite under protection as a California State Reserve was not good enough. Muir would write two articles for *Century* magazine. Johnson would lobby friends in New York and Washington. Together they would campaign to create something better, something outrageous: Yosemite National Park.

And so Muir wrote, but he was tired. He had a deep bronchial cough and nervous indigestion. He needed to get well. This to him meant only one thing: "mountain nourishment," his best medicine, another adventure north. California was his home and battlefield, but Alaska was his elixir, what he called his "Holy Land," the wildest place he knew. A single glacier in Alaska might contain more ice than all that existed in the contiguous United States, and Alaska had an estimated one hundred thousand glaciers. And bears, wolverines, wolves, and whales.

Up there, Muir could be Homer on the Aegean, Humboldt in the Amazon, Huck Finn on the Mississippi, never more alive; and like Mark Twain's Huck, he might lie on his back one night and look up at the cold, brittle, indifferent stars and wonder "whether they was made, or only just happened."

Go, Louie told him. *Go north.*

Stay, his doctor said. "If you go on this journey in your condition, you'll pay for it with your life."

"If I don't go," Muir said, "I'll pay for it with my life."

They debated.

Muir went.

ON JUNE 14, 1890, he sailed from San Francisco on the steamer *City of Pueblo.* In no time Muir engaged a Scandinavian sea captain he described as "an interesting old salt, every sentence of his conversation flavored with sea-brine, bluff and hearty as a sea-wave, keen-eyed, courageous, self reliant and so stubbornly skeptical he refused to believe even in glaciers." The Scandinavian said he was headed north to have a boat built in Port Blakely.

Muir recommended that after he finished his business, "you had better go on to Alaska and see the glaciers."

"Oh, I haf seen many glaciers already."

"But are you sure you know what a glacier is?"

"Vell, a glacier is a big mountain all covered up with ice."

"Then a river must be a big mountain all covered up with water."

Muir educated him and got him excited, telling him "he must reform, for a man who neither believed in God nor glaciers must be very bad, indeed the worst kind of unbeliever."

In Port Townsend, Muir met his friend Henry Loomis, with whom he had climbed Mount Rainier in Washington two years earlier. They sailed for Glacier Bay on the steamer *Queen*, Captain James Carroll commanding. It rained up the British Columbia coast and Muir didn't mind as he described scenery "delightful even in the dullest weather." In Fort Wrangell he watched passengers mob the waterfront shops and pay "high prices for shabby stuff manufactured expressly for tourist trade ... Most people who travel look only at what they are directed to look at. Great is the power of the guide-book-maker, however ignorant."

He missed his friends Reverend Young and Lot Tyeen, who were out of town. Continuing north, Muir studied passing glaciers from every viewpoint, and he noted with pleasure the many stranded icebergs off the LeConte Glacier, and again at the mouth of Sumdum Bay (today's Tracy Arm). Captain Carroll then steered the *Queen* up Taku Inlet so the 180 passengers, according to Muir, could see the Taku and Norris glaciers "in the flesh."

In the gold-fever town of Douglas, they toured a large mill where six hundred tons of low-grade quartz were crushed every day. Westbound one day after the summer solstice, they crossed Lynn Canal, where "there are now two canneries," Muir wrote. "The Indians furnish some of the salmon at ten cents each." The weather was perfect that night, and Muir noted how everybody stayed on deck "to see the midnight sky. At this time of year there is no night here, though the sun drops a degree or two below the horizon. One may read at twelve o'clock San Francisco time."

———◆———

HOW MUST IT have felt for John Muir, fifty-two that summer, when on June 23, 1890, the *Queen* entered Glacier Bay and steamed directly to his namesake glacier, a massive wall of ice some three hundred feet high, two and a half miles across, thundering icefalls into the bay, a luminous tidewater glacier proclaimed by some as the Eighth Wonder of the World?

Today's demographers have estimated that of the roughly 110 billion people who have lived on earth the last 50,000 years, only a small fraction have achieved age fifty and beyond; of those, half are alive today. In other words, Muir was already the beneficiary of a relatively long life. He was famous, yet fame didn't interest him. He shied away from leadership, carried not an extra ounce of fat, and grew his beard down to his chest. For all her attempts to civilize him, Louie had failed. At his core, he was still a tramp. With regard to his influence as a writer, he was just getting started.

In the next two months, July and August, *Century* magazine would land on the doorsteps of 200,000 American homes with two back-to-back articles by Muir in defense of his California home. Appeals to Congress would flood into Washington, and by the end of the year, Yosemite would be a national park.

But in the summer of 1890, he had a spirit to revive, a theory to test, a cough to kick. New friends to make. How best to find the boy inside the man? How best to get well? Go north. Travel on a glacier. Sleep on the ice.

CHAPTER SIX

no lowland grippe microbe

THE WORLD is the geologist's great puzzle box; he stands before it like the child to whom the separate pieces of his puzzle remain a mystery till he detects their relation and sees where they fit, and then his fragments grow at once into a connected picture beneath his hand.
—LOUIS AGASSIZ, 1866

By 1890, when John Muir arrived in Glacier Bay for the third time, sixty years had passed since the publication of Charles Lyell's premier edition of *Principles of Geology*, which introduced the literate world to uniformitarianism and deep time: an earth shaped by slow-moving forces still under way today, an earth not thousands of years old, but millions—perhaps billions—of years old. Forget religious dogma. The world was a puzzle indeed, dynamic, ever-changing, no longer adequately explained by Old Testament text.

It was instead fleshed out by creative speculation, rigorous field studies, and careful analysis of landscapes and rock types of vastly different ages by men who accepted the constructive criticisms of their peers. As such, they fine-tuned their ideas through the scientific process until they made sense, and a new science was born, the study of the earth called geology, and its subset study of ice as an earth-shaping force: glaciology.

It was a delightful coincidence for Muir that his life should parallel the formative years of the science of glaciology. So much had been unveiled, yet so many questions remained. How did glaciers work? What secrets did they hold? Why did they advance and retreat, surge and collapse?

How extensive had they been in the earth's past, and for how long? And how might they shape—or be shaped—by the future?

MUIR AND LOOMIS had been in Glacier Bay for a week, undaunted by the rain, camped on their nine-foot-by-nine-foot-square tent platform near the calving, thundering tidewater face of Muir Glacier, icebergs stranded on shore like diamonds in the rough. At four o'clock in the morning of July 1, 1890, a whistle awakened them. It was the steamer *George W. Elder*. Muir went out and stood atop a lateral moraine and waved; the *Elder* tooted its whistle in response. A party came ashore lead by Harry Fielding Reid, professor of geology at the Case School of Applied Sciences in Cleveland.

"Are you Professor Muir?" he asked.

While Muir made no pretense to be an academic, many in academic circles admired him. Outside of his 1870s debate with Josiah Whitney over the shaping of Yosemite Valley, wherein time would prove him right and Whitney wrong, Muir would make no major peer-reviewed contributions to the science of glaciology. But he would popularize glaciers unlike anybody else, and be to glaciers what Jacques Cousteau would be to the oceans and Carl Sagan to the stars.

Conservation was fast becoming his primary aim. In their brief time together, Muir had described himself to Robert Underwood Johnson as an amateur scientist, nothing more, a "self-styled poetico-geologist" who found scientific discourse too dominated by "angular factiness." Better to write from the head *and* the heart. The Greeks knew this: pathos, ethos, logos. Leave no part of one's humanity untouched. According to the British teacher, critic, mountaineer, and poet Terry Gifford, Muir would achieve more in America's conservation politics "precisely because he declined to adopt the discourse of the professional scientist." His alliance with Johnson and *Century* magazine was already bearing proof.

It took Muir and Professor Reid no time to strike up a friendship, given their shared fascination with natural history in general and glaciers in particular. Reid had come to Glacier Bay to conduct serious studies; he wasn't traveling alone, or unencumbered. Half a dozen students joined him. The *George W. Elder* dropped anchor and off-loaded the party's instruments, tents, personal baggage, and other provisions. Seven to eight tons of freight, Muir estimated. Reid wrote of Muir and Loomis:

> They had come also to study the glacier, and added much to the pleasure of our stay. We immediately set to work to put up our tents, and before evening everything was in good shape. We brought boards from Juneau for flooring, tables, etc., which added materially to our comfort and convenience. A book-shelf held our small library of works on glaciers, logarithmic tables, etc. A gasoline stove enabled us to cook our meals with ease, and campstools permitted us to eat them in comfort. This was to be our base camp and, in honor of Professor Muir, we named it Camp Muir.

Wrote Muir, "I am delighted to have companions so congenial—we have now a village."

Four years earlier, Reverend George Frederick Wright of the US Geological Survey and Oberlin Theological Seminary had visited Muir Glacier and set stakes across its vast surface to find its rate of flow at seventy feet per day in the middle and ten feet per day on its margins, not unlike a river, where friction slows down the current. The fact that it wasn't advancing, but instead retreating, meant that Muir Glacier was experiencing a net loss of ice. It was starving. Snow accumulation in the mountains had decreased while melting and calving at the glacial terminus had increased. Muir Glacier, according to Wright, must be losing some 200 million cubic feet of ice per summer day, ice discharged off its tidewater face into the sea, a staggering number.

Wright's findings, published in his 1889 book *The Ice Age in North America, and Its Bearings upon the Antiquity of Man*, were severely criticized by other academics, perhaps justifiably. But Muir and Reid knew there was no snobbery like academic snobbery. Perhaps Wright hadn't been so wrong. It was time to find out.

For days Muir and Reid tramped about, taking measurements, making observations, sometimes together, sometimes each off on his own, or accompanied by Loomis or Reid's students. Muir discovered what he called "fossil wood" on the west side of the glacier, concentrated in a stratum of sand and clay. He later found "a large grove of stumps in a washed-out channel near the glacier-front but had no time to examine closely. Evidently a flood carrying great quantities of sand and gravel had overwhelmed and broken off these trees, leaving high stumps."

He had seen stumps like these on previous adventures in Glacier Bay, and puzzled over them. Later, he again discovered a stand of what he called "monumental stumps in a washed out valley of the moraine. . . . The largest is about three feet in diameter and three hundred years old." But when had they died? And how exactly? "How these trees were broken off without being uprooted is dark to me at present," Muir observed, his keen mind already at work to unveil the geological history of Glacier Bay. It was like old times when he hiked the High Sierra and probed its mysteries, or when he first came to Alaska, a place he found "abounding in beginning lessons on landscape making."

One week after Reid's arrival, the steamer *Queen* returned and disembarked many of its 230 passengers, who mobbed Camp Muir. "What a show they made with their ribbons and kodaks!" Muir observed,

All seemed happy and enthusiastic, though it was curious to see how promptly all of them ceased gazing when the dinner-bell rang, and how many turned from the great thundering crystal world of ice to look curiously at the Indians that came alongside to sell trinkets, and how our little camp and kitchen arrangements excited so many to loiter and waste their precious time prying into our poor hut.

Earlier that day, knowing the *Queen* would leave with outgoing mail, Muir composed a letter.

To Mrs. Muir. Glacier Bay. Camp near eastern end of ice wall.

Dear Louie:
The Steamer Queen is in sight pushing up Muir Inlet through a grand crowd of bergs on which a clear sun is shining. I hope to get a letter from you to hear how you and the little ones and older ones are.

Tourists off a steamship admire icebergs stranded at low tide near the face of Muir Glacier, in Glacier Bay.
PHOTO COURTESY OF THE NATIONAL SNOW AND ICE DATA CENTER

I have had a good instructive and exciting time since I wrote you by the Elder a week ago. The weather has been fine and I have climbed two mountains that gave grand general views of the immense mountain fountains of the glacier and also of the noble St. Elias Range along the coast mountains, La Perouse, Crillon, Lituya, and Fairweather. Have got some telling facts on the forest question that has so puzzled me these many years, etc., etc. Have also been making preliminary observations on the motion of the glacier. Loomis and I get on well, and the Reid and Cushing party camped beside us are fine company and energetic workers. They are making a map of the Muir Glacier and Inlet, and intend to make careful and elaborate measurements of its rate of motion, size, etc. They are well supplied and will no doubt do good work.

I have yet to make a trip round Glacier Bay, to the edge of the forest and over the glacier as far as I can. Probably Reid and Cushing and their companions will go with me. If this weather holds, I shall

*not encounter serious trouble. Anyhow, I shall do the best I can. I mean
to sew the bear skin into a bag, also a blanket and a canvas sheet for
the outside. Then, like one of Wanda's caterpillars, I can lie warm on
the ice when night overtakes me, or storms rather, for here there is now
no night. My cough has gone and my appetite has come, and I feel
much better than when I left home. Love to each and all.*

Ever thine, J. M.

⚊〰

MUIR WENT ALONE. He probably never intended to have companions on his journey into the white unknown of Glacier Bay, but his letter
to Louie said otherwise to set her mind at ease. Loomis and two Indians accompanied him early on to help haul gear over the moraine. With a
handshake they turned back, and Muir was gone. He pulled a three-foot-
long wooden sled "made as light as possible," loaded with a sack of hardtack, pemmican and nuts, a little tea and sugar, his caterpillar sleeping bag,
and a meager change of clothes. He held an alpenstock, a long wooden pole
with an iron-spiked tip used in the Alps since the Middle Ages for travel
on ice and snow. He moved with confidence and chose his route carefully.

Crevasses everywhere. Seracs, moulins, moraines. Nunataks in the
distance. Meltwater running atop and throughout the glacier; the ice
itself alive, moving. Everywhere a profound, embracing quiet. Stillness.

There was no place he'd rather be. Alone on a vast Alaskan glacier.
More than a few people thought him a crank, a kook.

⚊〰

CONSIDER the European occupation of America, a sweep of history
beginning with William Bradford, who described a "hideous and desolate wilderness" when he stepped off the *Mayflower* in 1620. Thus began
what historian Roderick Nash would call, "a tradition of repugnance." The
America that lay before Bradford and his fellow Pilgrims was no paradise,
wonderland, or national park. Such concepts were unthinkable back then.
Wild America was a threat to their survival, an alien place filled with
wolves, thieves, and the unknown.

In Middle Ages Europe, dark forests had always been dangerous. Mountains were evil. Landscape art did not exist. Goodness and spiritual guidance were found in churches and cathedrals, not in the woods. Wilderness was good for one thing only: to be transformed into civilization. Nash observed: "Anticipations of a second Eden quickly shattered against the reality of North America. Soon after he arrived, the seventeenth century frontiersman realized that the New World was the antipode of paradise . . . If men expected to enjoy an idyllic environment in America, they would have to make it by conquering wild country."

And conquer it they did. By 1820, two hundred years after the Pilgrims landed, the virgin hardwood forests of New England were gone, and Americans were moving west with Old Testament fervor and insatiable appetites for raw land. Calls from the pulpit exhorted that those lands be "brought under the axe and plow."

Small criticisms began to surface, mostly from Europeans with Romantic tastes such as François-René de Chateaubriand and Lord Byron, who confessed in 1816:

> There is a pleasure in the pathless woods,
> There is a rapture in the lonely shore.
> There is society where none intrudes . . .
> I love not man the less, but nature more.

IN 1823, fifteen years prior to John Muir's birth, James Fenimore Cooper became an American literary hero with the publication of his third novel, *The Pioneers*. In this and his next four novels, published over eighteen years, Cooper created Natty Bumppo, a native protagonist who found purity in the wild, deceit in the city. With this likeable, admirable character, Cooper, according to Nash, "discovered the literary possibilities of the wilderness. Wild forests and plains, as Cooper both knew and imagined them, dominate the actions and determine the plots of these novels . . ."

No major writer had ever done this, made wild nature *itself* a character with depth and tone. As such, Natty Bumppo, also known as Leatherstocking, found clarity and strength from what Nash called the "holiness of wild nature . . . Indeed Natty is his own best evidence, since lifelong exposure to the woods has given him an innate goodness and moral sense." Nash concluded, "Both Natty and Cooper believed in the 'honesty of the woods!'"

Traveling through America in 1831, French aristocrat Alexis de Tocqueville observed that many Americans saw the pioneer as the point of the spear of progress; the plow as God's trowel. "Democratic nations . . .," Tocqueville wrote, "will habitually prefer the useful to the beautiful, and they will require that the beautiful be useful." Utility was everything. If a man struggled to survive in the wilds and didn't know what he was doing, he'd always fight nature instead of learn *from* it, or live *with* it, as Natty did. Nature would be his adversary. In the end, man would lose. He'd lose his soul, his humanity, his grace; he might get rich and live in a big house, but he'd lose the vibrant, bountiful world around him. He'd inevitably lose the clean sky over his head.

How to stop this? We must transcend ourselves; move away from our materialism and back into the essence of our humanity. If any single moment in the history of the United States best voiced this call for transcendentalism, it came twenty years after Tocqueville's visit, in 1851 (the year Cooper died and Herman Melville published *Moby Dick*), when a thirty-four-year-old, slightly built pencil maker named Henry David Thoreau, having spent twenty-six months living at Walden Pond in a cabin he had built himself, stood before the Lyceum Society in Concord, Massachusetts, and announced, "In wildness is the preservation of the world." His point: Men are seduced by material gain and trivial sport. "For one that comes with a pencil to sketch or sing, a thousand come with an axe or rifle." The challenge was to moderate, simplify; find the Leatherstocking in each of us, a woods-wise goodness combined with the better refinements of civilization.

It was no surprise that Thoreau became an activist, a writer-moralist jailed for a single night because he opposed slavery and refused to pay taxes to support America's war with Mexico. "Henry, what are you doing in there?" Ralph Waldo Emerson allegedly said upon visiting him. Thoreau responded, "Ralph, what are you doing *out there?*"

How can you not be an activist?

The world was coming undone.

When Emerson visited Muir in Yosemite in 1871, the old man spoke at length about his protégé, Thoreau. Intrigued, Muir read *Walden* the next year, and for the rest of his life he would encourage friends and acquaintances to read anything by Thoreau. It would be no surprise to many when Muir himself became a writer, a moralist, and an activist.

But at this point, in 1890, he was an explorer, perhaps remembering his Thoreau: "be . . . the Lewis and Clark and Frobisher of your own streams and oceans; explore your own higher latitudes."

EVERY DAY would be a big adventure. Muir's goals on this solo trip were straightforward: lose the nagging cough he'd had for three months and explore his glacier and its seven major tributaries. Quickly, his investigative mind went to work, noting trees "storm-bent" from southeast winds; "margin terraces" composed of "grist of stone . . . rolled and sifted;" water trapped in crevasses that refroze to create "irregular veins seen in the structure of the glacier."

Early on he observed the powerful force of glaciers against the mountain flanks: "Nothing could be more striking than the contrast between the raw, crumbling, deforested portions of the mountain, looking like a quarry that was being worked, and the forested part with its rich, shaggy beds of cassiope and bryanthus in full bloom, and its sumptuous cushion of flower-enameled mosses."

He observed mountain goats, ravens, and ptarmigan and heard marmots and wolves. He called flowers by their scientific names, but ptarmigan he generalized. All his life Muir would show more scientific interest in flowers than birds, except if the bird were a favorite, like his beloved water ouzel of Yosemite.

On the morning of day four, he arose early to hear wolves in a place he called Howling Valley. During breakfast the wolves sounded nearer; Muir feared "they had a mind to attack me." He took shelter against a large boulder where he could use his alpenstock to defend against a "frontal attack." The wolves never appeared; Muir moved on. He gave many places names: Snow Dome Mountain, Nunatak Islands, Divide Glacier, Girdled Glacier, White Glacier, Braided Glacier, Berg Lake, Howling

Interglacial stumps from an old spruce-hemlock forest sheared off by advancing glaciers thousands of years ago in Muir Inlet
PHOTO BY FRANK LAROCHE, COURTESY OF THE NATIONAL SNOW AND ICE DATA CENTER

Valley, Granite Canon Glacier, Gray Glacier, Dirt Glacier, and Quarry Mountain. Only a few of these exist on maps today.

Though the exact route of Muir's ten-day journey in July 1890 is somewhat guesswork, it's safe to say that all the places where he walked on glacial ice are now ice-free. Muir Glacier today, only a fraction of its size in 1890, now rests at the head of Muir Inlet, some thirty-plus miles farther north, and is no longer tidewater. Neither are any of its tributaries except one: McBride Glacier. The glaciers of Muir Inlet, on the upper east side of Glacier Bay, are today vestiges of what they used to be.

Process, process, process. How? And why? Muir wanted to know *how* water and ice shaped the land, *why* this flower grew here and not there. "How often and by how many ways are boulders finished and finally brought to anything like permanent form and placed in beds for farms and fields, forests and gardens."

Across his boyhood haunts of Scotland and Wisconsin Muir had seen—but not fully understood, until now—the handiwork of glaciers, the clues left for those with keen eyes willing to slow down and look around. Out here Muir could develop his imagination, think about the *how* and the *why* of things, be on fire with excitement, and get well.

He slept on his sled and made little fires from fossil wood to heat his tea. At one point, with no fossil wood, he shaved off portions of his sled to make kindling.

He wrote in his journal: "It has been a glorious day, all pure sunshine. An hour or more before sunset the distant mountains, a vast host, seemed more softly ethereal than ever, pale blue, ineffably fine, all angles and harshness melted off in the soft evening light."

After a dinner of hardtack, he felt he could climb a mountain a second time, but pulling the sled had tired him.

Glissading down a steep slope, he hit blue ice and skidded out of control but landed without injury:

Just as I got up and was getting myself oriented, I heard a loud fierce scream, uttered in an exulting, diabolical tone of voice which startled me, as if an enemy, having seen me fall, was glorying in my death. Then suddenly two ravens came swooping from the sky and alighted on the jag of rock within a few feet of me, evidently hoping that I had been maimed and that they were going to have a feast. But as they stared at me, studying my condition, impatiently waiting for bone-picking time, I saw what they were up to and shouted, "Not yet, not yet!"

As day six ended he curled into his sleeping bag and wrote of "soft, tender light . . . cozy and comfortable resting in the midst of glorious icy scenery." The next day was equally sunny, "a glorious and instructive day." His shoes were nearly worn out, his feet wet every night . . . "but no harm comes from it, nothing but good." Day eight he awoke feeling tired, but after a meager breakfast he began to sketch and look about and soon felt he could climb five thousand vertical feet. "Anything seems easy after sled-dragging over hummocks and crevasses, and the constant nerve drain in having to jump crevasses . . ."

After so many sunny days, he admitted, "my eyes are much inflamed and I can scarce see." He had snow blindness. All the lines he sketched appeared double. "Nearly blind," he began his journal on day nine. "The light is intolerable and I fear I may be long unfitted for work." He improvised a poultice (what he called "wet bandages") and admitted that this was the first time in Alaska he'd experienced too much sunshine. Clouds moved in later that day, to his great relief. He made a pair of snow goggles but was afraid to wear them against his inflamed face. His eyes improved the next day, and he made many observations on the workings of Muir Glacier. A hummingbird twice visited his camp, attracted to the red liner of his sleeping bag.

While making his way across the glacier, he fell into a concealed crevasse and plunged into icy water that was over his head. He climbed out and hurried to a protective cliff, where he stripped down, threw the wet clothes into a "sloppy heap," and climbed into his sleeping bag to shiver through the night and finally sleep.

On July 21, he awoke to rain and found putting on his wet clothes "a miserable job . . . far from pleasant." But he was healed. "My eyes are better and I feel no bad effect from my icy bath. The last trace of my three-month's cough is gone. No lowland grippe microbe could survive such experiences." After dinner, as Muir was going to bed, he saw his friends Reid and Loomis walking over the moraine, coming to ferry him back across the inlet.

In Camp Muir he wrote, "I had a good rest and sleep and leisure to find out how rich I was in new facts and pictures [sketches] and how tired and hungry I was."

MUIR WOULD NOT head home to California for a month after this. He savored his time up north, for once he returned he knew his life would be busy in a way it never had been before.

In late July the *Queen* arrived with a load of dimension-cut lumber for a cabin. During a rainy spell, Muir and the others erected it, putting in two windows, a door, and a stone chimney. Wrote Reid, "Prof. Muir takes his meals with us and we use his house to sit in. The fire-place is

John Muir (far left) with Harry Fielding Reid (far right) and Reid's geology students at the cabin they built in August 1890, at Muir Point, Glacier Bay
PHOTO COURTESY OF THE US NATIONAL PARK SERVICE

progressing; in the meanwhile, we have built a fire on some sand in the middle of the floor, which warms the house but causes a good deal of smoke."

From their vantage on a beach terrace near Muir Inlet, with the glacial terminus not a mile away, they saw ptarmigan, oystercatchers (nesting on the shore), harbor seals, and, out beyond the icy waters, an occasional humpback whale. "And at odd moments," biographer Donald Worster would write, "some great jewel of ice would break away from the crystalline wall and plunge noisily into the sea, sending spray hundreds of feet high. Here was danger, but here also was knowledge and radiance enough to satisfy Muir's insatiable appetite."

Inspired by the country and also Muir's own exploits, other members of the party pushed themselves deep into rugged terrain, over rock and ice and crevasses that plunged into blue oblivion, in some places roping up and ascending slopes as steep as fifty degrees. Reid and two others climbed Pyramid Peak; mountaineer Dave Bohn would one day observe: "[I]t was the first roped ascent in that country. There would not be another for forty-one years."

On August 22, Muir, his cup full, finally boarded the *Queen* back home for California. The wilderness had nourished and fortified him. He had walked the "crystalline prairies" of ice far away from what Worster called "the heat and smoke of politics."

Muir was healed. He was a new man.

At home, with high winds ravaging the grapevines, and ground squirrels doing their usual damage, and only four Chinese laborers to do the fieldwork, and Wanda and little Helen with rotting teeth (Helen had had two extracted; the girls would brush better once John got home), Louie had written to her husband, "… the good Father above will not fail to lead you, His own dear child, in safety through all the darkness of Alaskan storms." Her enduring image of Alaska was of one fraught with bitter cold and ferocious storms.

Reid and party stayed in Muir Inlet a while longer to do their scientific work by water in a sixteen-foot rowboat and a three-man dugout canoe, attempting to measure the glacier's movements by setting stakes across its breadth near the tidewater face, a dangerous job. They never quite succeeded. Reid would leave Glacier Bay determined to return.

⌐•⌐

MUIR ARRIVED HOME in September to what must have been a glorious reunion with his girls, Wanda, age nine, Helen, four. Excitement brewed on many fronts. His articles in *Century* magazine had stirred the American public beyond his wildest dreams. The commercial and selfish exploitation of his temples of Nature had become so egregious that people were waking up and taking action, some loudly, others quietly, but action nonetheless, broad, swift, and deep.

Louie gushed, "Many good Californians are rejoicing over the beginning of success for your noble effort to save our Sierra woods and gardens from the hands of manifold destroyers."

Letters flooded into Congress and democracy worked. A bill proposing a "Yosemite National Park" was adopted by the House Committee on
Public Lands, which stated:

> The preservation by the Government in all its original beauty of a
> region like this seems to the committee to be a duty to the pres-
> ent and future generations. The rapid increase of population and
> the resulting destruction of natural objects make it incumbent on
> the Government in so far as may be to preserve the wonders and
> beauties of our country from injury and destruction, in order that
> they may afford pleasure as well as instruction to the people.

The bill passed the House and Senate, and on October 1, 1890, it was
signed into law by President Benjamin Harrison. That same season Congress created another national park in California, later named Sequoia, to
protect the world's largest living organisms.

The mood was contagious. In a nation where bison were slaughtered
by the tens of millions and Indians hoodwinked off their lands if not mur-
dered in their tents, national parks were catching on. Before the end of
the century, Mount Rainier National Park would be added in the Pacific
Northwest. And in the first decade of the next century, a naturalist/
hunter/conservationist named Roosevelt would occupy the White House
and do things that were still unimaginable in the 1880s. Yellowstone, created in 1872, was no longer *the* national park.

Something amazing was happening.

In the final decade of a century that saw a blistering expansion of
civilization, the accumulation of great wealth and urbanization of abject
poverty, a stupendous growth in industry, and the accelerated plunder-
ing of natural beauty from coast to coast, America held up a mirror and
asked some hard questions. It began to save the best of itself. Just in time.
This was no insignificant act, moralists knew. They wondered: Could this
nation, still young and bountiful, stand before that bounty and practice
restraint? Leave the apple unpicked? Improve on the progress of man?

No, said one writer.

Yes, said another.

CHAPTER SEVEN

moneyfest destiny

ALWAYS A PROVOCATEUR, Mark Twain, Muir's contemporary, called it like he saw it. The truth about America was not the glittering patriotism, prosperity, and virtuous hard work so often cherished and recited by businessmen and civic leaders. The real deal was darker, he said: a tawdry, opportunistic land-grab money-grub dressed up by boosters and boomers as righteous manifest destiny. "Truth is stranger than fiction," Twain famously quipped, "but it is because fiction is obliged to stick to possibilities; Truth isn't."

Muir biographer Donald Worster observed that Twain's novel *The Gilded Age* (coauthored with Charles Dudley in 1873, a book that would give the second half of the century its name) portrayed America's noble experiment in liberal democracy as "a farce," wherein the authors, "poked wicked fun at the something-for-nothing attitude that seemed to have driven out all virtue and sincerity." Mark Twain was the quintessential writer-as-critic: witty, wry, wise, lyrical, bitter, and unapologetic, challenging America's cherished myths. For that's all they are, he said: myths.

America's favorite novelist didn't wade into the shallow end of the pool of truth where others made a sport of self-congratulation; he dove into the deep end that had no hard bottom and swam to the unpopular conclusion that mankind was not so kind. Man was, in fact, "not made for any useful purpose, for the reason that he hasn't served any; that he was most likely not even made intentionally; and that his working his way up out of the oyster bed to his present position was probably [a] matter of surprise and regret to the Creator."

Twain's bitterness would grow when he lost his beloved daughter Susy to meningitis when she was just twenty-four. "It's one of the mysteries of our nature," he would write, "that a man, totally unprepared, can receive a thunderstroke like that and live."

John Muir never suffered such loss. Where Mark Twain saw hopelessness—even despair in his later years—Muir saw hope. The successful campaigns of 1890 to create Yosemite and Sequoia National Parks were beacons of inspiration. Think of it: A magazine story appears in August, citizens write letters, Congress responds and passes a bill in September; the president signs it into law in October. Man could and would improve upon himself, Muir believed. Though, in a sobering paradox of his own making, it would not happen until his back was against the wall and he faced destruction on all sides.

But last-minute revelations and resolutions were better than none at all. According to historian William Cronon, Muir was "a kind of ecstatic holy man" who found God in nature and goodness in men. Not all men, but enough of them. What society needed every so often was a catalyst, a Wordsworth, Emerson, or Thoreau to turn things around. Little did Muir know that his name would one day belong in that same pantheon, that he too would speak for the voiceless and change the way we see the world.

IN SOME RESPECTS John Muir never left Scotland, and this benefited him; it gave him emotional distance from the more unsavory aspects of America, something Mark Twain, raised in Missouri, never had. All his life Muir held dear his childhood home in Dunbar, on the Firth of Forth, roughly forty kilometers east of Edinburgh. He'd confess, "My love of my own Scottish land seems to grow with every pulse so that I cannot see the name or hear it but a thrill goes through every fibre of my body."

According to Muir biographer Steven J. Holmes:

Muir's notes on Scotland contain very little reference to agriculture, which would have been the dominant influence on the landscape around Dunbar. Although this omission was partly grounded in the relative weight of his childhood impressions, it also probably reflected his own impatience with and rejection of the farming life he had experienced in Wisconsin. Scotland could function as a powerful symbol and ideal for Muir only if it were not associated with the pains and struggles of the present—but it still had to carry the power and emotion of the past.

The highlands and the coast, the historic castles and winding roads and Edinburgh itself, seat of the Scottish Enlightenment and its great university (which once had more students than Oxford and Cambridge combined)—this was Muir's Scotland, a vanishing point, a place where he could disappear into the mists of time.

This affinity for his homeland de-Americanized him enough to reject militarism in general and the American Civil War in particular. A young pacifist with no fixed identity in the grinding world of machines and men, he had buried himself in his university studies in Wisconsin, then went to Canada for two years.

Before the war, Emerson said:

[W]e valued ourselves as cool calculators; we were very fine with our learning and culture, with our science that was of no country, and our religion of peace;—and now a sentiment mightier than logic, wide as light, strong as gravity, reaches into the college, the bank, the farm-house, and the church. It is the day of the populace.

Muir cared little for "the populace." Wisconsin in the 1860s was a sleepy western nebulae compared to New England, New York, Pennsylvania, Maryland, Virginia, South Carolina, and Georgia, those tight bustling spiral galaxies of the known eastern universe where young men picked up arms and onlookers jumped into carriages, and they headed off to Bull Run as if to partake in a sporting event.

Back then, the war excited Muir not at all; he didn't even want to talk about it. What excited him was Emerson's science of no country. God's splendors. Nature without borders.

Rather than take the entire curriculum at Madison, Muir said he "picked out what I thought would be most useful to me, particularly chemistry, which opened a new world to me, and a little Greek and Latin and Botany and Geology, and when I got apparently all I could get from the University, I quietly walked off without saying anything about a diploma—without graduating."

Twain, two and a half years older than Muir, walked away as well. After enlisting in a local Confederate unit in Missouri in 1861, he lasted only two weeks and headed west to California, apparently charmed not one bit by others' zeal for fighting and boasting.

———

PRIOR TO THE CIVIL WAR, America's self-identity was largely measured by how the new nation distanced itself from Europe and European influences. The war fractured that image into many sharp pieces to create a new America, war-torn but ambitious, John Muir's America. It was a nation still in search of what it was and could be, flexing new muscles, evangelical and egalitarian, reaching west into the frontier, inventive and insatiable, enamored with industrial progress yet also shaken and looking back to ask what exactly happened, and why.

The Civil War was—and to this day remains—the most traumatic and transformational event in US history. More than 625,000 dead. Families and communities ravaged. An entire Southern culture and way of life, gone, in some places burned to the ground. And in the aftermath, a time called the "reconstruction," a nation attempted to rebuild.

"In the devastated South," author David Von Drehle would observe, "writers and historians kindled comforting stories of noble cavaliers, brilliant generals and happy slaves, all faithful to the glorious lost cause." People everywhere seemed to forget what Abraham Lincoln said in his second inaugural address: the entire nation, North and South, profited greatly from slavery and then paid for it. Slaves in 1860 contributed more to the US economy than America's railroads, factories, banks, or ships. In what the South called "The War of Northern Aggression," an entire economy was brought to its knees because it was based on something immoral; built on the subjugation of one race by another. It had to end.

The Founding Fathers knew they had planted a time bomb in the US Constitution when they failed to address slavery. It took seventy-five years to explode. And now a nation ravaged by war was expanding west and casting itself anew, displacing tribes and stringing barbed wire and calling it good, getting something for nothing. The nation was warming itself yet again, Mark Twain would say, with comfortable stories of savage Indians and innocent pioneers. All lies.

———

EVERY TEN YEARS, beginning in 1790, the Superintendent of the Census counted the US population and mapped areas of "settlement" from east to west. Beyond those areas lay the "frontier," delineated by a line running north–south. In the beginning the frontier stretched all the way to the Pacific. Exactly how far, nobody knew. This was sixteen years before Meriwether Lewis would return from his epic expedition and confer with Thomas Jefferson in the White House, astonishing the president with William Clark's "memory map," drawn to within 1 percent accuracy for distance. To qualify as a "settled area," the land needed six people or more per square mile, all "tax-paying non-Indians."

In 1800 the frontier began along the crest of the Appalachian Mountains. In 1810 it retreated west beyond the Ohio River Valley. In 1850 it lay entirely west of the Mississippi River. By 1880 it began in western Nebraska and Kansas. And in 1890, a century after the census began, the map showed no more frontier, due in large part to a growing spider-work of railroads and, according to the census, "to towns and cities that occur regularly enough to disrupt the appearance of a clear, unbroken line separating the generally settled area from the frontier." In effect, the American frontier was gone. The land was settled.

What did this mean?

Prior to 1890 there had always been another horizon to chase, a new field to plow, a valley to settle, virgin forests to fell. This "next ridge syndrome," as some historians have called it, gave Americans a great sense of opportunity, even urgency, as they moved west. While some wanted to just "get by," many wanted to "get rich." How exactly? "Dishonestly if we can; honestly if we must," wrote Mark Twain in a scathing newspaper essay lamenting the loss of morality in America.

More than a few thinkers, writers, artists, and educators deplored the elimination of wilderness from the American landscape, but they did little to stop it. The economic juggernaut was too powerful and immense, always expanding, growing and feeding on everything, including itself. Americans routinely patted themselves on the back with one hand while swinging an axe with the other, convinced they were doing the right thing, making the world a better place, a utopia perhaps, Thomas Jefferson's pastoral ideal, a place without poverty and hunger.

MORE THAN one hundred years earlier, political economist Adam Smith had introduced his notion of "the invisible hand of the market"—each man out to maximize his own gains would benefit society as a whole. This central justification of laissez-faire economic philosophy said self-interest would generate socially desirable ends through fair competition, lower costs, and better markets. Vigorous Economic Growth Forever became the great American secular religion. Never mind that the world was only so big, or that economies grow while ecosystems do not. Economists would find a way around that.

John Muir called it the "gobble, gobble school of economics," and added that "nothing dollarable is safe."

Muir's fellow critic Mark Twain was more sarcastic and direct: "Money is God. Gold and greenbacks and stock—father, son, and the ghost of the same—three persons in one: these are the true and only God, mighty and supreme."

While Mark Twain wrote his best novels in the 1880s and would later have financial difficulties of his own, John Muir amassed significant wealth getting his hands dirty growing and selling fruit. By the end of 1890, back from Alaska, with the national park campaigns behind him, according to historian Donald Worster,

> [Muir] wanted to spend the remainder of his days teaching Americans to take a new attitude toward nature. He hoped to bring greed under the control of ethics, aesthetics, and enlightened self-interest, and his strategy for doing so was to join the movement to conserve nature and natural resources, one of the great reforms of the so-called "Gilded Age" that Twain neither acknowledged nor appreciated.

IN 1891, with urging from influential members of the Boone and Crocket Club (a New York City–based organization of gentlemen hunter/naturalists founded by Theodore Roosevelt and George Bird Grinnell), an amendment to a general land law glided through Congress authorizing the president to create "forest reserves" by withdrawing federal land from public domain. President Benjamin Harrison immediately put the law to work.

In May of 1892, two professors at the University of California, Berkeley, organized a meeting in an attorney's office in San Francisco and sent out invitations "for the purpose of forming a 'Sierra Club.' Mr. John Muir will preside." They would model themselves after the Appalachian Mountain Club. While Muir typically shied away from formal leadership, he accepted the title of president, a position he would hold the rest of his life. He returned home ecstatic, where a supper guest said, "I had never seen Mr. Muir so animated or happy before. Hitherto, his back to the wall, he had carried on his fight to save the wilderness. In the Sierra Club he saw the crystallization of the dreams and labor of a lifetime."

In less than a month the Sierra Club was fighting a bill financed by the timber industry to open more forests to commercial logging by reducing the boundaries of Yosemite National Park. Muir complained, "this formal, legal, un-wild work is out of my line." But the stakes were too high for him to ignore. This was his new life: making appointments, calling meetings, writing letters, winning votes. The glaciers of Alaska would have to wait.

Soon Muir's little club had two-hundred-plus members and was on its way to becoming one of the largest and most effective conservation organizations in the world. Muir would exhort his troops to marshal on, for this was the good fight, "part of the eternal conflict between right and wrong, and we cannot expect to see the end of it." This, too, was a war about moral justice, one worth fighting. For John Muir, the greedy destruction of the natural world was just as criminal as slavery, perhaps more so.

Rudolf Diesel patented his new internal combustion engine that same year; Walt Whitman and Alfred Lord Tennyson, two literary giants, died. Tchaikovsky wrote *The Nutcracker*, and a Swedish physicist/chemist

named Svante Arrhenius began to speculate on the "hydrocarbon problem": the worldwide effects of burning coal, and later, oil. He spoke of
Europeans "evaporating our coal mines into the air" since the beginning
of the Industrial Revolution in the early 1700s. Would such burning,
increasing every year with population and industrialization around the
world, add to the amount of carbon dioxide (CO_2) in the atmosphere?
And would that atmospheric CO_2 act as a greenhouse gas to trap long-
wave solar energy (as heat) and raise the surface temperature of the Earth?

Arrhenius thought it might.

HARRY FIELDING REID returned to Glacier Bay that summer and
occupied Camp Muir for two months, the cabin still standing. Accompanied by two hired hands, he explored the west arm of the bay where John
Muir, S. Hall Young, and five Tlingits traveled by canoe in 1879. Since
then, Grand Pacific Glacier had retreated roughly four miles on its eastern face to unveil most of Russell Island, and eight miles on its western
flank, where it had separated into a second glacier that Reid named for his
alma mater, Johns Hopkins University.

The trip was not without adventure. Reid and his party lost their boat
three times to twenty-foot tides that floated it away; each time somebody
had to swim for it in ice-choked waters barely above freezing. The rain
seldom relented. "It is now half-past nine and raining pretty hard," Reid
wrote. "We have concluded that there are many infallible signs of rain in
this region. If the sun shines, if the stars appear, if there are clouds or if
there are none; these are all sure indications. If the barometer falls, it will
rain; if the barometer rises, it will rain; if the barometer remains steady, it
will continue to rain."

Schooled in math and physics but deeply interested in the dynamics
of glaciers, Reid created dozens of detailed sketches, made many photographs, and over time would produce twenty-four notebooks of his fieldwork in Glacier Bay. He closely measured the rates of ice flow, and he
developed a theory on how tidewater glaciers maintained their terminal
shapes while losing mass. He explored areas of ice loss along the eastern
flank of Muir Glacier (that would one day open into Adams Inlet) and

Inspired by the writings of John Muir, many scientists and photographers visited Glacier Bay in the 1880s and 1890s, documenting the positions of glaciers. They created records that today are an important contribution to our understanding of glacial history in Alaska.
PHOTO COURTESY OF THE NATIONAL SNOW AND ICE DATA CENTER

did measurements on rates of flow that disagreed so widely with G. F. Wright's work of 1886 that Reid called them "irreconcilable . . . either that one set [of measurements] was in error or that there was a remarkable change in the motion of the glacier between our visits."

Reid consulted with Captain Carroll, who visited Muir Glacier every summer. Carroll said, "For the years 1890, 1891, and 1892 there was more ice coming from Muir Glacier than there was in any of the seven years previous to 1890. I never saw so much ice coming from the glacier, before or since, as there was in that year (1890)."

We can imagine Reid applying his mathematical mind to the dynamics of Muir Glacier, any glacier for that matter. Why did rivers of ice retreat and advance at inconsistent rates, speed up, slow down, speed up again? Did it have to do with weather, climate, topography, bathymetry?

Why did tidewater glaciers actively calve ice on some days but not on others? Did it have to do with temperature, tides, rainfall? Did ice waves pulse through a glacier? If so, at what speed? And what propagated them? Why did glaciers rule much of the terrestrial high latitudes long ago, cover most of Canada and mainland Europe, then retreat only to advance again, and retreat again, and advance and retreat over and over many times? Why these cycles? These oscillations?

What excited Reid and other scientists about glaciers was elemental: They were beautiful, dynamic, mysterious, and perhaps sensitive; they responded to things we couldn't see or fully understand. They had their own language, rhythms, and behavior; their own secrets to tell. Secrets about our world and how it worked. Secrets too compelling to ignore.

ONE THING was certain, John Muir and his glacier had changed America's image of Alaska from one of a frozen wasteland to that of a shimmering beauty. Aside from Muir himself, no single person was more responsible for this than Captain James Carroll. Already successful at transporting fish, lumber, mining equipment, gold ore, and liquor (most of it smuggled) between the Pacific Northwest and Alaska, Carroll had read Muir's early magazine stories of Glacier Bay, consulted with Muir, and decided to add excursionists to his list.

When in July 1883 he sailed the steamship *Idaho* into Glacier Bay, bringing people face-to-face with a living ice age, landing them on shore and naming the great gleaming glacier for John Muir, he effectively launched a new industry in Alaska: tourism. A little more than a century later, Southeast Alaska, crowned by Glacier Bay with its glaciers, whales, and bears, would be the most popular cruise ship destination *in the world*, with some vessels carrying as many as four thousand people.

In 1884 Carroll steered the side-wheel steamer *Ancon* into Glacier Bay but the paddle wheels got "badly smashed" by the floating ice. Thereafter he mostly used the magnificent 330-foot *Queen*. Historian Theodore Catton would write, Captain Carroll, "brought more excursionists in subsequent years, and built a small dock in Muir Inlet and boardwalk over the moraine to the glacier's surface . . ." where guests could climb up and walk atop the ice river dressed in their Victorian finery. By the early 1890s,

> [T]he Pacific Coast Steamship Company had three vessels, George W. Elder, City of Topeka, and Queen, sailing fortnightly from Tacoma and Portland to southeast Alaska during the excursion season of May through September. The package tour included a night in Victoria, followed by twelve days on the steamer. The highlight of the trip was Glacier Bay where the excursionists came "face to face with Muir Glacier."

According to author/photographer Dave Bohn, Captain Carroll was noted as a genial host who "constantly regaled his passengers with stories of the bay and his narrow escapes from collisions with icebergs . . ."

When Carroll picked up Harry Fielding Reid at Camp Muir in September 1892, Reid told him about the retreat of Grand Pacific Glacier in the west arm of the bay, Russell Island emerging from under the ice, and Johns Hopkins Glacier, once a tributary of Grand Pacific, now spilling down from the highest peaks of the Fairweather Range, standing on its own and calving ice like crazy. Always up for an adventure, Carroll sailed the *Queen* into uncharted waters, naming today's Queen and Rendu Inlets, and proving, according to Catton, "that large passenger vessels could maneuver in the confining fiords."

Missing on the *Queen* that trip was one of Captain Carroll's favorite guests, journalist/adventurer Eliza Scidmore, who at age twenty-six first sailed with him to Glacier Bay on the momentous trip of July 1883, and again in 1884, and three more times after that. She would become the first female writer/editor at a new magazine called *National Geographic*, and over the next four decades she would travel the world, living at times in Switzerland and Japan. Her writings had done much—second only to John Muir—to warm the American public to a new, inviting Alaska.

At Muir Glacier she had written:

> *The crashes of falling ice were magnificent at that point and in the face of keen wind that blew over the icefield we sat on the rocks and*

97

From about 1,800 feet up the western slope of Mount Wright, Muir Glacier in 1893 makes an impressive sight. Over the next one hundred years it will retreat thirty-plus miles. The site of Muir's cabin, built in 1890, is barely visible far below, near where icebergs are stranded on Muir Point.

MUIR GLACIER

272 MUIR GLACIER, ALASKA

A steamship off Muir Glacier. The adjacent slopes, recently deglaciated in
1896 when this photo was taken, are today covered in a forest dominated by
Sitka spruce.

Summer tourists stand atop Muir Glacier enjoying what journalist Eliza Scidmore called "the wondrous scene."

watched the wondrous scene. The gloomy sky seemed to heighten the grandeur, and billows of gray mist, pouring over the mountains on either side, intensified the sense of awe and mystery.

On her final trip in 1891, she had occupied the cabin at Camp Muir (the summer after it was built) and brought a female companion, an artist, a sportsman, a small boy and his dog, a Russian hunter, and a maid. All were awakened by icefalls throughout the night. And every day, Scidmore filled her journal with vivid impressions.

She wasn't alone. Sometime in the mid-1880s Muir Glacier had been established as a wonder of the world, and according to Dave Bohn, "descriptions of it became more and more complicated and ponderous. In other words, Scidmore's evaluations had been mild and straightforward compared to what followed."

Alaska was for sale and other steamship companies were about to cash in, if they could. But this was nothing compared to the rush that would soon transform Alaska forever, when gold was discovered on the Klondike River, an upper tributary of the mighty Yukon that flowed 1,400 miles from Canada across Alaska into the Bering Sea.

But that was later. By this point Alaska remained in the past, an afterimage of the ice age, beautiful, alluring, but in the past nonetheless. Though it had tough competition: the future.

——◆——

NOWHERE was America's industrial optimism and emerging exceptionalism on greater display than in Chicago in the summer of 1893, at the World's Columbian Exposition to commemorate four hundred years of progress since the European discovery of the New World. The "Chicago World's Fair," as it was called, introduced people to a new sandwich called a hamburger, a new music called ragtime (played by young pianist Scott Joplin), and a belly dancer named "Little Egypt" doing the hootchy-kootchy. People could ride camels, donkeys, and a breathtaking, 264-foot-tall new machine called a Ferris wheel.

A dazzling blend of education and entertainment, the fair rose like a dream on the shore of Lake Michigan, a city within itself, the so-called

"White City," as many of the buildings were made of white stucco and designed the way a city should be, said architect Daniel Burnham. Along with landscape architect Frederick Law Olmstead, cocreator of New York City's Central Park, Burnham aimed for the beaux arts principles of design, using French neoclassical architecture based on symmetry, balance, and splendor. Covering more than 600 acres with 200 buildings, canals, and lagoons, and hosting 50,000 exhibits from 46 nations, the fair was magic. More than twenty-seven million people attended from May through October.

One of them was John Muir.

Dear Louie . . . I have been at the [World's] Fair every day, and have seen the best of it, though months would be required to see it all.

You know I called it a 'cosmopolitan rat's nest,' containing much rubbish and commonplace stuff as well as things novel and precious. Well, now that I have seen it, it seems just a rat's nest still, and what do you think was the first thing I saw when I entered the nearest of the huge buildings? A high rat's nest in a glass case about eight feet square, with stuffed wood rats looking out from the mass of sticks and leaves, etc., natural as life. So you see, as usual, I am "always right."

I most enjoyed the art galleries. There are about eighteen acres of paintings by every nation under the sun, and I wandered and gazed until I was ready to fall down from utter exhaustion . . . The view outside the buildings is grand and also beautiful . . . Last night the buildings and terraces and fountains along the canals were illuminated by tens of thousands of electric lights arranged along miles of lines of gables, domes, and cornices, with glorious effect . . ."

He went on to say how much he wished Louie and the girls could be with him, though little Helen, always frail, might "have been made sick with excitement . . ."

This was the new world, illuminated not by General Electric's prohibitively expensive direct current, but by Nikola Tesla's alternate current, made available by George Westinghouse at less than one-fourth the cost. For many people who attended the Chicago World's Fair, it became a touchstone they would remember the rest of their lives, informing their values and faith in the future. Among them were a young L. Frank Baum, who'd one day create an Emerald City in the Land of Oz, and Walt Disney, who'd create his theme parks, and Henry Ford, who upon seeing an internal combustion engine dreamed of creating something truly outrageous: a horseless carriage affordable for the average man, one per family, maybe two.

Miles away, in the brown Chicago tenements, soot-faced children collapsed after working fourteen hours a day, six days a week, in coal-fired factories and meatpacking plants.

A smallpox epidemic originated at the fair and spread through the city; it coincided with an economic panic with working-class people sinking into urban poverty and starving in the streets—not just in Chicago, but in gritty, dirty cities around the country—all while corporate captains gained wealth and power. Two days before the fair ended, the mayor of Chicago was assassinated, and the closing ceremonies became a memorial. Then a fire swept through the fairgrounds (started by disgruntled workers) and destroyed most of the buildings.

Nowhere in the entire fair was there a single tribute to wild nature, or any overt mention of the "cost" of four hundred years of progress, as though there was none. Nowhere was there an accounting of the continent-wide destruction of habitat and wildlife, the poisoning of water and soil, the displacement of rich cultures, entire nations; the fencing of open space. One man, however, a young historian named Frederick Jackson Turner, as bold and original as Thoreau forty-two years earlier, did present a thesis that would have scholars talking for a long time: *With the American frontier gone,* Turner asked, *who are we? What will we become?*

John Muir caught a train to New York City, so he missed Turner's presentation. Had he heard it, we can only imagine the letter he would have written to Louie.

CHAPTER EIGHT

that masterful grasp of material things

FREDERICK JACKSON TURNER, thirty-one years old, fiercely intelligent, neatly dressed, and wearing a nicely trimmed moustache, looked every bit the young academic when he stood before the American Historical Association's annual meeting at the Chicago World's Fair. He was there to deliver a provocative essay he called, "The Significance of the Frontier in American History"; today, it is known simply as "Turner's Frontier Thesis."

Born to a newspaper family in Portage, Wisconsin, Turner had no doubt walked the same muddy boardwalk streets in his youth as John Muir did after Muir's father gave up farming and moved his family there. Turner had earned his doctorate in history from Johns Hopkins University and returned to Madison to begin teaching at the University of Wisconsin. He would later move east to Harvard and there finish his academic career.

The West, not the East, he said, was where the unique American character was forged in a fluid, exciting margin between civilized settlement and savage wilderness. Here a new citizen emerged, as if by alchemy, made of strength and individuality, a can-do spirit and resourcefulness that would color the world. The farther west the American moved, Turner said, the less he relied on European traditions, institutions, and ideas. Here, in the mountains, canyons, deserts, grasslands, and plains were golden opportunities masquerading as insurmountable problems.

Early in his thesis, Turner quoted John C. Calhoun's 1817 appraisal of a young United States, "We are great, and rapidly—I was about to say fearfully—growing!" Where better to grow and expand than to the west.

"So long as free land exists," Turner said, meaning the frontier, "the opportunity for a competency exists, and economic power secures political power. But the democracy born of free land, strong in selfishness and individualism, intolerant of administrative experience and education, and pressing individual liberty beyond its proper bounds, has its dangers as well as its benefits."

Free land doesn't last forever. Frontiers close, they disappear, as this one had, in 1890. The bottomless basket had a bottom after all. Turner asked: Would the best of America disappear with it, "that practical, inventive turn of mind, quick to find expedients; that masterful grasp of material things, lacking in the artistic but powerful to effect great ends; that restless nervous energy . . .?"

WHILE TURNER and his academic colleagues looked west, John Muir went east by train to New York City. He was astounded at the receptions he received by creative, inventive, intelligent people, most of them wealthy; they treated him as a peer, a celebrity, even. This was a far cry from his penniless walk to the Gulf of Mexico when he slept on the ground and befriended former slaves. Now, bathed in adulation, he wrote to Louie, "I had no idea that I was so well known considering how little I have written."

Robert Underwood Johnson, prestigious editor of *Century* magazine, who in Muir's later life had become what Jeanne Carr was in his earlier life—Muir's ambassador to the learned world—ushered Muir from one social gathering to another: dinners and parties in Washington Square, West Point, and Gramercy Park; animated, impromptu meetings in the offices of *Century*, where Muir thought he'd do some writing but was too busy to do so. Everywhere he regaled listeners with stories garnished with his Scottish accent, most notably his adventure with the little dog, Stickeen, on the Brady Glacier. As the story progressed, audiences would grow to where hotel and restaurant staff would tarry and listen from behind serving doors, not wanting to miss a word.

Muir met John Burroughs, the celebrated nature writer, and found in him a kindred spirit, a lover of botany and birds, white-haired and white-bearded like himself. The "two Johnnies" they'd be called six years later on a remarkable journey north, Burroughs's first and only trip to Alaska, Muir's seventh and last.

Muir also met Nikola Tesla (in his laboratory), Mark Twain, Rudyard Kipling, and lumber merchant James Pinchot and his son Gifford, who'd recently returned home from studying forestry in Europe. An ambitious young man, then age twenty-seven, with his own emerging ideas about conservation, Gifford Pinchot would soon antagonize Muir unlike anybody else had.

With a little free time, Muir squirreled himself off to Central Park. He found glacial erratics there that thrilled him; some were marked by striations, like the granite boulders of the High Sierra he'd once used to deduce the geologic processes that shaped Yosemite Valley. Obviously, a glacier had once occupied the Hudson River Valley, flowing from north to south, and must have terminated far down the valley.

From New York, Johnson ushered his prized author to Boston for more dinners and stories among the intellectual elite: scientists, professors, historians, authors, and philosophers. In Concord, as if on a pilgrimage, Muir visited the gravesites of Emerson and Thoreau, and he made his way to Walden Pond, where in the mid-1840s Thoreau had renounced the commercial serfdom of civilization and lived alone for twenty-six months. "I'd rather sit on a pumpkin and have it all to myself," Thoreau had said, "than be crowded on a velvet cushion."

Nearly fifty years later, the pumpkin was still there; Muir loved it, the relative tranquility, the power of Thoreau's words, ideas, and deeds. Unlike Emerson and Thoreau and most of the distinguished people he'd met on this trip east, Muir had never received a formal school education. He had had the Bible pounded into him by his father, and he'd learned to read literature at his mother's side, which he did with great intensity. Now he would embark on his next big challenge: to be a good writer.

It didn't come easy. Crumpled pieces of manuscripts often littered his "scribble den" in his Martinez home as he worked and reworked a paragraph. His magazine pieces had proven wildly successful, first in the *Overland Monthly* in the 1870s, with feature articles on his early theories on glaciology, and later in *Century*, in the 1890s, as a voice for wild lands appreciation and conservation. *Now it was time to write a book,* Johnson told Muir. *You have it in you. Cobble together your early magazine work and field notes, and some new material.* Muir wanted to spend more time in Concord, but his companions whisked him away, not without irony—Emerson had been whisked away from Muir's company in a sequoia grove twenty-two years earlier.

He crossed the Atlantic for the first time since coming to America in 1849, landed in Liverpool, and headed straight for Edinburgh and Dunbar, his homecoming, keen on reclaiming his Scottish identity. The gray skies and blooming heather reminded him of Alaska, though not as wild—sans bears, wolves, mountains, and glaciers. He stayed in Dunbar for ten days, visited long-ago family friends who'd read his articles in *Century*, and walked the crumbling castle grounds and wild coast and breathed deeply the cool sea breeze. He wrote to Wanda, "The waves made . . . grand songs, the same old songs they sang to me in my childhood, and I seemed a boy again . . ."

In Grasmere village, in the Lake District of England, he visited the gravesite of William Wordsworth, buried next to his beloved sister, Dorothy. Again, deep emotions washed over Muir. He wrote in his journal of the poet's unpretentious resting place, the simple headstones while "maple, yew, pine and ash hold boughs over them. A robin came and sang on the maple as I stood with damp eyes and lump in my throat. What a pity it is that Wordsworth, with his fine feeling for nature, died without knowledge of the glacial gospel."

IF ANY ONE MAN could wear the mantle of first expressing the need for public lands that would belong to everybody and nobody, a new space to protect nature and renew the human spirit, it would not be a priest, a scientist, or a politician, but a poet: William Wordsworth. In 1805 he described the Lake District as a "sort of national property, in which every man has a right and interest who has an eye to perceive and a heart to enjoy."

Likewise in America, the first call for establishment and protection of public lands came from an artist, George Catlin. In 1832, while traveling up the Missouri River and witnessing depraved white men pay Mandan Indians whiskey money for buffalo hides, Catlin, his heart breaking, wrote of saving "by some great protecting policy of government . . . a magnificent park . . . A nation's park, containing man and beast, in all the wild and freshness of their nature's beauty."

Forty years later, we had Yellowstone. That was just the beginning. A century after that we'd have Earth Day, the Clean Air Act, the Clean Water Act, and, most remarkable of all, the Endangered Species Act.

As a young man Muir had written that all the inventors of letters "receive a thousand-fold more credit than they deserve. No amount of word-making will ever make a single soul to *know* these mountains . . . all that is required is exposure, and purity of material. The pure heart shall see God." This sentiment echoed the opening lines of *Tao Te Ching*: "The Tao that can be told is not the eternal Tao. The name that can be named is not the eternal name." And yet words did have undeniable influence and power. Jeanne Carr had said so, as had Emerson.

Standing at Wordsworth's simple headstone, Muir knew what he had to do. He had to write. Not write to say something, but write because he had something to say. Write to make things right, if only by small degrees. The world changed slowly, but it did change. It would be hard work, writing; he'd never shied away from hard work, physical, mental, spiritual. He'd been raised on it, toughened to it. And he'd prospered. He had to write, and write more after that . . . and more after that.

In mainland Europe he admired the Matterhorn in the Swiss Alps and loved seeing old people hiking alpine trails; he visited the haunts of Louis Agassiz and found evidence of glaciers in retreat as they were in America, the world appearing to warm up year by year. He spoke French so poorly, he said, "Even the dogs didn't understand it as I speak it and refuse to wag their tails at my 'Bon chien, bon chien.'"

In the Italian Alps, he carefully observed Lake Como "hemmed in by lofty sharp glaciated mountains . . . the depth [of the lake] is governed by the down-thrust of many small glaciers . . . not a single glacier is visible now from the lake . . . once there were hundreds." He marveled at the beautiful dark-eyed children and women who dressed with "exquisite taste."

Back in England, London flummoxed him with what biographer Donald Worster would describe as, "a synthetic wilderness of intricate streets, clubs, and social classes that he could not read or navigate . . . traveling alone, feeling like an inferior provincial in the seat of world empire, a Scots-American who belonged on the margins of civilization, Muir was eager to leave the place behind."

It was the same for him in all large cities. *Get away.*

He wrote to seven-year-old Helen that Westminster Abbey was "A grand church full of curious-looking, old fashioned people made out of stone," and the Tower of London was "a huge grim castle full of guns and swords and shields and armor and a thousand queer things I have no room to write about."

The famous Kew Gardens pleased him, especially in the warm hospitality of his old friend Sir Joseph Hooker. But he longed to be home. He recrossed the Atlantic, and after more time with his champion, Robert Underwood Johnson, and a quick visit to Washington, DC, to lobby for Yosemite, he took a train west and arrived in Martinez in mid-October. The fall harvest was easy work compared to pulling together his magazine articles and field notes and two new essays for his book.

As an editor Johnson rode him hard, telling him to steer away from rhapsody. And no manuscript left the house before being approved by Louie, his toughest critic.

Published in 1894 and called *The Mountains of California*, Muir's first book focused on the Sierra Nevada Range but also wandered, as the author once had, north to the glaciers and forests of Alaska. He wrote lyrically on the beauty of snow and ice, from the smallest snowflakes and ice crystals ("snowflowers") to the largest glacier ("a current of ice derived from snow"), how they shaped and reshaped the land, enriched the soil, fed the rivers, colored the meadow, and played a grand role in the great cycle and connectedness of all things.

We only need baptize ourselves in the glory of the natural world, he said, to see it and understand it, and from that understanding will come reverence and respect, an abiding regard, a deep peace. He encouraged readers to find joy and love in the wilderness, and to express it. He warned of entire worlds, millennia in the making, now disappearing before "the fire and steel of man."

Muir may have been the first naturalist to ascribe glacial retreat to global warming. He wrote:

The glaciers of Switzerland, like those of the Sierra, are mere wasting remnants of mighty ice-floods that once filled the great valleys and poured into the sea. So, also, are those of Norway, Asia, and South America. Even the grand continuous mantles of ice that still cover Greenland, Spitsbergen, Nova Zembla, Franz-Joseph Land, parts of Alaska, and the south polar region are shallowing and shrinking. Every glacier in the world is smaller than it once was. All the world is growing warmer . . .

In other words, he said, "the crop of snow-flowers is diminishing . . ." Where once it snowed, now it rained.

Muir made no pretense at being a neutral journalist. His first book was a paean to God's creation, a polemic to some degree, and a preview of things to come. According to biographer Linnie Marsh Wolfe, the book "met with immediate and far-reaching success. It rallied and solidified the conservation sentiment for the entire nation, leading directly to a new upsurge of determination to preserve the forests . . . It also aroused the opposition, and during the nineties the care and protection of the forest reserves became an increasingly sore problem."

In Washington, DC, commissions formed and lobbyists lobbied while out west corporations employed rackets of cover men to assert fake forest claims on large tracts that would be logged to the last tree. America was full of scoundrels, Mark Twain had warned. John Muir was about to learn just how full.

———

BUT PREMONITIONS came first. Early one June morning John had a sudden urge to return to Wisconsin to see his mother. This had happened before, with his father, in 1885, when Louie was pregnant with Helen. John felt that the old man was dying. Long separated from John's mother and the rest of the family so he could go evangelizing in Canada, Daniel Muir was old and frail and living with Joanna, the youngest of the Muir children. She had written to John, "He will not listen to reason . . . he must have his way about *every* thing."

For three months John traveled by stagecoach and rail, first to Yellowstone National Park, then Wisconsin to see his mother and siblings and other relations (for the first time in eighteen years), then to Kansas City, where Joanna had moved with her family. When John greeted his father, now enfeebled in bed, the old man didn't recognize him. John spoke "broad Scotch" and Daniel responded, "O yes, my dear wanderer." Joanna told John that earlier that year their father had expressed regrets about his harsh words and manner back when John was a boy. Daniel advised Joanna to treat her own children better than he'd treated his, raise them with devotion and love. A picture of forgiveness, John lay down beside the old preacher and held his hand for long hours, and he stood over him with six of his brothers and sisters, teary-eyed, when he died.

Now eleven years later his mother was dying. Nobody had to tell him, by letter or telegram. John just knew, as he had with his father. "Oh, John," his sister Sarah cried upon seeing him arrive in Portage, "surely God has sent you. Mother is terribly ill!" After half a day with John in her presence, telling her stories of his time in Scotland, she revived to where she could sit up. Soon John had her laughing. Feeling she was out of danger, he left for Harvard to receive an honorary degree. While back east, he received word that she had died in her sleep. He immediately returned home for her funeral.

Louie's mother had died the year before, leaving her parentless as well. Such a turn of fate. The onetime wanderer and tramp who befuddled his siblings with a casual disregard for money was now more financially solvent than all of them. He'd inherited a ranch and estate worth $235,000, much of it due to his hard labors and keen business acumen throughout the 1880s. He and Louie belonged to the landowning elite of the Alhambra Valley, but John was seldom there. He traveled often and campaigned hard for conservation.

Through his high-voltage magazine articles and leadership in the Sierra Club, his connections back east, and his influence on an important forestry commission tasked with surveying specific forests and making recommendations for their protection and use, John perched alone as the nation's preeminent voice in wild lands protection. When an editor at *Atlantic Monthly* asked Charles Sprague Sargent, Harvard botany professor and chairman of the Forestry Commission, who best to hire to write a series of articles on forest conservation, Sargent replied, "There is but one man in the United States who can do it justice, and his name is John Muir."

He was America's nature prophet, a bird with a song in his heart and thorn in his chest.

Soon after his mother's funeral, Muir met the Forestry Commission in Chicago. They traveled to Yellowstone, the Black Hills, Idaho, and Washington State, then Crater Lake, where they witnessed meadows devastated by sheep grazing; grasses and perennial flowers chewed down to nothing by "hoofed locusts," said Muir. In California they found entire mountains stripped of trees, blackened stumps as far as the eye could see; "the work of ruin going on." At the Grand Canyon, Muir cautioned Gifford Pinchot against killing a tarantula; it had as much right to be alive as they did.

At first the two men got along well. Each admired the other's love of the outdoors. Pinchot described Muir as "in his late fifties, tall, thin, cordial, and a most fascinating talker." An avid fisherman, Pinchot was amazed that Muir "never carried even a fishhook with him on his solitary explorations. He said fishing wasted too much time." Muir's role on the commission was in an ex officio capacity of his own choosing, but he had the ear and sympathy of Charles Sargent.

After much hard-nosed debate, a good portion of it between Pinchot and Sargent, the commission made its recommendations in early 1897 that 1) fraudulent timber and mining laws be repealed; 2) new forest reserves be established; 3) the nation's forests be managed scientifically (protected by the military or a new federal agency); and, 4) new national parks be established.

President Grover Cleveland responded by executive order and set aside twenty-one million acres of forest reserves in eight states in the American West.

According to Linnie Marsh Wolfe:

[T]he lumber, stock and mining syndicates . . . flew into a mighty rage. Wires sizzled with telegrams. Congress was bombarded with screaming "memorials" . . . The "Cowboy Senators," hearing from their masters, assembled in hysterical turmoil to undo this "outrage." Wildly they bleated that the whole idea was promoted by "a few zealots, Harvard professors, sentimentalists and impractical dreamers."

For two days they worked to impeach the outgoing president but dropped the matter when Congress recessed.

John Muir's 1897 article in *Atlantic Monthly* began: "The American Forests, however slighted by man, must surely have been a great delight to God; for they were the best he ever planted. The whole continent was a garden, and from the beginning it seemed favored above all the other wild parks and gardens of the globe."

Robert Underwood Johnson might have discouraged Muir to write such a rhapsodic lead, but according to biographer Gretel Ehrlich, Muir's rhapsody "turned to elegy and elegy to polemic in this smoldering essay."

Muir outlined his plan to save the forests of America, and ended: "Any fool can destroy trees. They cannot run away; and if they could, they would still be destroyed—chased and hunted down as long as fun or a dollar could be got out of their bark hides, branching horns, or magnificent bole backbones."

Muir found time to visit Alaska in the summers of 1896 and 1897, first traveling with Henry Fairfield Osborn of the American Museum of Natural History, and second with Charles Sargent and fellow botanist William M. Canby. Both times were on the steamer *Queen,* with Captain Carroll commanding. Both times included a visit to Glacier Bay, where Muir noted the terminus of his namesake glacier shrinking back each year. He offered lively lectures to the guests but rested as much as anything else, exhausted from his duties as an outspoken critic of "Those western corporations with their shady millions," as he'd written to Johnson . . . those moneymen that "seem invincible in the Senate. But the fight must go on!"

Gold fever was hot and heavy beginning the summer of 1897, help-ing to lift the nation out of a staggering depression. In July, steamships arrived in San Francisco and Tacoma carrying rags-to-riches prospec-tors with suitcases stuffed with gold. "GOLD, GOLD, GOLD, A Ton of Gold from the Klondike!" exclaimed one newspaper. Tens of thou-sands of men (and a few women) dropped their lives to go north and start over. Salesclerks left their counters, doctors left patients, preach-ers abandoned their pulpits. Within four days, a dozen members of the Seattle police force were headed north. The mayor of Seattle wired in his resignation, and a former Washington governor quit a senatorial race.

"North to Alaska, the Last Frontier," announced storefront signs. "North to the Future."

America suddenly had another frontier.

In heavy rains that summer, Muir visited the gold mines of Juneau and Douglas, near where he had camped in 1880 and later passed along his suspicions that gold could be found in great quantities. He was right. The Treadwell Mine alone was producing ten million dollars per year; Muir wanted none of it. He could have made millions, but to him all gold was fool's gold. In Skagway he watched desperate men—"a wild, discouraging mess"—struggle through the mud to make their way over the mountains and into the Klondike. The rush was on.

Homeward bound, Muir happened upon Gifford Pinchot in a Seattle hotel lobby and confronted him. The young forester, for whom forestry was not just a science but a religion (he always capitalized Forestry), had been quoted in newspapers saying that sheep grazing in Crater Lake did no substantial damage to the meadows, forests, and soils. Muir thrust the printed page in front of him and asked, "Are you correctly quoted here?"

Pinchot admitted he was.

"Then if that is the case," Muir said, his Scotch ire rising, "I don't want anything more to do with you. When you were in the Cascades last sum-mer, you yourself stated that the sheep did a great deal of harm."

From this single flash point, historians have mapped the beginning of a great rift in conservation in America. On the one side stood Pinchot with his tenets of utilitarianism, first articulated a century earlier by the

British philosopher and social reformer Jeremy Bentham, and summed up in the maxim, "The greatest good for the greatest number." Forests were to be *used,* Pinchot argued. The notion of a preserved wilderness was not compatible with productive forest management.

On the other side stood Muir with his preservation principle of "Let it be." Nobody can improve upon a tree. Need was one thing, but greed was something else. Follow the money. Who did the powerful speak for in America? The people, or themselves?

While Pinchot echoed political economist Adam Smith's belief that each man's self-interest would benefit those around him, Muir shook his head and echoed Thoreau: "A man is rich in proportion to the number of things he can afford to let alone." Pinchot winced at intangibles; Muir marveled in them. Where Pinchot saw economics, Muir saw aesthetics; where Pinchot saw lines, Muir saw cycles and flow, everything on its way to being something else. Where Pinchot capitalized Forestry, Muir capitalized Nature.

Where Pinchot saw trees as timber to be managed for the wise use and greatest benefit to the people, Muir saw trees as a forest temple of greater value left standing than felled. Each man begged the question: Who are the forests for? And each was about to discover that the other could be an effective publicist and formidable adversary.

In *Harper's Weekly*, Muir wrote,

> *Much is said on questions of this kind about "the greatest good for the greatest number" . . . but the greatest number is too often found to be number one. It is never the greatest number in the common meaning of the term that make the greatest noise and stir on questions mixed with money . . . Complaints are made in the name of poor settlers and miners, while the wealthy corporations are kept carefully hidden in the background.*

Businessmen, according to historian Stephen Fox, "were concealing their simple greed behind democratic sentiment. The public should not be deceived, said Muir; every acre of the remaining federal forest land not suitable for farming needed permanent protection."

A keen political player, Pinchot wanted a top job in Washington and more; he wanted personal control over the nation's forests. He befriended senators, representatives, and cabinet secretaries and would soon have direct access to the White House. Muir meanwhile had little appetite for politicking. He worked more as a writer and grassroots activist. Upon meeting a Pasadena banker (and amateur nature photographer) interested in joining the Sierra Club, Muir urged him to write to politicians and "make their lives wretched until they do what is right by the woods."

British statesman/historian Lord James Bryce had visited America and witnessed industrious men everywhere nearly drunk on the wholesale destruction of nature, busily building this and that. "Gentlemen," he pleaded,

why in heaven's name this haste? You have time enough. No enemy threatens you. No volcano will rise from beneath you. Ages and ages lie before you. Why sacrifice the present to the future, fancying that you will be happier when your fields teem with wealth and your cities with people? In Europe we have cities wealthier and more populous than yours, and we are not happy. You dream of your posterity; but your posterity will look back to yours as the golden age, and envy those who first burst into this silent splendid nature, who first lifted up their axes upon these tall trees and lined these waters with busy wharves. Why, then, seek to complete in a few decades what the other nations of the world took thousands of years . . .? Why do things rudely and ill which need to be done well, seeing that the welfare of your descendants may turn upon them? Why, in your hurry to subdue and utilize nature, squander her splendid gifts? Why allow the noxious weeds of Eastern politics to take root in your new soil, when by a little effort you might keep it pure? Why hasten the advent of that threatening day when the vacant spaces of the continent shall all have been filled, and the poverty or discontent of the older states shall find no outlet? You have opportunities such as mankind has never had before, and may never have again.

MUIR WAS TIRED and unwell and unable to fully rest at home, busy with obligations in his scribble den. The grippe was back. The bronchial cough, too. His second *Atlantic* article appeared in early 1898; it dismissed Pinchot's wise-use utilitarian argument as anything but wise. Muir was the point of the spear, "the authentic voice of conservation," Linnie Marsh Wolfe would say, "speaking high above the babel of tongues, clearing the public mind of commercial propaganda." His writing increased the *Atlantic*'s circulation "enormously," according to his editor, and would soon help to bring about policy change in President McKinley's Washington.

The son of immigrants, Muir was hardly ignorant about the hardscrabble life; he knew what it meant to go hungry and get his hands dirty, to sleep in winter clothes and slip on frozen boots. He acknowledged the abundance and richness of the New World, and the benefits that came from settling it, turning forests into fruit orchards and farms. But must we settle and cultivate it all? Let not selfish people subdue every acre beyond its ability to regenerate, he would say. To which Pinchot would agree.

But while Pinchot saw forests essentially as tree farms to be carefully managed, Muir did not. Forests to him were churches, some cathedrals, the best God ever made. If busy man can take one day a week and not work, and let deeper, greater values direct him, can he not take one seventh of the land and regard it differently as well, with greater honor and restraint? This "Sabbath for the Land," as writer Scott Russell Sanders would one day call it, was Muir's entire point. Why hurry our way into Heaven? It's right here before us.

Slow down. Look around. Nature's beauty is everywhere, as essential as bread.

Again, he needed mountain nourishment, and he got some with a summer jaunt through Canada, in some places picking up his old draft dodger's trail, followed by an autumn trip into the "leafy" Appalachians of North Carolina and Tennessee with his good botany friends Charles Sargent and William Canby. The South troubled him, to see it still on its knees and hardly reconstructed, more than thirty years after the Civil War.

A letter from Louie encouraged John to stop in Washington to speak with President McKinley or with whomever he might gain an audience.

"Think of the beautiful woods being left with nothing mightier than Pinchot's *little plan* between them and destruction," she pleaded. The daughter of a botanist and horticulturalist, Muir's wife was always more fond of flowers and trees than glaciers and rocks. John ended up going to Washington but hurried home by way of Florida and Texas; he was unaware that he'd soon receive two invitations that would give him unprecedented access into America's corridors of power: one industrial, the other political.

EDWARD H. HARRIMAN, America's so-called "New Colossus of Roads," president of the Union Pacific, Southern Pacific, and Illinois Central Railroads, the Pacific Mail Steamship Company, and Wells Fargo Express Company, was one of the wealthiest men in the United States at the close of the nineteenth century. Mustering all his energy in the last six years, he'd shaped a sloppy, haphazard national transportation system into a model of efficiency and profitability. But at a cost. Keep working like you are, his doctor said, and you'll be more rich than you already are, but you'll fall over dead of a heart attack. The doctor's advice: take a vacation, a sea cruise perhaps. Fine, Harriman said. Incapable of doing anything in a small way, he charted the steamship *George W. Elder* for the summer of 1899 and invited a "who's who" of America's top scientists, explorers, artists, natural historians, and writers to travel with him and his family and his servants.

His destination? The future, of course. Alaska.

PART THREE

1899–1906

CHAPTER NINE

author and student of glaciers

IN TRUTH, Harriman wanted to shoot a bear.

Promptly at twelve noon on May 30, 1899, his special train—"the most velvety and superb train I ever saw," said Muir—arrived in Seattle from New York. John Muir was there to greet him, having traveled up from California with Charles Keeler, a poet and director of the museum of the California Academy of Sciences. A smallish fifty-five-year-old man with a large ginger-colored moustache, Harriman had a high brow and keen, penetrating eyes. Somewhat cold, humorless, and aloof, he could make a poor first impression. But Muir would come to like him, even admire him. "To him I owe some of the most precious moments of my life," Muir would write.

Harriman had dropped out of school at age fourteen, gotten work in the New York Financial District, and skyrocketed from there on supreme talent, drive, and business sense.

Upon first hearing from his doctor that he should take a vacation, Harriman had considered a western hunting adventure, the kind made famous by Teddy Roosevelt in the Dakotas. Then came the even better idea of shooting a famous Alaska brown bear. And if he were already taking a trip to Alaska, why not go all out and make it a grand scientific expedition at his personal expense? Be a philanthropist like Andrew Carnegie.

In early March, rather than issue the invitations himself, Harriman paid an unannounced visit to Dr. C. Hart Merriam, head of the Biological Survey (today's US Fish & Wildlife Service). Blowing like a typhoon into Merriam's office, he told him his plan and asked Merriam if he would recruit scholars for the expedition party. Was this a prank? A man of science, not industry, Merriam had never heard of Harriman. A quick check proved he was real, and serious.

Follow-up meetings in Manhattan's Metropolitan Club and Washington's Cosmos Club quickly cemented the deal. Merriam's list included: William Healey Dall, paleontologist of the US Geological Survey; Bernhard Fernow, dean of the School of Forestry at Cornell; Henry Gannett, chief geographer of the US Geological Survey; Grove Karl Gilbert, geologist with the US Geological Survey; George Bird Grinnell, editor at *Forest and Stream;* Robert Ridgway, curator of birds at the US National Museum; William E. Ritter, president of the California Academy of Sciences; Frederick Colville, curator of the National Herbarium and botanist of the US Department of Agriculture; Edward Curtis, promising young Seattle photographer; Louis Agassiz Fuertes, bird artist; Frederick S. Dellenbaugh, landscape artist. And others.

When Muir first heard about the trip, he was skeptical and unwilling to accept any favors that would leave him indebted to a railroad czar. According to historians William H. Goetzmann and Kay Sloan:

> Only after Merriam explained that the voyage would explore areas of the Alaska coast that even the adventurous, well-traveled Muir had not seen did the seasoned explorer agree to sign on. Muir was not the only guest whose scientific credentials did not conform to the scientific mold. When the pastoral John Burroughs agreed to serve as the expedition's historian, he lent a sentimental appreciation of nature to the fact-finding mission of the scientists. Burroughs' many nature books had struck a receptive chord in the American public, and in 1899 he was a popular national figure.

While the scientists signed the ship's guest log as distinguished professors and heads of museums and scientific academies and government agencies, Burroughs signed in as "Ornithologist and Author"; Muir signed as an "Author and Student of Glaciers."

The two Johnnies resumed their friendship in Seattle. Only one year apart in age, with Burroughs grounded in the East, Muir in the West, they admired and needled each other. Muir felt Burroughs squandered his stature as America's most beloved nature writer by writing nothing about the destruction of America's forests and wild lands, and our collective responsibility to protect them. Chagrined at Muir's love of glaciers, Burroughs called him "Cold Storage Muir," and added, "He is a poet and almost a seer . . . He could not sit down in the corner of the landscape, as Thoreau did; he must have a continent for his playground."

Then would come the needle: "In John Muir we had an authority on glaciers, and a thorough one—so thorough that he would not allow the rest of the party to have an opinion on the subject." Deep into the expedition, Muir would tease and torment Burroughs about his homesickness and seasickness.

On the westbound train journey, Harriman and the highbrow scientists had devised a way to manage the expedition activities. An executive committee would be chaired by Harriman, followed by committees on routes and plans, zoology, botany, geology, mining, geography and geographic names, big game, lectures, library, literature and art, music, and entertainment. Muir would chair none of them. Despite his Alaska experience (exceeded only by that of William Dall), he remained something of what he'd always been, an outsider, a tramp.

THE *George W. Elder* departed Seattle on the last day of May 1899. In heavy seas she'd be called the "George W. Roller," and during lectures, a "floating university." At 1,709 tons and 250 feet long, 38 feet at the beam, black below and trimmed white above, she was a beauty. The ship was refurbished and outfitted at Harriman's expense with a piano and organ, packhorses and hunting rifles, a library containing more than five hundred volumes, and state-of-the-art audio and visual equipment. Below decks was a full wine and champagne cellar and a stable of animals (steers, sheep, turkeys, chickens, and a milk cow), should the hunting prove unsuccessful. Twin masts stood fore and aft, twice as tall as the central smokestack; lifeboats rested on the upper hurricane deck.

Beyond the scientific party of 25 were 2 photographers; 2 stenographers; 3 artists; 1 surgeon and his assistant; a trained nurse; a chaplain;

11 hunters, packers, and camp hands; Harriman and 13 others who were members of his extended family, or their servants; and 65 bridge officers, engineers, and crew, for a total compliment of 126.

The objective: sail the northwest coast from Seattle to Wrangell, Juneau, Glacier Bay, Yakutat Bay, Prince William Sound, Cook Inlet, Kodiak, the Aleutian Islands, the remote islands of Bering Sea, and the Russian Far East, and back, all while seeing, documenting, and learning as much as they could.

"All along the Alaska coast," Alaskan Nancy Lord would observe,

> there were distances to be measured, tree rings and fish streams to be counted, worms to be collected. There were Indians eating gull eggs and boiled marmot and Eskimos who paddled skin boats. And there were, all around, strange new vistas to admire, photograph, paint and describe . . . Who would not have begged to have been invited on such a trip, to witness Alaska at the century's cusp, when it and the world were still so new? When so much was possible? It was the age of innocence, still ruled by infectious Victorian optimism, and Alaska in 1899 was—and perhaps still is—a place of promise.

MUIR wasted no time befriending the five Harriman children. The three older girls, together with their cousin, he called the "Big Four"; the younger two boys, proudly dressed in their sailor suits, he called the "Little Two." Muir softened toward their father early in the trip upon seeing him play with little Roland, the youngest boy, "the Admiral," helping him pull a toy train across the spacious decks. The older boy, eight-year-old Averell, poised and self-assured, would one day become US ambassador to the Soviet Union, governor of New York, and one of President Kennedy's "Wise Men."

Something of a perennial child himself, filled with wonder, Muir was forever drawn to young people. During his epic 1879 Alaska canoe journey, when he slept on the ground and paddled in the rain and gloried in blue gleaming glaciers all around, he'd impressed Missionary Young and others when he helped nurse a Tlingit baby back to health with warm milk. And with his own girls, now teenagers (the "Big Two," he called them), he'd attended to their needs with love and sacrifice, especially little Helen, so frail at birth. While traveling he wrote as many letters to them as he did now to Louie.

In more recent years, each of his seven siblings had come to depend upon John for financial help and spiritual guidance. Even young Joanna, who'd once criticized him in a letter for saying he found God in the woods. ". . . you naughty bad boy!" she wrote. "What could the world in general do without churches and Sunday schools? You know that they who are not pure in heart cannot see God in his works, they see only sheep and firewood . . . So you must be good, and not talk like that anymore."

Now with the Harriman children as his new disciples, and still preaching his glacial gospel, John would offer this: "Kill as few of your fellow beings as possible and pursue some branch of natural history at least far enough to see Nature's harmony."

— ◆ —

VANCOUVER ISLAND made for a short but pleasant first port-of-call, where Dall and Grinnell found enough time to discover what they suspected was ancient woolly mammoth dung encased in deep shore ice. They hauled it aboard as the expedition's first specimen. As the ship moved north through Seymour Narrows everybody fell into casual routines of sightseeing and storytelling. Loquacious as ever, Muir found keen competition in the yarn-spinning department from Yale meteorologist William Brewer.

At Lowe Inlet, on the British Columbia coast, they visited a salmon cannery worked hard by local Indians and Chinese, and they walked through the temperate rain forest thick with understory and spongy moss, not a rewarding experience for the expedition artists who attempted to haul their cumbersome gear. They didn't get far.

With every nautical mile the ship moved north, the country got more wild and exciting, peopled here and there in little spores of civilization, nothing more, as if it were America all over again, a land of new beginnings. The misty mountains and green, shaggy forests seemed to go on forever, laced with deep inlets and dark-water fjords. Already it felt like a journey through time as much as space.

Not a churchgoing man, Muir made an exception on the Sunday he and his shipmates spent in New Metlakatla, on Annette Island, their first stop in Alaska. It was there that Muir's fellow Scot, a short, gray-bearded clergyman named William Duncan, had created what the ship's chaplain, Dr. George F. Nelson, described as a unique experiment in "civilizing the savages" that merged religion with capitalism. Formerly of the Episcopal Church of British Columbia, Duncan had gotten in trouble there after he refused to serve wine in the sacrament, saying the taste of alcohol would corrupt the childlike Indians. Refusing to conform, he left Canada with his flock and resettled on Annette Island to supervise the construction—and manage the profits—of a new church, salmon cannery, sawmill, schoolhouse, and town hall.

Grinnell wrote of the Indians:

Whatever they are today, Mr. Duncan has made them, and he himself and no other is responsible for the change in the individuals that have been born and lived and died, and still live in this colony during the period of his wise and beneficent influence over them. He has kept them by themselves, teaching them to live as the white man lives, and yet not letting the white man come in among them. They govern themselves in town-meeting fashion, consulting Mr. Duncan frequently as to what they ought to do.

Grinnell and the others, raised and schooled in Victorian America, enamored with imperialism and the Americanization of Indians, observed Duncan's accomplishments with fascination. They sat in the church with the Indians to hear Nelson's preamble followed by Duncan's fiery sermon.

Muir slipped away quickly to walk in the woods with Burroughs. Earlier in the trip, when Chaplain Nelson had offered a service in the saloon and few people showed up, Harriman had sent a ship's steward to herd the scientists and artists into service. The steward found the two Johnnies sunning themselves on an upper deck. "Well," Burroughs asked his friend, "are you going to obey orders?"

"No," Muir said, "I'll be damned if I do."

But Muir did love to sing. After emerging from a hymnal session down below, he ran into Burroughs, who'd been enjoying beautiful alpenglow topside from the bridge. "You ought to have been here fifteen minutes ago," Burroughs told Muir, "instead of singing hymns in the cabin."

"Aye," Muir fired back, "and you, Johnny, ought to have been up here fifteen years ago, instead of slumbering down there on the Hudson."

ALWAYS ready with an opinion, especially on matters of natural history, Muir antagonized those around him even more than they antagonized him. Jeanne Carr had introduced him thirty years ago by saying, "He is as modest as he is gifted." But he was sixty-one now, more like his proselytizing father than he probably cared to admit, a battle-hardened activist who wouldn't hold his tongue in the company of educated men who offered no hard position on conservation, though they considered themselves conservationists; or worse, in the company of greedy men everywhere who, while deaf to the forest music of birds and trees, could hear a dollar bill fall on pavement.

Muir worried aloud that gold prospecting—followed by large-scale industrial mining—would soon despoil Alaska as it had California, ravage streams and mountainsides, poison water, and bring out the worst in men.

According to historians Goetzmann and Sloan, the Harriman Expedition sailed in "an age of strange binocular vision that was at times replete with irony;" the participants "saw two Alaskas—one, the stunning, pristine land of forests and mountains and magnificent glaciers, the other, a last frontier being invaded by greedy, rapacious, and sometimes pathetic men, often living out a false dream of success."

Muir would echo Thoreau by writing of "A fearful smell, a big, greasy cannery," and claiming, "Men in the business are themselves canned."

Himself a study in contrasts, Muir could be playful too, as in Wrangell, when he spotted botanist Alton Saunders probing along Tlingit dugout canoes at low tide, hunting for algae specimens. "Seaweed Saunders," he called him.

Muir's cabinmate, California poet Charles Keeler, described Wrangell as a "dirty, miserable" town. But his spirits brightened—everybody's did—when the ship transited Wrangell Narrows and offered clear views of Patterson Glacier spilling down from the Stikine Icefield. But here again Muir irritated his shipmates by boasting in yet another spontaneous lecture that what they were seeing was nothing compared to what awaited them: his own glacier, Muir Glacier, nestled in Glacier Bay, so large it contained more ice than all the glaciers in Switzerland *combined*.

PRIOR to their arrival in Juneau, the Harriman participants heard an onboard lecture from Coloradoan Walter Devereux on mining technology, how new equipment enabled companies to extract world-famous profits—three to four dollars per ton of rock—from previously low-grade, gold-bearing quartz. Juneau had roughly two thousand residents, most of them Indians, and was growing fast. In another seven years it would become the territorial capital of Alaska. A few gift shops catered to the expeditioners, while across Gastineau Channel, in the town of Douglas, the Treadwell Mine boomed and thundered. At one point a single blast was so loud that Dellenbaugh, in his stateroom, thought somebody had fired a cannon on the upper deck. Upon visiting the mine, he and his shipmates found it unbearable, the miners so far below, miniscule, at times knee-deep in water and mud, toiling hard for three dollars a day while the corporation made millions. And the noise, the dust, the filth . . .

Many in the Harriman party left early. Some were stunned and saddened to see men ravaging the forest and despoiling clean water for a soft yellow metal that made nice jewelry and not much else. It was as disheartening as the destructive millinery industry in the eastern states, where men killed egrets and robbed heron rookeries by the thousands for feathers to make fashionable women's hats. Among well-educated men such as these, more than a few burdened by an ecological conscience, it triggered questions asked to this day: When does an environmental issue become a social justice issue? And who writes the definitions of progress?

UP LYNN CANAL, the gold-fevered boomtown Skagway offered further testimony to the transformational power of gold. Here every man was for himself. No corporation, no big boss, no steady paycheck, small though it may be. Men dreamed big as they slogged their way over the mountains, following great silt-laden rivers into the interiors of Canada and Alaska. Two years before, as news of "Gold in the Klondike" had burst upon the world, all the best claims were already staked. Still, men came. Fathers, brothers, and sons, a young writer named Jack London, a future shoe and clothing merchant named John Nordstrom.

Finding no good color in the Klondike, many would move on to other promising strikes in Fairbanks, Kantishna, Eagle, Iditarod, and finally Nome. Rumors said gold nuggets lay scattered in Nome like confetti on the beaches of the Bering Sea. Those in Skagway who fared best mined the miners: clothing and equipment merchants, boot repairmen, saloon and hotel owners, prostitutes, and scoundrels. A wild, unruly town where street boys shouted out hotel costs and women flaunted themselves in billowy "bicycle suits," Skagway was nothing like Metlakatla. John Burroughs and others stared with astonishment through their eastern sensibilities.

John Muir dreaded seeing Skagway again but also looked forward to a reunion with his friend, S. Hall Young, whom he last saw here in 1897. With so much depravity found in gold-rush towns, Young felt his calling was to move north to help protect downtrodden Tlingits and other victims indentured into semi-servitude by gold fever, many toiling in the rutted streets or lawless slipshod businesses for low wages and no respect. Muir had described the scene to Young as "a nest of ants taken into a strange country and stirred up by a stick," an impression that remained unchanged, though Skagway was larger and slightly more orderly than before.

The narrow-gauge White Pass Railroad had been completed to the top of the pass, and Harriman secured passage for himself and his distinguished guests. As the little train chugged upslope, the tracks biting into bedrock, Burroughs noted how recent dynamite blasting had revealed the "ribs of the earth." Soon the railroad would reach all the way to Lake Bennett, providing a much easier and safer route into the Klondike. But by then the rush would be over; Nome would be the new El Dorado.

On the return downhill trip, the train passengers witnessed solitary stampeders trudging upslope, burdened by massive packs, their expressions tired, wistful. Only just beginning and late for any promise of gold, they put one foot in front of the other and climbed nonetheless into the great unknown with their thinning hopes for a better life.

While the entire scene disgusted Muir, the contemplative Dall puffed away on his pipe and predicted that the railroad, while late for the gold rush, would one day contribute to another economic boom: tourism. People will come to Alaska in great numbers, he said, to see the country, the history, the authenticity. Gannett agreed: "Alaska's grandeur is more valuable than gold or the fish or the timber, for it will never be exhausted. This value, measured by direct returns in money received from tourists, will be enormous."

Gannett further wrote:

There is one word of caution and advice to be given those intending to visit Alaska for pleasure, for sight-seeing. If you are old, go by all means; but if you are young, wait. The scenery of Alaska is much grander than anything else of the kind in the world, and it is not well to dull one's capacity for enjoyment by seeing the finest first.

For the one Yosemite of California, Gannett concluded, Alaska has hundreds. Little wonder that John Muir kept coming back.

—◦—

MUIR GLACIER was indeed large—its icy terminus roughly two hundred feet high and two miles across—and had a lot to say the day the *George W. Elder* arrived off its face to search for good anchorage. It thundered with massive icefalls and frightened the Harriman children. Burroughs described it as a "new kind of Niagara," saying nothing about the cheap commercialism that had recently defiled *the* Niagara Falls, a loss that could have been prevented had he worked to make it a national park, as Muir and Johnson had done with Yosemite. This was Muir's new political realism: In the face of gobble-gobble economics, Nature cannot take care of itself. It needs defenders. It needs strident writer-activists and activist-writers.

Muir noted that the tidewater face of his glacier had retreated about four miles since his first visit in 1879. If the terminus were to retreat to where it no longer had a stabilizing anchorage on an underwater recessional moraine at the mouth of Muir Inlet, then Muir Glacier would back off into deeper water, destabilize, and in years ahead enter a phase of catastrophic retreat and calve ice faster than it already was.

THE EXPEDITION spent five days in Glacier Bay, by far the most time in any one location. Harriman wanted to bag a bear. John Muir had just the place for him. "Howling Valley," he said with the rueful grin, where wolves howled by the hundreds and you'd find big game . . . magnificent bears and such. He'd traveled there alone and pulled a sled over his glacier, and found it so wild and healing that he'd kicked a bad bronchial cough. He'd also returned snow-blinded, bruised, hungry, and wet—information he did not share.

All business, Harriman took Muir's recommendation and organized a hunting party fit to slay a mammoth. Six packers left first, carrying camping and cooking equipment, followed by Harriman with Merriam and Grinnell and the ship's physician and his assistant, plus Captain Luther "Yellowstone" Kelly, a former cavalry scout for General Custer. All six men carried Winchester rifles.

As Muir watched them move over the icy terrain and shrink into the distance, other members of the expedition explored Camp Muir—the 1890 cabin still standing and in good shape—and walked the rudimentary boardwalks built over the moraine for the benefit of summer tourists. Eager to get the best photos possible, Edward Curtis used a canoe to access multiple angles and vistas. All that night, the glacier calved and the *George W. Roller* rocked everybody in and out of a fitful sleep.

The next day Muir hiked with the Harriman girls and regaled them with Alaska stories, while the indefatigable Curtis and his assistant canoed off the face of the glacier. Several times they paddled for their lives into massive percussion waves created by large calvings, their little boat rising cork-like over the crests, surrounded by floating ice, pieces large and small. To the astonishment of others watching, the two men

Edward Curtis's assistant approaches the tidewater face of Muir Glacier before a large icefall sends him rocking in June 1899.

PHOTO BY EDWARD CURTIS, COURTESY OF THE ALASKA STATE LIBRARY-HISTORICAL COLLECTIONS

survived; some of Curtis's large-format photographic plates, soaked in salt water, did not.

After twenty-four hours, the big-game hunters returned from Howling Valley exhausted, blistered, battered, cold, and—as Muir had hoped—empty-handed. Eighteen miles out and eighteen back. This would have bothered Muir little, if at all, were it not for the sight of Merriam, his benefactor, the gentleman-biologist who'd invited him on this expedition, hobbling down the beach, knees stiff by arthritis, hands cut and bruised by rock and ice. Muir and two others hurried out to take his pack and help him. That night the hunters fell into bed. Hearing of their woes, of the vast stretches of snow and ice, of them having to rope up to cross crevasses, and slipping and falling and sleeping hardly at all, and seeing no sign of bears or any other big game, Burroughs wondered if "all the howling" had been only in Muir's imagination.

At their farthest point out, the hunters had stood atop a ridge and looked into a valley silent and still. One hundred years later Alaskan Nancy Lord would write:

The comforts of the ship were far behind. The men were surrounded by wilderness still locked in winter, dangerous and unforgiving. I imagine a chill passing through them, through even the experienced packers and old scout. There was no romance to be found in the obscurity of white, in the cold. A person didn't stroll about here and admire the views; a person stood in awe, had to feel his smallness, his insignificance. He had to know there was something greater than himself, beyond all his control.

Perhaps this is what Muir wanted. In lieu of big game, let them find human smallness, humility. Not that he had mastered it himself. It was a journey, a lifetime endeavor, longer for some than for others. Of the hunters' failure, Muir would only write, "No bears, no bears, O Lord! No bears shot. What have thy servants done?"

Harriman would get his bear elsewhere.

The remaining three days in Glacier Bay found the expedition participants scattered about, eager in their pursuits. At Point Gustavus, in the lower bay, scientists collected birds and plants and were visited by Tlingits who taught them their own names for each species. In the upper bay, Curtis and Merriam photographed Tlingit sealing camps, Burroughs and Keeler climbed high for panoramic views; with help from Harriman's daughters, Gannett set up his plane table and made measurements. Dellenbaugh sketched a distant Mount Fairweather while Fuentes, the bird artist, hiked into a spruce forest in search of a bird he could hear but not see; it called and called, he said, like something out of a Grimm's fairy tale, pulling him deeper into another world.

Muir, Gilbert, and Harvard mineralogist Charles Palache (who'd been intrigued by the Treadwell Mine) hiked and camped on the glaciers of Hugh Miller and Reid Inlets, and no doubt talked geology; Muir, the least credentialed, did most of the talking. As the *George W. Elder* approached to pick them up, an amused Muir watched his shipmates stand atop an iceberg and wave, "wild to get on the steamer." Three days wasn't enough time in the wilderness for Muir, who in a letter to S. Hall Young would lament that he "longed to break away from the steamboat and its splendid company, get a dugout canoe and crew of Indians and, with you as my companion, poke into the nooks and crannies of the mountains and glaciers which we could not reach from the steamer."

MORE GLACIERS presented themselves in stunning majesty up the coast, first in Yakutat and Disenchantment Bays, where beneath the St. Elias Range, some of the highest coastal mountains in the world, Harriman failed again to get a bear, and in Prince William Sound, where again, no bear, but glaciers cascaded down from their mountain battlements. The expedition members named College Fjord and its many glaciers after their alma maters. Captain Doran consulted his chart and said the shore was solid bedrock and glaciers. Yet a thin dogleg inlet, visible from a certain angle, suddenly opened into a mysterious place no white man knew. Getting the 250-foot-long steamship in there would be a risk. A safety-minded guest-captain whom Harriman had invited on board agreed; it is not the purpose of a fine steamship to charge recklessly into "every little fish pond." One uncharted rock could sink the *George W. Elder* in less than

Tlingit sealers in their dugout canoe. Muir and other members of the 1899 Harriman Expedition admired the dignity and resourcefulness of the Huna Tlingit, and their connection to Glacier Bay as an ancient homeland.

COPYRIGHT
1899
E.H.HARRIMA

an hour. As if the physical world like the business world was his to will into obedience, Harriman insisted they push on. He'd take full responsibility. The rocks could move.

Like most of his gambles, this one paid off. The fjord was a magic kingdom of glaciers and peaks unknown and unnamed, ribbons of ice flowing from mountaintops into the sea. Dazzled and charmed, the scientists insisted that the new fjord, and the large glacier at its head, be named for their patron. It would be the expedition's most important discovery.

In time they left behind the tall coastal peaks of the Fairweather Range, and the St. Elias, Wrangell, and Chugach Mountains, and approached the long arc of the Aleutian Chain, known more for its fierce winds and live volcanoes than lofty realms of ice and snow.

On Kodiak Island, Harriman got his bear, more by guile than stealth. While several members of the expedition surrounded Harriman and waited at the bottom of a narrow draw with rifles, others above drove a mother bear and her cub into the trap. Harriman shot the oncoming mother, Yellowstone Kelly shot the cub, and everybody was happy, almost. Upon seeing the dead bears stuffed into a rowboat, Muir called them "mother and child."

Fourth of July in the little Russian-flavored town of Kodiak lifted spirits. The graphophone belted out John Philip Sousa's "Stars and Stripes Forever." Brewer spoke on America as a beacon for humanity and freedom around the world while Keeler, the iconoclastic poet and Muir's cabinmate, condemned recent acts of American imperialism. Canoe races followed, with much whooping and shouting. The entire time Muir sat apart and visited with an old mountaineer and glacier lover who'd sought him out to share stories.

Down the Alaska Peninsula and into the Bering Sea, the expedition headed for the mysterious Russian Far East, driven, many suspected, by Harriman's grand vision to build a tunnel under— if not a bridge across— the Bering Strait; to encircle the world with a railroad. Change "Seward's Icebox" into "Harriman's Crossroads." Now that he had his bear, it was time for Harriman to get back to railroads, venture capitalism at its best.

After visiting the Shumagin Islands and Bogoslof Island, they visited the Pribilofs, where the slaughter of northern fur seals brought to mind the fate of bison in the American West. The expedition then landed at Plover Bay, in Siberia, "the most barren and desolate place of its size," Merriam said he had ever seen. In ferocious winds beneath a gray, undertaker sky, he and his colleagues were greeted by an image from the Pleistocene: Chukchi in reindeer-skin parkas and sealskin boots, little changed from their ancestors of ten thousand years ago.

AFTER A SHORT VISIT to Port Clarence, their northernmost stop, the expedition turned south on July 13. While hiking on St. Lawrence Island, the Harriman girls shouted "Bears!" at white spots in the distance. Their father headed over the windswept tundra, shotgun ready, his dutiful hunting guides tagging along, only to discover the strange animals were swans. On St. Matthew Island, the expedition members found old sod houses and heard a story from William Dall about Russian hunters living through the winter there, going crazy, and killing each other.

Again and again, when members of the expedition returned from their hunting forays with dead birds or foxes, Muir was disheartened. In all his time in the Sierra Nevada, when he made many field trips over many years to learn about flowers, trees, and animals, he'd never killed a thing.

"I DON'T GIVE A DAMN if I never see any more scenery," Harriman grumbled as the *George W. Elder* passed the Fairweather Range en route south. Rather than take deck chairs facing the mountains, as others had, Harriman and his wife took a pair facing west, on the seaward side of the steamer. Merriam had sought him out to tell him about the view, the best of the trip. But by now the railroad man was missing his exciting world of big business and corporate deal-making. He wanted to be back in New York.

Despite his differences from John Muir, the two men had come to respect each other. After hearing of Muir's claim that he (Muir) was richer because he had all the money he'd ever want and Harriman did not, the railroad man found Muir one night after dinner to respond. "I never cared for money except as power for work," Harriman explained. "What I most enjoy is the power of creation, getting into partnership with Nature in doing good, helping to feed man and beast, and making everybody and everything a little better and happier."

Biographer/historian Donald Worster would write:

> [Harriman] did not accept the notion that there should be a limit to acquisitiveness, but he gave capitalism a moral purpose— promoting the welfare of both nature and humanity. His expanding railroad network, in his eyes, was intended to enhance the earth as well as make the nation bigger and better. Muir sensed that his host was quite sincere, and from that moment on, bear hunter though he might be, Harriman was seen as a well-meaning friend and potential ally of the conservation movement.

Critics feed on the rich, and Harriman was prime rib. Although the *New York Daily Tribune* called the trip "an entire success," Harriman's Alaska expedition would be seen by some as an escapade, a junket, a feasibility study for a grand railroad scheme. To prove otherwise, Harriman subsidized the production of thirteen scientific monographs. When the steamship docked in Seattle on July 30, having covered nearly 9,000 nautical miles in two months, parts of the expedition were just beginning. Many of the participants had much writing and summarizing to do; Merriam would spend the next dozen years organizing, compiling, and overseeing the publication of the monographs into the most comprehensive official report of its kind, a scientific treasure.

Discovered on the slopes of Mount Rainier and tagged to come along at the last moment by George Bird Grinnell, the young photographer Edward Curtis would become a giant in his field. Bernhard Fernow, the Cornell forester trained in Europe, as Pinchot had been, would be proven wrong when he predicted that the temperate rain forests of southeast Alaska, being so remote, would never be heavily harvested. One hundred years later, those same forests would be checker-boarded with clear-cuts, with some cuts down to the shoreline and along stream edges, leaving no buffer zones for salmon protection.

The single most significant contribution would be in glaciology, and it would come not from Muir but Grove Karl Gilbert, the tall, bearded, methodical scientist with the US Geological Survey. Like Muir, he was passionate about glaciers and glacial ice, but he expressed himself differently. Steeped with experience in the Rocky Mountains, he saw ice as an expression of water, and glaciology as another branch of hydrology. The temperature of the ocean, more than the air, he said, dictates the change in climate and behavior of coastal glaciers. Multiple causation was the key. Many small, complex sets of variables come into play with each glacier, some that cancel each other, some that compound each other, all of which can be seen only by the empirical observer. General theory, Gilbert said, should be applied with great caution. He even reconstructed an ice age landscape and performed experiments to determine how large masses of moving ice behaved in salt water. According to Goetzmann and Sloan, "Gilbert's work was really the exemplification of a team effort: he needed Harriman's boat and library; Gannett's maps; Muir's experience; and the photographs of Curtis, Merriam and others."

In the century ahead, not only would glaciers become living barometers in a changing world, but glacial ice itself would provide a looking glass into the past in ways not even Gilbert could predict.

As for John Muir, he'd never see Alaska again. Yet his influence in the American conservation movement had yet to peak. Soon, the new president would come calling.

CHAPTER TEN

bully

THEODORE ROOSEVELT had his own way of doing *everything*.

He became president of the United States in September 1901 when a crazed anarchist shot and killed President William McKinley in Buffalo. He had never cared much for McKinley, a tactless, ruthless man, but the assassin's act enraged Roosevelt as "an assault on representative government and civilized order," according to biographer Edmund Morris. Roosevelt had been a six-year-old boy when Abraham Lincoln was assassinated; he'd watched the funeral procession from his upper-story apartment window in New York City. Such a sight: thousands of somber people dressed in black, grieving the great man who'd preserved the union and freed the slaves. It made a strong impression on the boy, one he'd never forget.

Considering McKinley's assailant, and his own imminent ascent to supreme responsibility, Vice President Roosevelt claimed: "If it had been I who had been shot, he wouldn't have gotten away so easily . . . I'd have guzzled him first."

"Theodore Rex," writer Henry James would call the new president.

He'd grown up a sickly, asthmatic child, and overcame every obstacle, Roosevelt said of himself, by "practicing fearlessness."

He embraced life with both hands, both fists. "Experiences had flashed by him in such number," Morris would write of Roosevelt's early years, "that he was obviously destined to travel a larger landscape of life than were his fellows." At eighteen, he'd been a published author; at twenty-two a husband; at twenty-three a respected historian and New York State Assemblyman; at twenty-five a father and widower; at twenty-six a rancher, hunter, and horseman in the Dakotas; at twenty-seven a candidate for mayor of New York City; at twenty-eight a husband again; and at thirty a Civil Service Commissioner of the United States. "By then," Morris would add, "he was producing book after book, and child after child, and cultivating every scientist, politician, artist and intellectual of repute in Washington."

One of those scientists was George Bird Grinnell, nine years Roosevelt's senior. Grinnell was the editor of *Forest and Stream,* and he would found the National Audubon Society, help establish Glacier National Park in Montana, and be labeled by the *New York Times* as America's "father of conservation." Grinnell had reviewed and commended Roosevelt's book *Hunting Trips of a Ranchman* (1885) for its "freshness, spontaneity, and enthusiasm," but then damned him with faint praise:

> Mr. Roosevelt is not well known as a sportsman, and his experience of the Western country is quite limited, but this very fact in one way lends an added charm to this book. He has not become accustomed to all the various sights and sounds of the plains and the mountains, and for him all the difference which exists between the East and the West are still sharply defined . . . We are sorry to see that a number of hunting myths are given as fact, but it was after all scarcely to be expected that with the author's limited experience he could sift the wheat from the chaff and distinguish the true from the false.

Stung by the review, Roosevelt stormed into the offices of *Field and Stream* and demanded a meeting with Grinnell. Always a gentleman, Grinnell assuaged Roosevelt's ego, engaged him in lively banter—not difficult with the young sportsman—and soon the two men found themselves talking natural history in great detail. They would go on to form a friendship that would serve each other well for decades.

Grinnell wrote of Teddy Roosevelt:

> Though chiefly interested in big game and its hunting, and telling interestingly of events that had occurred on his own hunting trips, Roosevelt enjoyed hearing of the birds, the small mammals,

the Indians, and the incidents of travel of early expeditions on which I had gone. He was always fond of natural history, having begun, as so many boys have, with birds; but as he saw more and more of outdoor life his interest in the subject broadened and later it became a passion with him.

The same could be said of John Muir. As a Wisconsin teenager, birds were what interested him most. In his twenties, while footloose in Canada, and during his thousand-mile walk to Florida and the Gulf of Mexico, botany was his love. As he moved west into the high country of California, and later north to Alaska, glaciers became his obsession.

Grinnell started with birds as well. How could he not? When he was seven, his family moved into Audubon Park, the magnificent thirty-acre estate in upper Manhattan that had been the great ornithologist's last home. Here young Grinnell found the walls adorned with paintings and hunting trophies, the old barn filled with specimens, the nearby Hudson and Harlem Rivers rich with eagles and other birds. As an undergraduate at Yale, he had suffered in the classroom just as Roosevelt had at Harvard; both longed to be outdoors.

"This cannot last," John James Audubon had written in 1843, lamenting the slaughter of buffalo during his journey up the Missouri and Yellowstone Rivers. "What a terrible destruction of life, as if it were for nothing . . . as the tongues only were brought in, and the flesh of these fine animals was left to beasts and birds of prey, or to rot on the spots where they fell. The prairies are literally *covered* with the skulls of the victims."

Audubon's lament became Grinnell's call to action. For Roosevelt, it was his ranch time in the Dakota Territory in the 1880s that gave him the same sense of urgency. Only strict and immediate government conservation policies could save the American landscape and its rich panoply of wildlife.

ROOSEVELT STORMED into the White House just as he'd entered Grinnell's office sixteen years earlier, with equal parts bluster, charm, and pluck. He quickly caused a national sensation by inviting Booker T.

Washington as an official dinner guest to the White House—the first time a black man had been given the honor. He spearheaded landmark antitrust legislation, infuriated Wall Street (where he was labeled "an extremely dangerous man"), liberated Cuba, determined the route of the Panama Canal (so the United States could have a two-ocean navy), mediated the great Anthracite Strike, and secretly defused a crisis in Venezuela that likely prevented war between the United States and Germany. Bold moves for a man who had not been elected to the presidency.

But his greatest legacy had yet to begin. In the spring of 1903, shortly after he'd established by executive order the nation's first bird preserve in Florida, the indefatigable Roosevelt embarked on an unprecedented 25-state, 14,000-mile cross-country tour (that would see him give 5 major speeches and 260 stump speeches) to better understand how to save America from foolish, greedy Americans without jeopardizing the nation's moral and economic progress. Could he balance pro-growth with pro-preservation? He aimed to give it a try.

With his good friend John Burroughs, who lobbied him not once during the trip, he visited Yellowstone, where the year before he'd won an appropriation to make the park's bison wards of the federal government; this time, to the dismay of his handlers, he spent a Sunday hiking by himself. Like Jefferson and Lincoln, Roosevelt sat a horse well and wrote his own material. He was a thinker, a scholar, a lover of history and keenly aware of his place in it.

Inspired and rejuvenated yet again in the world's first national park, he wrote:

> *Every man who appreciates the majesty and beauty of the wilderness and of wild life, should strike hands with the far-sighted men who wish to preserve our material resources, in the effort to keep our forests and game-beasts, game-birds, and game-fish—indeed all the living creatures of prairie and woodland seashore—from wanton destruction. Above all, we should recognize that the effort toward this end is essentially a democratic movement. It is entirely within our power as a nation to preserve large tracts of wilderness, which are valueless for agricultural purposes and unfit for settlement, as playgrounds for rich*

*and poor alike . . . But this end can only be achieved by wise laws and
by a resolute enforcement of the laws.*

The Grand Canyon, which would not become a national park until
1919, stunned him. "I don't know exactly what words to use in describing
it. It is beautiful and terrible and unearthly." Upon hearing that the Santa
Fe Railroad had declined to build a hotel on the rim, he beseeched his
listeners, "Leave it as it is. You cannot improve on it. The ages have been at
work on it, and man can only mar it—keep it for your children, and your
children's children, and for all who come after you."

California beguiled him with its trees, flowers, and pretty girls. When
he saw a stately redwood with calling cards and posters pinned to its
trunk, giving it an "air of the ridiculous," he complained; the clutter was
quickly removed, the tree restored to its original majesty. "There is nothing more practical in the end than the preservation of beauty," Roosevelt
declared the next day at Stanford University. "I feel most emphatically
that we should not turn into shingles a tree which was old when the first
Egyptian conqueror penetrated to the valley of the Euphrates."

But where exactly Roosevelt would land in the debate between preservation and utilitarianism in the sticky, tricky issues ahead, with Gifford
Pinchot whispering in his one ear and George Bird Grinnell in the other,
remained to be seen. The president was a study in contrasts, a hunter who
loved animals, an imperialist who brokered peace, an expansionist who
believed, according to historian Douglas Brinkley, that national parks
"were the rightful trophies of expansionism." At a dinner overlooking the
California coast he vowed, "the aboriginal American spirit toward the
wilderness had to flourish in the twentieth century. Nature was the great
replenisher for the American people."

His next stop was Yosemite, where he'd asked for the company of
only one man.

❦

WITH THE NEW CENTURY John Muir could feel his life changing;
he likened himself to a glacier, breaking into smaller pieces. The writing process, he said, was one long grind. In 1901, Houghton-Mifflin

published his second book, *Our National Parks*, after Muir complained to Harvard botanist Charles Sargent that Robert Underwood Johnson, while a good mentor and friend, edited him with a heavy hand. Sargent recommended that Muir change publishers, which he did. Losing Muir, Johnson would say, was like having a child abducted.

No sooner had Muir and Sargent arranged a grand botany trip around the world (Europe, Russia, and Australia) when a message arrived in March 1903 from Washington. The president, an admirer and good friend of John Burroughs, had heard much about one Johnny from the other, and from Grinnell and Merriam as well, and was now coming to Yosemite. He wanted the incomparable John Muir for a guide. "I do not want anyone with me but you," TR wrote, "and I want to drop politics absolutely for four days and just be out in the open with you."

With blessings from Sargent, Muir changed his travel plans. In mid-May he was headed to San Francisco, where the most powerful man in America would arrive by train. Muir bought a new suit, too short in the arms and legs, and a new tie, and told reporters of his intentions with the president. "It is only a little trip," he said. "You can't see much of the Sierras in four days . . . after we get to the valley, the President and I will get lost." Meaning Muir intended to get TR away from all the bustle and prattle.

"NOW, THIS IS BULLY," Roosevelt exclaimed as he breathed in the smell of hot coffee over an open fire on Glacier Point, high above Yosemite Valley. The previous night he and Muir had camped beneath the great sequoias of the Mariposa Grove, with Roosevelt announcing he was "as happy as a boy out of school." The next morning, when the rest of the party departed in coaches for the valley, the two men dropped the official itinerary and rode horses up an old Indian trail, accompanied by two park rangers, two packers, and three mules. Five feet of snow still lay on the ground in some places.

Muir made beds of ferns and cedar bows, built a fire (with help from the rangers, who made themselves as invisible as possible), and bantered with Roosevelt late into the night. One of the rangers discreetly observed that both men wanted to do all the talking. It was East meets West; Boone and Crockett Club meets Sierra Club; hunter-conservationist meets biosphere activist. Roosevelt hoped to absorb some of Muir's prophetic aura; Muir hoped to make political hay, mostly on issues of forest preservation. They agreed on everything except on Gifford Pinchot, with Roosevelt's admiration far exceeding Muir's, and on sport hunting, which Roosevelt found "ideal training for manhood," and Muir found vulgar, a "murder business."

"Mr. Roosevelt," he asked, "when are you going to get beyond the boyishness of killing things . . . are you not getting far enough along to leave that off?"

"Muir," the president replied in an uncharacteristically soft voice, "I guess you're right."

Roosevelt was reportedly astounded to find that Muir, while a keen observer of trees and rocks, offered little commentary on common birdsong. But the old Scot, twenty-one years Roosevelt's senior, might have lost some of his higher-frequency hearing. Regardless, he could read landscapes like a book, and this impressed the president. According to Douglas Brinkley, "Muir had an ethereal quality and his erudition was simultaneously bold and profound. Roosevelt immediately admired him. Muir's eyes were deep blue . . . and his attitude was life-affirming. While Roosevelt thought in terms of Americanism in nature, Muir thought about the planet in peril."

That same year, 1903, Svante Arrhenius, who ten years before had predicted global warming due to humans burning coal on an industrial scale, won the Nobel Prize for chemistry for his work in conductivity. When he began it, the work earned him only derision, like his prediction of climate change. That same year, the Wright brothers introduced America to aviation, making a single twelve-second flight of 120 feet at Kitty Hawk. Regular trans-Atlantic radio transmissions began between the United States and Britain. And Jack London published *Call of the Wild*, about a dog, Buck, stolen from his pastoral existence in California and taken north to work brutishly in the Klondike goldfields. The bestseller explored the paradox between the primal and the civilized, and it made London the nation's first millionaire novelist.

The median annual income for a family of four was little more than $500 in 1903. One hundred years later it would be $40,000, an eighty-fold increase. How long could such vigorous expansion continue? Economies grew, ecosystems changed. The planet was only so big. Forests regenerated, but there was only so much productive land, so much good soil and water. "Whiskey is for drinking," men quipped in the arid West, "water is for fighting over."

Like Twain, Muir questioned the seemingly universal assumption that growth was progress, and such progress made us happy. He ate little, and often low on the food chain (though at the president's insistence, he joined him in eating an inch-thick steak). He knew that economic growth, while good in many respects, like lifting people out of poverty, was also destructive and addictive. It plundered Nature and raised pampered people into absurd realms of excess, as those same people responded not with gratitude, but by jealously guarding their wealth and wanting more.

After tens of thousands of years hunting, gathering, settling, planting, sowing, and reproducing, struggling through famine, fire, disease, war, and drought, the human race had reached a global population of around one billion in the year 1810. By 1930 it would be two billion. Every fifteen to twenty-five years thereafter would add another billion, with each generation living longer, consuming more, and sending greater and greater amounts of carbon dioxide and other greenhouse gases into the atmosphere, first by burning coal, then oil and natural gas. No human society had ever experienced vigorous and sustained economic growth without burning fossil fuels. Now, at the beginning of the twentieth century, such accelerated burning was becoming the norm. It's what everybody expected.

"Disturbing as it sounds," historian Steven Stoll would write, "growth on the scale known to industrial societies over the last two centuries is a historically exceptional condition that carries with it all sorts of doubtful ideas about the relationship between society and nature."

Over the next five years, 1903 to 1908, President Roosevelt would protect 230 million acres of federal land (in 53 wildlife reserves, 16 national monuments, and 5 national parks), an area larger than California and Texas *combined.* He had the long view, the courage to take criticism, and the wisdom to hear sage whispers among the howling dogs. He often spoke of society's responsibility to "future generations," of restraint as an essential ingredient in manly virtue. He would never stop hunting, but in the years ahead would carry his camera more often than his rifle. Powerful and calculating, he'd charm and inspire Muir but later disappoint him, seeing things more as Pinchot did, through the wide lens of utilitarianism. A forest, while beautiful, Pinchot had declared, was also a factory for trees. We can have both, he argued: beauty and utility.

They had a grand time together, Roosevelt and Muir, the president fit for a Kipling novel, dressed in his khaki jodhpurs and a Rough Rider hat like he'd worn storming up San Juan Hill, a soiled bandana around his neck; Muir in his loose-fitting suit, the hobo intellectual, a sprig of cedar poked through a buttonhole.

Waking up atop Granite Point the last morning, beneath a dusting of new snow, the president exclaimed, "This is bullier yet. I wouldn't miss this for anything."

Riding into the valley that afternoon and dismounting at the Sentinel Hotel, Roosevelt and Muir were swallowed by a crowd. Governor George C. Pardee was there, as were members of the Yosemite Park Commission. Extravagant plans had been made to entertain Roosevelt.

"We slept in a snowstorm last night . . ." TR told them, "just what I wanted." Later he added, "This has been the grandest day of my life. One I shall long remember." So grand that he and Muir mounted their horses to ride away for yet another night together of camping, storytelling, and philosophizing. The commissioners begged him to stay; they had a searchlight show planned for him. "Nature faking," Roosevelt called it. He wanted the real thing. "John Muir talked even better than he wrote," Roosevelt said, adding that camping "amid the pines and the silver firs in Sierrian solitude, in a snowstorm, too, and without a tent," was one of the greatest experiences he'd ever had.

So he and Muir left behind the flabbergasted dignitaries once again, left them quietly cursing Muir and his Druid spell over the president. The two new friends camped in Bridalveil Meadow and let the dusky sunset surrender into a million winking stars in the great dome of embracing night sky.

"GOODBYE, JOHN," the president said the next morning. "Come and see me in Washington. I've had the time of my life!"

Roosevelt had done what Emerson's handlers forbade him from doing with Muir thirty-two years earlier among the great sequoias: He slowed down and stayed awhile. Became a sequoia himself. Slept among his brethren. In a letter to Louie, John wrote, "I never before had so interesting, hearty and manly a companion. Camping with the President was a remarkable experience. I fairly fell in love with him."

Muir later told his friends about his remarks to Roosevelt on federal protection for Yosemite Valley (still within the state's jurisdiction) and the need for strident forest preservation, adding, "I stuffed him pretty well regarding the timber thieves."

Would it be enough?

"We are not building this country of ours for a day," Roosevelt announced in Sacramento, after his time with Muir. "It is to last through the ages."

As much as he championed the bully pulpit and loved his time with Muir, the president couldn't stay there. He lived in a world of political compromise. He believed Americans could and should have it both ways: preservation and growth, city and farm, forest and factory . . . and forests *as* factories if that's what moved America forward into its rightful ownership of the new century. With one hand he'd preserve the past, with the other he'd grab the future.

Muir had his own contradictions; he fought for forest preservation while living in a large house made of wood and on land once Eden-like with flowers and trees, before industrious men put it to work as a commercial fruit ranch. He knew the road from idealism to practicality was rocky and long; that all great institutions and new ways of thinking suffered through adolescence, a difficult coming-of-age into maturity. He'd covered a great distance in his own personal journey, leaving behind the shadow of his father's Calvinism to embrace a brighter world wherein men of greatness and leadership operated out of civic virtue, not personal greed, and did the right thing for the right reasons. In effect, Muir

John Muir and Theodore Roosevelt standing atop Granite Point, high above
Yosemite Valley, May 1903
PHOTO COURTESY OF THE LIBRARY OF CONGRESS

believed in the power of government to save the American landscape, and
thus America itself. He kept a photograph of Roosevelt on his wall in his
scribble den, but Muir would never visit him in the White House.

TWO WEEKS after his time with Roosevelt, Muir began his epic round-the-world botanizing trip. With all its logistics, baggage, clutter, and confusion—beginning with his friend Charles Sargent losing their passports (they slipped into the lining of his suitcase and would not be found until his return to Boston)—Muir did not at all enjoy the early part of the trip. In fact, it made him sick. In Europe he plodded through an endless parade of urban gardens, stuffed museums, and the shallow trappings of the aristocracy.

The capital of Russia, St. Petersburg, dispirited him with its "huge yellow public buildings, war memorial, barbaric colored churches & cathedrals & palaces full of armor jewelry & some fine paintings." To Robert Underwood Johnson, he wrote, "I'm still alive after this monstrous dose of civilization—London, Paris, Berlin, etc. with their miles of art galleries, museums full of old armor and murder implements . . . Glad to leave holy Moscow, Kremlin, and all."

A short distance away, in Finland, he encountered "the tallest and most uniform patch of manufactured forest I have seen," and while the trees lifted his spirits, the forest itself haunted him as the kind of monoculture Muir feared would one day cover America if Gifford Pinchot got his way: forests as farms; trees as crops in tidy rows like consumer products.

In Chechnya, he'd fallen ill after eating bad food in bad hotels. Now day after day crossing Russia on the incomplete 6,000-mile Trans-Siberian Railway found him taking morphine and brandy to fight abdominal pains from ptomaine poisoning, his weight falling below one hundred pounds while he and Professor Sargent (and the professor's son) never got off the train, the wheels clacking, the forests flashing by. Stands of spruce and "indomitable birch" intrigued Muir and compelled him to stay, but the professor had them on a tight schedule, moving, always moving. Muir wrote how Sargent "never seemed to think of me sick or well or of my studies only of his own until he feared I might die on his hands & thus bother him."

From Vladivostok, they sailed down the Korean coast, where Muir's spirits brightened, first to be off the train, second to stand on deck and admire mile after mile of glacial topography: finely sculpted mountains above elegant fjords. He parted company with the Sargents in Shanghai, cabled his friend Edward H. Harriman for help with steamship arrangements, and was soon sailing the China coast for India, home of the Himalaya. "I feel alive with mountains in sight once more," he wrote to Louie. "Glad to be free . . ."

Every morning in Darjeeling he would climb a ridge or a hill to watch dawn play its symphony on the highest mountains in the world, the mighty melting glaciers feeding the rivers of the Himalayan Plateau that ran into China and India and sated the thirsts of tens of millions of people. Soon Muir's appetite returned, and he was well again among the banyans and monkeys and gilded temples, the dark-faced women in their colorful saris, the rich people with faces furrowed, always worried about money, while the poor people smiled all the time, knowing they'd never be rich. A premonition vexed him that Helen, his youngest, now eighteen yet always a bit weak and prone to pneumonia in a time before antibiotics, had fallen terribly ill and needed him. He cabled home and received a stoic reply from Louie: "All's well."

Relieved, he berated himself as an old worrywart and bought a ticket to Egypt, telling Louie by cable, "There are a few more places I should see before I die."

DEATH was no longer an abstraction—if it ever had been, given Muir's pioneer upbringing with its share of sickness, toil, and disease. Jeanne Carr, after years of dementia in a nursing home, died that winter while Muir was overseas. One biographer noted that Muir should have dedicated his first book to her (he dedicated it to nobody), the woman who "had once befriended, taught, loved and inspired him . . . for more than anyone else she had encouraged him to write down his thoughts and share his passion with nature with the public."

Two years before, in 1901, the deaths of other friends had rocked him, together with the loss of his unmarried sister, Annie, his only sibling left in Wisconsin. The geologist Joseph LeConte died of a heart attack during the Sierra Club's first big annual camping trip to Yosemite's Tuolumne Meadows. A professor at the University of California, Berkeley, LeConte had explored the Sierra Nevada with Muir in the early 1870s and acknowledged the young Scot as the discoverer of many glaciers, albeit small ones, where none were thought to be. A gracious man, LeConte had taken special care to give credit to Muir, who alone had ventured into the high country, followed silt-laden streams to their source glaciers, and used wooden stakes to measure the movements of the glaciers at about one inch per day during summer. Muir had recommended to the US Coast & Geographic Survey that the southernmost tidewater glacier in North America (near present-day Petersburg, Alaska) be named after his benefactor and friend.

MUIR LEFT INDIA and sailed west to Africa. Skipping the Holy Land due to a cholera epidemic, he focused on the "dusty antiquities" of Egypt, where he found the pyramids and the Sphinx impressive in their size and proportions, and enjoyed sailing up the Nile on a steamer. One night while back in a Cairo hotel, as he regaled three sisters from Philadelphia about the mighty sequoias of the Sierra Nevada, an Englishwoman overheard him and interrupted to ask if the wood of the sequoia made nice furniture. "Would you murder your own children?" Muir shot back. She quickly left, casting a dark eye over her shoulder at such a madman.

Homeward bound, he sailed east for Australia and New Zealand, intrigued by every new landscape and its geology and botany, the finer features that gave it character. With fellow botanists he spent four months Down Under collecting specimens (more than one hundred new species), taking notes, and having the time of his life. If he had thought sheep were a scourge on the native vegetation of California, it was nothing compared to what he witnessed in Australia and New Zealand. He put on his old weight and made many new friends. After a jaunt north to the Philippines, Hong Kong, and Japan, he crossed the Pacific, stopped in Hawaii, and arrived in California to the warm greetings of his family. He'd been gone a full year. He weighed nearly 140 pounds and pulled pranks and danced about the home as if he were young John back on the farm making his mother and sisters laugh. Only this time it was his wife and daughters, an even greater delight.

Though tourism was beginning to spread its wings as an international phenomenon in the early 1900s, it still belonged to the wealthy. Less than

Muir (l) and Burroughs (r), the "two Johnnies," admirers and critics of each other
PHOTO COURTESY OF HOLT-ATHERTON SPECIAL COLLECTIONS, UNIVERSITY OF THE PACIFIC

1 percent of 1 percent of Americans had been around the world. America's largest cities were crowded, dirty, smelly, mean, and corrupt—and only getting worse. People worked long hours for meager pay, including school-deprived children condemned to the sweat and grime of factories, foundries, and slaughterhouses. The Boer War had ravaged South Africa. And Imperial Japan, beginning to flex itself into mainland Asia, had already provoked war with Russia. As the Victorian era ended, with its strict rules, formal manners, and pious conventionality, Sigmund Freud published *The Interpretation of Dreams* (1900), and then *The Psychopathology of Everyday Life* (1901).

Meanwhile, John Muir extolled his fellow man to get back to Nature, our ancestral home. As the world seemed to bifurcate into realms of rich and poor, hope and despair, altruism and selfishness, many people nonetheless believed in a bright future that was already showing itself, where buildings got higher, bridges stronger and longer, ships larger, medicine better. Life, in general, improved. Every year brought new revelations in science, industry, and exploration.

WHILE Muir returned from his epic overseas journey, Robert Falcon Scott returned from Antarctica, completing the first British expedition into that icy realm since the 1840s when James Clark Ross discovered the sea and ice shelf that would one day bear his name. We can only imagine how Muir would have responded to Antarctica, home to 90 percent of the world's ice. In Alaska, he'd found a mountainous landscape punctuated by glaciers; in Antarctica, Scott found an icescape punctuated by mountains. Antarctica was Alaska twenty thousand years ago. It was the Ice Age itself.

"Terra Australis Incognita," said the early maps that hypothesized the continent's existence, anchored somewhere at the bottom of the world. Men had been going there since James Cook first circumnavigated it in the 1770s but never actually sighted the mainland. But with Scott's 1901 to 1904 expedition, men began to probe the interior. Scott launched the "Heroic Age" of exploration in Antarctica that would star himself as the eloquent loser, Roald Amundsen as the tragic winner, and a strong supporting cast of Ernest Shackleton, Frank Wild, Douglas Mawson, and others. While the Arctic was an ocean surrounded by continents, Antarctica was a continent surrounded by ocean—big, mysterious, and bitter cold.

Both poles had yet to be claimed. Scott had attempted to reach the South Pole and didn't get remotely close. Traveling with two companions, he nearly died and never got off the Ross Ice Shelf, a massive coastal body of ice the size of France, the largest of many ice shelves that embroidered Antarctica. Next time, his pride and poor judgment would get him killed; he'd freeze to death in his tent. Everything in Antarctica was a superlative: the highest, driest, coldest, windiest, and loneliest place on Earth, filled with glaciers that throughout the next century would render many secrets about the past and help foretell the future with things called ice cores, thin slices, and isotopes.

Perhaps a man could be transformed by travel only when he was young, as Scott was in Antarctica. For John Muir, now thirty years older than Scott, Yosemite had once been his transformation, back when he was young, and Alaska his terra incognita. But by the time Muir traveled around the world from 1903 to 1904 as an older man, he'd calcified into who he was, as most old men do. If anything, overseas travel confirmed his prejudices rather than shattered them. "Going around the world had not changed Muir's thinking substantially," Donald Worster would write:

> He had added to his herbarium, his stock of impressions, his long list of friends and colleagues, but he came home with no new large insights into nature or society. Nothing in his journal suggests that travel had helped him see the world, himself, or his adopted country more profoundly. Had he walked the whole distance, it might have been different.

FOR ALL HIS passion and vigor, Muir often sniffled and coughed his way through winter. Built like a heron, thin and slight, he carried no fat on his lean frame. He could work and worry himself into a tizzy, fretting over his daughters or some conservation issue, a difficult-to-write book chapter, a magazine article. These traits, together with his keen intellect and love of words, he'd passed on to Helen, which vexed him but also excited him; he thought she might one day carry the mantle of activist/writer when he was gone.

Now almost twenty, his younger daughter had grown into a willful woman who regardless remained frail and homebound while her older sister Wanda attended the University of California at Berkeley. Now with another damp winter upon them, Helen was again pale and short of breath. She, her father, and her sister had recently visited the Grand Canyon and fallen in love with the colorful rimrock and dry heat of the desert southwest. While Louie stayed home, as always, to tend her flowers, John and Wanda took Helen back to Arizona, where her health improved immediately.

But then came dire news from Louie. She was gravely ill.

John Muir, his wife Louie, and his daughters Wanda (l) and Helen (r) at their Martinez home
PHOTO COURTESY OF HOLT-ATHERTON SPECIAL COLLECTIONS, UNIVERSITY OF THE PACIFIC

Muir had experienced earthquakes in his life, figurative ones: leaving his Wisconsin home without his father's blessing, losing his eyesight in the Indianapolis carriage factory, getting malaria in Florida. And literal ones: shaken out of bed in 1872 in Yosemite Valley, running around praising the power and beauty of Nature—shouting "a noble earthquake, a noble earthquake"—while massive granite boulders tumbled off the high cliffs. And in late summer 1899, a couple months after he'd departed Glacier Bay for the last time, a massive earthquake had rattled the glaciers and filled the bay with so much floating ice that for many years steamships could no longer approach the glaciers, killing the Alaska tourism industry. Muir Glacier began an accelerated retreat that during the next century would see it surrender its entire inlet to the sea, shrinking back to where it is today, only a small fraction of its original size, no longer tidewater.

Losing Louie was another earthquake. After a brief battle with lung cancer, she died at fifty-eight in August 1905. Muir was devastated and wracked with guilt by all the time he'd spent away from home, traveling afar, climbing glaciers, collecting plants. It all seemed trivial now, self-indulgent. Louie had given him two wonderful daughters, a path to financial security, and the freedom for him to travel in older age. According to Gretel Ehrlich, "She had learned that his love could be won only by letting him go his own wild way. In return he was loyal and grateful, an adoring father and husband, though an unwilling householder. She had been his critic, editor and helpmate, but she could never share his mountain joy."

President Roosevelt knew what it was to lose a wife. He wrote to Muir, "get out among the mountains and the trees, friend, as soon as you can. They will do more for you than either man or woman can." Muir went to Arizona instead, to soak in the heat with Wanda and Helen. He poked around the desert and let the intense sun dry his sorrows as he discovered pieces of petrified wood, reptile bones, and Indian ruins. He loved this desert time and enjoyed watching Helen's health improve. Back home, however, the tremors persisted. The next spring, California convulsed, unleashing an earthquake that would raise the stakes for everything: not just conservation policy in America, but Muir's own personal well-being.

PART FOUR

1906–1980

CHAPTER ELEVEN

a temple drowned

FOR MANY San Franciscans it was the longest moment of their lives, and for some, the last. The Great 1906 Earthquake, felt as far away as Germany, ruptured the San Andreas Fault just before five o'clock on Wednesday morning, April 18, catching people still in bed. An estimated 28,000 buildings were destroyed, if not by the earthquake that pancaked them to the ground, then by fires that ensued for three days and created their own wind, feeding on the ruins. More than half of the city's 400,000 residents were made homeless; 700 to 800 died, perhaps more. "Not in history has a modern imperial city been so completely destroyed." Jack London reported in *Collier's* magazine,

> San Francisco is gone. Nothing remains of it but memories and a fringe of dwelling-houses on its outskirts. Its industrial section is wiped out. Its business section is wiped out. Its social and residential section is wiped out. The factories and warehouses, the great stores and newspaper buildings, the hotels and the palaces of the nabobs, are all gone.

In Martinez, in the Alhambra Valley, at the north end of San Francisco Bay, the Strentzel house lost all five of its chimneys but remained intact, its foundation strong. Muir supervised repairs on the house but could feel cracks in the walls of his own life as time marched on. His beloved wife had died; for months he seemed lost, aimless. Wanda would soon marry a civil engineer he didn't much care for. Helen, for the sake of her health, would return to the desert again and again until finally settling there for good.

While still living at home and often struggling for a good deep breath, Helen convinced her father to take a much-needed vacation to the Sierra with his dear friend, the artist William Keith. She would stay back with their house servant, Ah Fong, to manage her cough and tend to chores as a capable horsewoman and buggy driver (like her older sister). En route to Hetch Hetchy Valley, in Yosemite National Park, Muir wrote to her, "The glory of the woods hereabouts now is the color of dogwood, glorious masses of red and purple and yellow . . . I can't get the sound of that cough out of my ears . . ."

The two men had a good time as they tromped about for a week and felt the wonder of their youth flood back into them. Of his friend, Muir wrote, ". . . after making about forty sketches, [he] declared with enthusiasm that although its walls were less sublime in height, in picturesque beauty and charm Hetch Hetchy surpassed even Yosemite."

On his return, Muir's heart sank. Helen had sent him away for his own health—like her mother, she knew when her father needed mountains—but her cough had worsened. John immediately summoned a specialist, who said Helen must move to a drier, warmer climate for two years, perhaps longer. It would be the beginning of the rest of her life. Always attentive, her father built her a sturdy cabin near the town of Doggett, in the Mojave Desert. Linnie Marsh Wolfe would write:

> Finding her a nurse and companion in the person of a Miss Stafford, whom he promptly nicknamed "Miss Sassafras," he left Helen comfortably settled, and returned to the lonely old house, now bereft for a second time of all cheer. Unable to resist the pleading eyes of her dog, Stickeen, he sent both him and her riding pony, Sniffpony, south to keep her company.

Like many fathers, Muir had harbored high hopes for his daughters, thinking they might follow his lead and become naturalists and writers, defenders of the defenseless. But those hopes, like so much else, slipped away as the girls chose more conventional paths. Wanda married the civil engineer who specialized in irrigation; Helen would follow her fortune-seeking husband into one scheme after another in the advertising business.

Being back in the "dismal old" Strentzel house, with its sixteen vacant rooms, gave Muir little comfort, working as he did in his scribble den, living alone with Ah Fong. "O dear these lonely days!!" he would write to his daughters as they all too quickly became independent women, "I must either get into consuming hard work or go up a canon."

———

SIX WEEKS after the earthquake, Gifford Pinchot, the nation's new chief forester, wrote to Marsden Manson, a San Francisco city water engineer, "I hope sincerely that in the regeneration of San Francisco its people may be able to make provision for a water supply from the Yosemite National Park . . . I will stand ready to render any assistance which lies in my power."

Plagued by water issues for decades, San Francisco found itself even thirstier as it rose from the ashes. Local politicians and water engineers had long coveted the snowpack of the Sierra, where high mountain basins could give their growing city a steady, year-round supply of drinking water and hydroelectric power. Top on the list was Hetch Hetchy Valley, in Yosemite National Park. Twice in the early 1900s, San Francisco had applied for the rights to dam the Tuolumne River and flood Hetch Hetchy, and twice Ethan Hitchcock, secretary of the interior, had said no. Soon after the earthquake, Pinchot's friend James Garfield replaced Hitchcock. That summer of 1906, while the Sierra Club leadership was in the mountains on its annual outing, Garfield blindsided them by holding a hearing in San Francisco filled with one-sided testimony.

With help from Robert Underwood Johnson, Charles Sprague Sargent, William Colby, and others, Muir got busy and wrote to President Roosevelt, saying of the dam proponents, "They all show forth the proud sort of confidence that comes of a good sound substantial irrefragable ignorance." If people across the country knew the facts, Muir said, "nine tenths or more" would oppose damming the Tuolumne River and drowning Hetch Hetchy. Roosevelt passed his sentiments along to Pinchot and Garfield and wrote back to Muir that in his experience the opposite was true; everybody he'd spoken to appeared to be in favor of the plan. He added, "and I have been in the disagreeable position of seeming to interfere with the development . . . p.s. How I do wish I were again with you camping out under those great sequoias or in the snow under the silver firs."

This fight, Muir confided to Johnson, "promises to be the worst ever."

Underpinning it all was a rift in the conservation community as deep as the San Andreas Fault: utility versus preservation, harness nature or let it run wild, dam a river or defend it. It all came down to money, Muir said. Men might speak of higher ideals, but don't be fooled; it's a ruse to mask simple greed. Little was said of the hydropower potential of Hetch Hetchy, where the big money was. The dam proponents wanted to avoid discussions of a generator plant and power lines that together with a massive concrete plug would further deface California's most famous national park. They harped instead on the drinking-water argument as if they were good guys coming to rescue the homeless of San Francisco. Such was the practiced art of Pinchot and others: to wrap the bitter pill of self-interest in the sweet butter of higher moral purpose. So as not to appear callous to the well-being of the people of San Francisco, Muir carefully proposed alternative sites (that would cost more but do less damage) and ascribed the Hetch Hetchy scheme to a few "mischief-makers and robbers of every degree."

It didn't work.

The mayor of San Francisco, James D. Phelan, wrote to Garfield, "John Muir loves the Sierras and roams at large, and is hypersensitive on the subject of the invasion of his territory. The 400,000 people of San Francisco are suffering from bad water and ask Mr. Muir to cease his aesthetic quibbling."

IF JOHN OF THE MOUNTAINS ever thought he'd turn seventy and look back over his life's accomplishments with satisfaction and a sense of ease, he was wrong. He was living alone and in the fight of his life to defend his spiritual home, the sister valley to Yosemite Valley, not as popular but every bit as enchanting. The wilds of Alaska must have seemed many thousands of miles away, something ethereal. Another lifetime when Tlingit Indians paddled dugout cedar canoes and rivers ran free and forests stood undefiled. The men who opposed Muir over Hetch

Hetchy seemed to regard only one thing as sacred: progress. And who wrote the definitions of progress? Men in power. And what paved the path to power? Money.

A few voices cried in protest, Muir's the most compelling among them. But the juggernaut was rolling. Every environmental defeat was final, every victory, provisional. A stay of execution. The dam might be defeated, but the dam site would still be there, whispering its temptations. That Muir's twilight years should find him with his back to the wall, according to biographer Stephen Fox, "made an ironic denouement to his life's work."

In May 1908, after Gifford Pinchot pronounced that damming Hetch Hetchy would in no way lessen the scenic quality of the Sierra, Secretary Garfield signed over to San Francisco the rights to develop the site. Only two hurdles remained: congressional approval and the president's signature.

Soon thereafter a "Conservation Conference" took place at the White House with neither John Muir nor Robert Underwood Johnson in attendance. They weren't invited, despite the fact that Johnson had proposed the conference months before, which Pinchot at the time called "impracticable." Now as the conference convened, President Roosevelt gave full credit to Pinchot, saying at one point, "In all forestry matters I have put my conscience in the keeping of Gifford Pinchot."

Muir was passionate and eloquent, but not a political player. He didn't horse-trade or smooth talk. He'd been a shrewd businessman in his day, but never greedy or easy prey to the subtle machinations of others. Money brought him his greatest pleasure when he gave it away to help relieve the troubles of his neighbors, even strangers. "He could squeeze a penny in a business deal as hard as the next Scotchman," Linnie Marsh Wolfe would write, "but he gave with prodigality. His files are filed with letters of gratitude from organized charities, relatives, friends, and needy people he had merely heard of."

Upon hearing of a woman who'd lost her husband and was struggling to feed and clothe her children, he traveled by buggy to deliver a small sack of heavy coins to get her through the winter. Again and again he did this sort of thing, and asked for nothing in return. Old Toyatte, the captain of his canoe in 1879, had told Muir of the Tlingit potlatch tradition: It isn't what we own that makes us rich, it's what we give away.

NOT ALL NEWS on the conservation front was dispiriting in Muir's final years. In 1906 Congress passed the American Antiquities Act, called by some "the greatest conservation act that nobody's ever heard of." Masterminded by Congressman John F. Lacey of Iowa, working closely and in private with President Roosevelt, the act gave the president the power to create national monuments by executive order, without congressional approval. Just a stroke of the pen, lickety-split.

While the act was designed to quickly protect small archeological sites from vandals and thieves, Roosevelt took it and ran with it, to Muir's delight. Many national monuments established by TR would later become national parks, and they were anything but small. Some were huge, such as 600,000-acre Mount Olympus National Monument (later Olympic National Park) and 800,000-acre Grand Canyon National Monument. Roosevelt took sharp criticism for this, but didn't care. Also in the mix was Petrified Forest National Monument, in Arizona, a favorite of Muir's after spending time there with Wanda and Helen; many times he'd lobbied Washington to preserve the area from the bottomless pockets of vandals. In the decades ahead, beyond Muir's life, other presidents would invoke the Antiquities Act to safeguard spectacular amounts of wild acreage, most notably in Alaska.

To measure a man's influence is no easy task. Drop a pebble into a pool and the ripples run to every shore, some near, some far. Muir's correspondence in his final years, written while he fought bronchial coughs and terrible headaches, often speaks to his ongoing, never-ending struggle to preserve wild Nature, and the full benefits that can only be measured in the years ahead. The future is out there, he said, looking back and judging us, asking hard questions about our worst habits, our insatiable appetites, our addiction to growth and always wanting more, and yes, our strokes of genius and compassion, our caring for other human beings and other species, our deep regard for the beauties of Nature and all life caught in the travail of time.

In early 1909 James D. Phelan, the former mayor of San Francisco, looking dapper and sounding suave, testified before Congress that as a new arrival in Yosemite Valley many years earlier, Muir "began his career . . . as an operator in a sawmill. Verily 'the lover of the tree destroyeth the tree.' . . . He is a poetical gentleman. I am sure he would sacrifice his own family for the preservation of beauty. He considers human life very cheap, and he considers the works of God superior . . ."

Such attacks appeared to upset Muir's friends more than they did Muir. To William Colby, he wrote, "Never mind, dear Colby, the present flourishing triumphant growth of the wealthy wicked, the Phelans, Pinchots and their hirelings, will not thrive forever . . . We may lose this particular fight, but truth and right must prevail at last. Anyhow we must be true to ourselves."

When William Howard Taft won the White House in 1908 and visited Yosemite the next year, Muir accompanied him with a gaggle of newsmen. A big, sweaty man who loved to tease and provoke others, Taft announced loudly that Hetch Hetchy Valley would make a good place for a farm, and there, at the entrance, would be a good place for a dam. Taking the bait, Muir said adamantly, "A dam! Yes . . . but the man who would dam that would be damning himself." Muir then caught himself and calmly explained that the valley was God's creation. Isn't a man allowed to lose his temper now and then as Jesus did upon finding moneychangers in the temple?

Muir shared with the president his detailed plan to promote tourism in the park via roads and trails designed to link four major features, Hetch Hetchy being one. This would work only if the valley remained in its pristine state, he said. Think of the pleasure it will bring all Americans for centuries to come. Taft quietly agreed.

Upon his return to Washington, he appointed a board of engineers to investigate Lake Eleanor as an alternate site to supply San Francisco with adequate drinking water. But water had never been the sole issue, even the biggest issue. San Francisco wanted the higher elevation site of Hetch Hetchy for its hydroelectric potential. Taft also discharged Pinchot from the directorship of the US Forest Service. According to one account, Pinchot responded with "attacks more violent than before."

In a 1909 review of an updated version of Muir's book *Our National Parks*, the *New York Times* wrote:

> It is all well enough to talk about preserving our natural resources, reforesting our plains and denuded mountainsides, and refilling our empty river basins; but we doubt very much that the masses of our people are vitally concerned in that aspect of conservation, which really seems most irrelevant to their interests. It is the sentimentalist like Muir who will rouse the people rather than the materialist.

In other words, according to historian Stephen Fox, "Pinchot spoke for political opinion. Muir spoke for public opinion."

While the well-moneyed stated their case for building the dam, letters poured into Washington, and a congressional minority committee report concluded, "there has been an exceedingly widespread, earnest, and vigorous protest voiced by scientists, naturalists, mountain climbers, travelers, and others in person, by letters and telegrams, and in newspaper and magazine articles." As a result, the House killed the bill. Again the promoters lashed out. The *San Francisco Chronicle* called the preservationists "hoggish and mushy esthetes," while in 1910, with the debate going into its fifth year, city engineer Marsden Manson wrote that the opposition was composed of "short-haired women and long-haired men."

What was the world coming to?

———

MARK TWAIN died that year, as he'd predicted, going out with Halley's Comet as he'd come in seventy-five years before. Glacier National Park was established in Montana, in large part through the efforts of Muir's friend George Bird Grinnell, while a massive fire burned through the forests of the American West, unprecedented in its intensity and scope. And glaciers around the world continued to recede. The next summer a heat wave pounded New England and the British Isles. New Hampshire recorded 106 degrees Fahrenheit, London reached an until-then-unimaginable 100 degrees. Droughts seemed more severe, winds stronger, rains heavier. So-called "century events" were beginning to happen every twenty or thirty years, as everywhere the weather became more unpredictable.

John Muir found valuable summertime months to return to his beloved Sierra to rest and heal. Again and again he'd inspire his Sierra Club friends with his compassion for all living things, and irritate them by refusing to sleep in a tent. Instead, he'd curl onto the ground, wrap himself around a rock or tree, with only his coat for a blanket, and cough through the night. He'd defeated a lowland microbe once before by sleeping on his namesake glacier in Alaska; perhaps he thought he could do it again. He shied away from formal leadership and public speaking until friends (or his daughters, who loved to camp with him) coaxed him into a campfire story.

He'd start out slow, as if intending to speak for only a minute, then gain momentum and soon be on his feet, animatedly moving about, his voice rising and falling as he held his audience rapt. An elder now, fence-post thin, his hair white, beard long, he remained a powerful orator, more than a shadow of the mighty ice-chief he'd been back when ferocious Chilkat and Chilkoot Tlingits put down their differences and sat atop their rooftops to hear his every word.

While staying with the Harriman family at their summer lodge on Pelican Bay, on Klamath Lake, in southern Oregon, Muir had proved himself such an engaging storyteller (his book *Stickeen*, about his "glacier adventure" with the little dog, had just been published) that Edward Harriman assigned his stenographer to follow Muir around and record everything. Muir wrote to Helen, "I've . . . been kept so busy, dictating autobiographical stuff, I'm fairly dizzy most of the time, and I can't get out of it, for there's no withstanding Harriman's stenographer under orders. I've never been so task-driven in a literary way before. I don't know when I'll get away from this beneficent bondage . . ."

The result would be a first draft, more than a thousand pages long, of a book he never intended to write but now felt compelled to cut and shape into *The Story of My Boyhood and Youth*.

The book that was most important to him, however, had yet to be written: the Alaska book. It pulled on him like a strong flooding tide in Glacier Bay, the wildest place he'd ever been; he had to get it just right.

John Muir at age
seventy-one, in
1909, the year
Houghton-Mifflin
published his book
about the little
dog, Stickeen
PHOTO COURTESY
OF THE LIBRARY OF
CONGRESS

Louie had encouraged him to write it for twenty years, knowing the longer he waited the more it would vex him.

As usual, she was right.

Under the Taft Presidency, the Hetch Hetchy debate cooled, and Muir took the time to organize his notes. He had wanted to write a dozen books or more, perhaps as many as twenty. Now he'd do well to finish three or four before his time ran out. He could feel the curtain coming down, "the dark ahead," he called it. He had so much he wanted to do, and he was running out of time. He wanted to see the mighty Amazon River as Alexander von Humboldt had, feasting on every mysterious detail; he'd dreamed of this for fifty years, since before his thousand-mile walk to the Gulf of Mexico.

Then came news that Edward Harriman had died. And soon other friends were gone, including William Keith, a great loss for Muir. He wrote to Helen, "I wonder if leaves feel lonely when they see their neighbors falling."

In April 1911 John Muir traveled by train to New York, where again Robert Underwood Johnson greeted him warmly and ushered him from one prestigious event to another. Muir campaigned for Hetch Hetchy and received many awards, including membership into the American Academy of Arts and Letters and an honorary doctorate from Yale. Squirreled away for months in friends' homes, he finished up a couple book projects and cut handsome royalties for himself from his publisher. All that remained unwritten was Alaska. Tired after so much politicking and deal-making, he sailed for Brazil in August, seventy-three years old and alone, determined to "vanish in the wilderness of the other America." Helen had suggested that her husband accompany him, should anything go wrong and he need assistance. Muir said no.

An amateur botanist once again, he boated up the Amazon River to Manaus, buried deep in the heart of the richest assemblage of species in the world: plants, insects, and birds of outrageous color and design. Trees interested him most as he made his way from tropical jungles to grassy tablelands to glaciated landscapes where men cut down entire forests and shipped them away. He traveled to Africa via the Canary Islands, and down the west coast to Cape Town, where everybody talked of diamonds and gold, as if money ruled the world. Which it did, of course. Muir could see that now.

He found a baobab tree that to him was the spirit of Africa, thousands of years old, all by itself where recently it had stood in the company of others. More than a tree, it was an ecosystem unto itself, its bark, he wrote, "like the skin of an elephant." Muir asked many questions and received eager, gracious answers from dark, smiling faces. So much toil and sweat. Here was imperialism and raw human industry on a much larger scale, larger than he had ever seen.

IN EUROPE, America, and parts of Asia, powerful nations faced what they regarded as a straightforward choice in the new century: modernize or be marginalized. Grow or die. Produce energy or control in some manner those who do. In London the new first lord of the Admiralty, Winston Churchill, had an ambitious goal: revamp the powerful British Royal Navy by making coal-burning ships into oil-burning ships, a huge and risky undertaking. England had lots of coal, and no oil. So why switch? Because burning a pound of fuel oil produced twice as much energy as burning a pound of coal. Oil was the future, Churchill knew; wars would be fought over it. And the future had to be won. Otherwise it made a dangerous enemy. Soon biplanes would be replaced by Spitfires, Harriers, and Boeing 747s, and entire empires would collapse and be partitioned and renamed to satisfy the appetites and whims of the victors.

Muir returned home nearly a year after he'd left. As with his previous trips overseas, he'd collected plant specimens and made new friends but acquired no material or ideas for a book. The "hot continents," as he called them, were fascinating but not his place. Instead, he buckled down to write about "the great thundering crystal world" of tidewater glaciers and Tlingit canoes: Alaska.

Teddy Roosevelt returned to politics in 1912 to challenge President Taft in his quest for a second term. The two Republicans cancelled each other and enabled the election of Woodrow Wilson, a former president of Princeton University and the first Democrat to occupy the White House in twenty years. When Wilson appointed as his secretary of the interior Franklin Lane, a San Francisco attorney and good friend of former mayor James D. Phelan, the Hetch Hetchy debate seemed lost. California congressman John Raker introduced a bill that gave San Francisco everything it wanted.

Muir fought on; he suffered a serious blow when several prominent members of the Sierra Club (including a cofounder) voted on behalf of the city. Gifford Pinchot, who had worked hard on the Roosevelt campaign, jumped back into the debate with full force; Robert Underwood Johnson would later comment that without Pinchot's influence the Raker Bill would probably have died.

It lived and gained momentum as the debate split California down the middle.

According to Donald Worster, "No one of substantial fortune came to the valley's rescue. All or Muir's moneyed friends either stayed indifferent or went over to the other side."

Teddy Roosevelt expressed sympathy for Muir and his allies but made no strong stand. John Burroughs wrote in favor of the dam, saying, "Grand scenery is going to waste in the Sierras—let's utilize some of it."

The Raker Bill passed through Congress in December 1913. President Wilson's signature would make it law. Robert Underwood Johnson beseeched him to veto it, saying, "God invented courage for just such emergencies. The moral effect of a veto would be immense."

Wilson signed.

"It is hard to bear," Muir told friends.

He would not live to see the valley drowned, or the new century descend into semipermanent war.

—◆—

THE NEXT SUMMER, a Bosnian Serb freedom fighter assassinated the heir to the Austro-Hungarian Empire, in Sarajevo, and madness consumed Europe. Nation after nation declared war on its neighbors. A pacifist all his life, Muir equated one tragedy with another: men at war with Nature akin to men at war with each other. He called it "desolation work." On both sides, young recruits entered the fray as if joining a sporting event, thinking they'd return home in weeks, victorious. What they found instead was hell on earth, an end of innocence, war on a scale nobody could have conceived, with poisonous gases, aerial dogfights, armored tanks, submarines, trench fighting, and shell-shocked field officers sending tens of thousands to their slaughter again and again, boys cut down like grass. "The Great War," people would call it. Great only in carnage and destruction.

Perhaps most egregious, the war would presage the rest of the new century with other massive conflicts and loss of life, a world Muir couldn't imagine if he wanted to or wouldn't want to if he could. The "war to end all wars" would end with the Treaty of Versailles in 1919, what one journalist called, "a peace to end all peace." It shattered liberal ideals about the inevitability of progress, ideals dear to Muir and those before him, men of the

Scottish Enlightenment and the American and French Revolutions who resisted feudalism and church authority; men who believed humankind would always improve itself through organized labor, universal education, due process, women's rights, and other just causes.

The war instead consolidated state and corporate power over economic, political, cultural, and social affairs; it created mass propaganda and the consumer society, the beginning of what critics would describe as the "cult of the self." In America the concentration of wealth and the rise of the corporate elite began to erode the liberal class that for decades had been the strongest defense against the worst excesses of power. Liberalism as founded by Thomas Hobbes and John Locke more than two centuries earlier would fade away.

As the war in Europe only grew worse, people settled into the drumbeat of despair. Not only did illusions die. So did the last passenger pigeon, in a Cincinnati zoo, bringing to extinction a species that had once colored the skies of Audubon's America. All news, it seemed now, was bad news.

Muir kept his head down, writing. He knew he had little time left. His former editor at *Atlantic Monthly*, Walter Page Hines, wrote to him, "California and Alaska will be here a long time after we're gone; but your books must be got ready for the long life that awaits them, for they must live as long as the country remains safe from the final clash of things . . ."

It was hard work, as always. How to capture Alaska without hyperbole and the syrupy language Johnson had criticized him of years before? He didn't have to say Alaska was magnificent; just say *Alaska*. The name itself was another language, another time, when risk was daily bread and he remembered drinking the cool air like water, and the glaciers—always the glaciers—grand rivers of ice that textured his mind with their crevasses and seracs. How frisky and rambunctious he'd been back then, forty-one going on fourteen, still boyish, a tramp, curious about everything, imaginative, free.

Busy now in his scribble den, he received valuable editorial assistance from a neighbor, Marion Randall Parsons, who reported in Muir "no trace of pessimism or despondency" after the Hetch Hetchy defeat. What wore him down, she said, was the "intense physical fatigue" brought on by the task of writing for long hours, day after day, month after month.

John Muir at his desk in his "scribble den," in Martinez, California. His home today is part of the John Muir National Historic Site, administered by the US National Park Service.

Fall brought a cool dampness that worsened. A week before Christmas, he gathered up his research and went south to stay in the desert with Helen. The dry air helped until the cough developed into pneumonia, his lungs filling with fluid. Helen sent him to a hospital in Los Angeles, accompanied by her husband. Muir went, but not without complaint. His two daughters joined him a few days later. On Christmas Eve, as both women stepped out of the room and no nurse was in attendance, the old naturalist, activist, and pacifist slipped away. On the table next to his bed was his last manuscript shaped into a book: *Travels in Alaska*.

Eulogies would pour in from Robert Underwood Johnson, S. Hall Young, and many others. For the *New York Evening Mail*, Charles L. Edson wrote a poem:

> John of the Mountains camps today
> On a level spot by the Milky Way;
> And God is telling him he has rolled
> The smoking earth from the iron mold,
> And hammered the mountains till they were cold
> And planted the Redwood trees of old.

THE SAME NIGHT Muir died, halfway around the world, battle-fatigued soldiers on the western front put down their weapons to celebrate a moment of peace. It began with German troops erecting Christmas trees topped with candles that caught the attention of the British, who shouted and clapped. Each side began lobbing chocolate cake and other treats over to the other side. Commanding officers, white flags in hand, met in no-man's land and agreed to a cease-fire, and soon thousands of men covering hundreds of miles came out of their trenches to share stories, food, and drink. The Germans sang "Stille Nacht (Silent Night)"; the British sang "O Come All Ye Faithful." One report called it an "unprecedented fraternization between enemy forces that has never been repeated on an equivalent scale." In some places it lasted only one night; in other places, up to a week.

The old pacifist would have smiled.

MORE THAN A FEW Muir scholars and biographers have written about his "cosmic connection" to family, friends, and the natural world; that he knew, somehow, when his father and mother were about to die, how he dropped everything to travel great distances to be with them; how his children received his greatest love and attention when they most needed it. Others have commented on his sensitivities to Native American spirituality and ways of life. They point to once-noble Tlingit Indians that Muir said were made "dirty" by white men's corruptible influences during the Klondike gold rush. They point as well to Cape Fox Village, a final stop on the Harriman Alaska Expedition, where Muir's shipmates assumed the village was abandoned, and so carried away a large number of totem poles and other collectibles while Muir stood back and called it a "robbery." The village was not abandoned, he knew; the residents were merely away, out in their summer fishing camps.

As Andrew Carnegie and John D. Rockefeller, born like Muir in the 1830s, happened along at the perfect time to make their fortunes and change American business and industry, Muir came along to change conservation and save the American landscape. He could have been a great inventor and made a lot of money, but he dedicated himself instead to saving Nature as a community to which we belong, not as a commodity we own. His timing, by luck or design, was perfect; his voice, unique. He knew what people wanted to hear, what they needed to see. Nature's beauty was not a side dish, he said; it was the main meal, the best nutrition out there. You didn't find God in Nature. God *was* Nature.

The loss of Hetch Hetchy created a "never again" chant among Muir's allies and disciples. Sierra Club members who had voted against the dam formed an ad hoc group, the Society for the Preservation of National Parks, and soon began to talk of a new federal agency to safeguard the best of America's public lands.

Muir had written to Johnson, "The long drawn-out battle work for Nature's gardens has not been thrown away. The conscience of the whole country has been aroused from sleep, and from outrageous evil compensating good in some form must surely come."

"The most significant thing about the controversy was that it occurred at all," Roderick Nash would observe. "One hundred or even fifty years earlier a similar proposal to dam a wilderness river would not have occasioned the slightest ripple of public protest . . ."

Many people were stunned to hear of Muir's death. He had always seemed so boundless, robustly alive, eternally young. Among those who knew him best, however, it was no surprise. Hetch Hetchy had wounded him gravely. That he should leave as he did, without fanfare—his final manuscript on the hospital table beside him, committed to the wild beauty of Alaska and the power of words—made a fitting end.

And a powerful beginning.

CHAPTER TWELVE

in perpetuity

IN THE SUMMER OF 1916, as a war-ravaged Europe staggered through zeppelin raids on Paris and the endless bloodbaths of the Isonzo and the Somme, President Woodrow Wilson ran for reelection on a platform of keeping America neutral, one that would win him a narrow victory. Everybody talked about Gil Anderson, who'd driven a Stutz more than 102 mph at Sheepshead Bay, New York. And about Margaret Sanger, who'd written *Family Limitation,* a lightning rod pamphlet (later a book) on contraception and population control: She would soon open the first birth control clinic in the United States (in Brooklyn), be arrested nine days later, and be jailed for a month.

The National Park Service was established as an agency focused on preservation and enjoyment and placed in the Department of the Interior, unlike the US Forest Service, a multiple-use agency that resided in the harvest-minded Department of Agriculture. And William Skinner Cooper, a thirty-two-year-old assistant professor of botany from the University of Minnesota, arrived in Glacier Bay to conduct field studies in primary plant succession, how a landscape returned to life after a cataclysmic event—glacial ice and retreat—had scoured it down to bedrock. Cooper had read *Travels in Alaska,* published only the year before (a few months after Muir's death). He'd studied the works of Muir, Harry Fielding Reid, Grove Karl Gilbert, and others who'd mapped the glacial footprints of Glacier Bay, the tracks of ice through space and time, the land and sea a living testimony to resilience, wildness, and change.

How many times had glaciers ebbed and flowed here? And why? What caused an ice age? What produced profound shifts in the Earth's climate over vast reaches of time? Seventy-five years had passed since Louis Agassiz first proposed that ice once ruled the higher latitudes and altitudes of the world. By 1916, scientists knew that the Pleistocene epoch, beginning roughly 1.8 million years ago and ending 12,000 years ago, was in fact a time of many ice ages, of major advances punctuated by relatively short interglacial periods. Glaciers came and glaciers went. Why?

ENTER MILUTIN MILANKOVITCH, a Serbian mathematician who specialized in astronomy and geophysics and believed the explanation lay in seasonal and latitudinal variations of solar radiation received by the Earth. Jailed by the Austro-Hungarian Army during part of the war, Milankovitch continued to make computations by hand, reaching back 600,000 years. He concluded that three cycles of different lengths combined to shift the planet's energy budget by as much as 20 percent, giving rise to the Earth's dynamic climatic regimes.

First, the shape of the Earth's ellipse around the sun stretched out from one position and back every 96,000 years. Second, the planet's axis tilt relative to the solar plane increased or decreased every 41,000 years. And last, the Earth did a complete wobble on its axis every 23,000 years, giving us different configurations of the Zodiac. As such, 12,000 years from now the North Star would not be Polaris. Through the millennia, Milankovitch said, these three cycles variously cancelled or augmented each other; this augmentation was enough to radically change the Earth's climate at times. Other variables also came into play: extreme solar and global volcanic activity, albedo, chaos, feedback loops, and local factors such as earthquakes and (over great distances of time) the rise of mountain ranges like the Himalaya. And if Svante Arrhenius were correct, human activity played an increasingly significant role as well, given our growing population and industrial footprint that each year pumped more carbon dioxide into the atmosphere.

Milankovitch would work for decades to fully develop his theory, yet already, by the time William Cooper arrived in Glacier Bay, his results were creating a stir among scientists. This was no small accomplishment;

academics made tough critics. Consider Milankovitch's fellow theorist Alfred Wegener, a German meteorologist and paleoclimatologist who the year before, in 1915, completed a bold and elaborate explanation of continental drift. Wegener provided compelling evidence on many levels, such as fossils, rock types, and coastline patterns. However, he couldn't explain the driving force behind the drift.

That force, convections in the Earth's semimolten mantle that floats plates of the crust in various directions, would not be discovered until after World War II. And so Wegener's theory, exquisite in its detail but lacking a key element, earned him a flood of derision, especially from the United States. If what he proposed were true, one geologist later announced, then geologists would have to "forget everything which has been learned in the last seventy years and start all over again."

Like Muir, Cooper found the truth at his feet, in little plants and subtle patterns that had stories to tell—for those willing to slow down and look. His father had exposed him to mountains at an early age—first in the Blue Ridge and Adirondacks; later the Colorado Rockies—and he came to love science and mountaineering. According to a friend, he also developed a passion for the kind of nature writing "strongly reminiscent of that of John Muir." At Johns Hopkins University, Cooper studied geology under Harry Fielding Reid, who had known the great "Professor Muir" in Glacier Bay. He transferred to the University of Chicago, where, according to historian Theodore Catton,

> Cooper studied under Professor Henry Chandler Cowles, whose seminal work on "successional development" in plant communities in the Lake Michigan sand dunes had helped establish the new school of "dynamic" ecology. Together with University of Nebraska ecologist Frederic Clements, whose grassland studies proceeded independently yet parallel to his own work, Cowles introduced the concept of successional stages of plant communities leading to a "climax community" or steady state . . . Walking his graduate students in their minds' eyes through these dunes, Cowles planted a seed that would eventually germinate Cooper's study of plant succession in Glacier Bay.

Cooper visited and photographed every glacier and inlet except Johns Hopkins that first summer, 1916, and made careful observations, and established nine permanent one-meter quadrats "in three sites of varying distance from the glaciers" that he would visit every five years or so to "make a close study of changing soil and plant composition." He described his work as "exceedingly modest."

The modesty would end, however, when Cooper, like his hero John Muir, transcended himself to find the writer and activist within, who would fight to save the wild country he loved. It was something—*somebody*—he never thought he'd be, but once committed he had no intention of backing down. Glaciers shape the land; the land shapes the man.

Since Muir's final visit, in the summer of 1899, and the massive earthquake that rattled the region that September, the glaciers of Glacier Bay had continued their retreats north, in some cases opening entire new waterways. To begin a journey in the spruce-hemlock conifer forest of the lower bay, deglaciated the longest, and to proceed north through successive stages of vegetation—the dominant plants of each stage getting smaller and smaller, from trees down to shrubs down to mosses and lichens near the tidewater ice fronts—was more than a journey through space, as Cooper had learned from Cowles. It was a journey through time, measured by changes on the land and in the sea, a bay coming back to life, a universe unto itself, a Tlingit homeland, a scientific laboratory, and one day a national park, an international biosphere reserve, and a world heritage site—if people sacrificed; if they fought for it. In a nation increasingly crowded, industrial, and dedicated to economic growth, where every man with a pencil, suit, shovel, or saw was what Frederick Jackson Turner called "an expectant capitalist," wild places didn't stay wild by accident. They had to be loved, honored, defended.

And so William Cooper, a modest plant ecologist, dug deep and found the John Muir within.

AT THE ANNUAL MEETING of the Ecological Society of America (ESA) in Boston in 1922, he presented his initial Glacier Bay findings from the field summers of 1916 and 1921. So excited were his colleagues, they began to talk of how Glacier Bay could be permanently protected, perhaps as a national monument, or even a national park.

"In the first case," wrote Robert F. Griggs, a fellow botanist, "it is necessary only to convince one man [the president] of the advisability of the action, while in the second six hundred, more or less [both houses of Congress], must be converted to the idea." Get the monument first, Griggs reasoned; the park will follow, though it may take years. Griggs had recently returned from expeditions to the Valley of Ten Thousand Smokes, in the Katmai region on the Alaska Peninsula, seven hundred miles west of Glacier Bay, and successfully campaigned for Katmai National Monument, established in 1918. The following year, the year Teddy Roosevelt died, Grand Canyon National Park was established after having been a national monument (created by TR) for more than a decade.

Disinclined toward boldness, or to assume leadership or take credit that belonged to others, Cooper would later say it was Barrington Moore, former president of the ESA, who first proposed that a committee be established to seek permanent protection of the Glacier Bay region. Perhaps. But the task of chairing that committee fell to Cooper, and from then on he was the point of the spear.

"A MONSTROUS PROPOSITION," announced the *Juneau Daily Empire*,

> It is said the proposed National Monument is intended to protect Muir Glacier and to permit the study of plant and insect life in its neighborhood. It tempts patience to try to discuss such nonsensical performances. The suggestion that a reserve be established to protect a glacier that none could disturb if he wanted and none would want to disturb if he could or permit the study of plant and insect life is the quintessence of silliness. And then when it is proposed to put millions of acres, taking in established industries and agricultural lands and potential resources that are capable if supporting people and adding to the population of Alaska, it becomes a monstrous crime against development and advancement. It leads one to wonder if Washington has gone crazy through catering to conservation faddists.

One observer would note that Cooper "defended the concepts of the proposed monument in the same newspaper . . . also pointing out all the things the newspaper had not bothered to ask him about."

THE SAME YEAR, 1922, Cooper assumed command of his committee to safeguard Glacier Bay from so-called "development and advancement," the famously private expatriate T. S. Eliot published *The Waste Land,* one of the most important poems of the twentieth century, wherein he said "I can show you fear in a handful of dust." Antarctic explorer Sir Ernest Shackleton died early that year. Never comfortable in flat, green, rainy England with all its starched Edwardian finery, he sailed back to South Georgia, the island he called "the Gateway to the Antarctic," suffered a major heart attack, and was buried facing south among Norwegian whalers in the land of ice where his greatness shone best. And Sigmund Freud, in *Beyond the Pleasure Principle* and his other writings, described modern man as little more than a zoo animal trapped in invisible cages of his own making, pacing between the wishes of the individual and the requirements of society, driven by dissatisfaction, always wanting more: more money, more freedom, more land, more time.

What was success, exactly? A ghost? A mirage? A bigger this, a faster that? A neurotic dog chasing his own tail? And once he catches it . . . then what? Who wrote the definitions of success, development, advancement? If Alaska needed more people, as some capitalists said it did, how many more? When did "more" become "too many"? At what point, if ever, did we awaken to see the futility of it all?

Scholars have pointed out that Eliot's poem, shifting as it does between satire and prophecy, speaks to the hopelessness and meaninglessness of our existence; after all, we all become dust. The rich might have nicer coffins than the poor, but in the end they're not aware of it and are no more comfortable. The choir sings about the kingdom of Heaven, not the gifts of the Earth. Thousands of flowering meadows become shopping malls and housing tracts, and millionaire developers want more, and children stay indoors to eat processed food and watch five hours of television a day. "Tell me, what is it you plan to do with your one wild and precious life?" poet Mary Oliver would ask.

John Muir had observed, "Thousands of tired, nerve-shaken, over-civilized people are beginning to find out that going to the mountains is going home; that wilderness is a necessity . . ."

We'd better think carefully about what we're doing.

One day in 1889 while walking on the California coast, Muir had struck up a conversation with a young amateur botanist and mountain guide named Enos Mills. Inspired, as were others by John of the Mountains, Mills buckled down and launched a campaign to safeguard his beloved Colorado from runaway development. Calling himself "the John Muir of the Rockies," he spearheaded a campaign to create Rocky Mountain National Park, no easy task. But all great opportunities mask themselves as insurmountable problems. In 1915, the year after Muir died, Rocky Mountain National Park was established. "I owe everything to Muir," said Mills, who'd lobbied for the park for more than a decade. "If it hadn't been for him I would have been a mere gypsy."

Two years later Mount McKinley National Park was established in interior Alaska, again through a decade-long effort, not of one man but two: Charles Sheldon, a wealthy hunter/naturalist in the tradition of Teddy Roosevelt, and Belmore Browne, a mountaineer/writer who in 1912 had come within one hundred meters of being the first man to stand atop Mount McKinley, the highest mountain in North America, with its seventeen glaciers spilling down magnificent granite gorges to braided rivers and the tundra below. Both Sheldon and Browne found strength and inspiration in the life and works of John Muir.

BY THE TIME William Cooper began his campaign to establish Glacier Bay National Monument a few years later, the US National Park Service had become a no-nonsense outfit headed by Stephen T. Mather, a Sierra Club member and arch-opponent of the Hetch Hetchy Dam and the utilitarian policies of the Forest Service. He'd made a fortune in borax mining and brought to his new job an authenticity some found refreshing, others threatening. Early on, he often used his own personal fortune to help finance the service, saying, "I got my money out of the soil of the country, so why should I not be praised for putting a little of it back? That's only decent acknowledgment."

Critics charged that the national parks were expensive irrelevances at best, communist enclaves at worst. Park advocates cried baloney, adopting a staunch defense. "Without parks and outdoor life," asserted Enos Mills, "all that is best in civilization will be smothered." He said the wilderness character of the parks are the best thing we have to "rebuild the past" and "keep our nation young," and will only grow in value over time, so long as we keep and protect them.

With America still recovering from the recent war, and the west largely undisturbed during those years, writer John C. Van Dyke (capitalizing the word "Nature" as Muir had) asked, "Was there ever a time in human history when a return to Nature was so much needed as just now? How shall the nations be rebuilt, the lost faith and hope renewed, the race live again through the Great Mother who we have forsaken?"

New voices began to speak out—Aldo Leopold, Robert Marshall, Benton MacKaye, Robert Sterling Yard, Olaus Murie—as vigorous defenders of the last wildernesses, each a disciple, in his own way, of John Muir. If these places disappeared, they said, we'd lose far more than we'd gain. Picking up on Frederick Jackson Turner's appeal to a national identity, Leopold, a Wisconsinite like Turner and Muir, wrote that,

> many of the attributes most distinctive of America and Americans are [due to] the impress of the wilderness and the life that accompanied it . . . if we have such a thing as American culture (and I think we have), its distinguishing marks are a certain vigorous individualism combined with ability to organize, a certain intellectual curiosity bent to practical ends, a lack of subservience to stiff social norms, and an intolerance of drones, all of which are distinctive characteristics of successful pioneers. These, if anything, are the indigenous part of our Americanism, the qualities that set it apart as a new rather than as an imitative contribution to civilization.

And how can we expect to preserve these institutions, Leopold concluded, "without giving so much as a thought to preserving the environment which produced them and which may now be one of our effective means to keeping them alive?"

Yes, these protected wild places were great for having fun. But as Roderick Nash would point out, they're much more: "They maintained the opportunity for successive generations of Americans to acquire the characteristics of pioneers and to acquaint themselves firsthand with the conditions that shaped their culture."

In other words, they're reference points, places to be quiet and acquire wisdom; to listen and give thanks.

As Leopold would one day declare, "I am glad I shall never be young without wild country to be young in. Of what avail are forty freedoms without a blank spot on the map?"

PRESIDENT CALVIN COOLIDGE signed the executive order that created Glacier Bay National Monument in February 1925. The Alaska economy did not fail. The monument was not a monster. The world continued to turn, the population of Alaska continued to grow, slowly; the glaciers continued to retreat, some quickly. And William Cooper, soft-spoken as ever, continued to visit the bay every five years or so to study the shimmering blue ice fronts and his little pioneering plants.

Accompanying Cooper on each visit was Tom Smith, a Juneau-based boat skipper who didn't like the monument, saying it locked up the land and restricted prospecting and the scrappy entrepreneurial spirit that made America great. The two men agreed to disagree and maintained a friendship, though Smith, according to most accounts, could never let it go.

Early in their adventures, he anchored off Rendu Glacier while Cooper went ashore to hike about. When the glacier calved and sent a large wave down the inlet, Smith's boat got so violently tossed about (with Smith hanging on tight) that he announced he would never again approach a tidewater glacier. Years later, however, when Johns Hopkins Inlet opened up behind the retreating glacier to become the wildest inlet in the bay, an icy inner sanctum embraced by peaks more than twelve thousand feet high—what John Muir would call "mountain nourishment" of the highest order—Smith couldn't help himself. He and Cooper once again approached a massive ice wall and had a grand time.

Elsewhere in the bay, Cooper investigated the interglacial stumps that had so perplexed Muir in his day. Later, radiocarbon dating would determine the stump was four hundred years old when it died some seven thousand years ago, on that same spot. Buried in gravel that was bulldozed by the advancing ice front before the tree was snapped off higher up, it became entombed under the glacier and exposed again after hundreds—maybe thousands—of years, when the ice retreated and meltwater carried away much of the gravel.

How many times glaciers had ebbed and flowed over this land was hard to say. Each ice advance largely obliterated the evidence of previous events. It made a powerful metaphor, how a resilient land attracts resilient people, and the pioneer destroys the thing he loves, just as the little strawberry flower, so tough but only so big, prepares the soil for the alder that displaces it, and the spruce and hemlock that in turn displace the alder.

"One does not ordinarily think of strawberries growing next door to a glacier," wrote Cooper. "But Alaska is full of paradoxes."

Tom Smith loved the land no less than Cooper, but he could never come to accept it as a national monument. Dave Bohn would write:

> And over and above the argument, the recurring paradox; namely that those who move away from the crowded centers of population— for many reasons but always at least to find more space for themselves, proceed not only to ruin the land for any who would follow, but also proceed to do their utmost to bring as many as possible to crowd the very space they sought. In the history of this country the multitude almost without exception has followed. And almost without exception the land has been ruined. But not always.

While enamored with prospecting, the thought of large-scale industrial mining frightened Smith. Could one be permitted without the other? The strawberry flower without the alder?

At one point Smith wrote a letter to Cooper:

Dear Bill:
Pleased to hear from you. I think you better be prepared for the worst
when you start for Alaska again. You may not be pleased with the
going ons in Glacier Bay. If the mineing company finds a large body
of nickel ore there, there will be a long, dirty greasy stinking cable
running from the Bradey Glacier right to the head of the bay—and
could be several thousand dirty mineres working there—and freight-
ers hundreds of feet in length with dirty black smoke roleing out of the
funnells—turning that beautiful blue ice into an awful color. Then
next would be a smelter and from past sad experience we know what
happened at Treadwell Mine on Douglass Island just killed all that
fine young groth of timber. The worst is yet to come. The Canadians
may open a port in the head of the Bay—and they would have dozens
of steamers plowing through the Bay—and hundreds of deck hands,
longshoremen, grease pots etc. It is really too awful to contemplate . . .
Hope you will excuse my punctuation, as I do not have the book larnin
that you have.
    Best regards to you and Mrs. Cooper.
    Tom Smith

A crew of mineral explorers working for the Fremont Mining Company did indeed find a promising copper-nickel deposit in a nunatak
(rock outcropping) in the Brady Icefield. The following summer Fremont
made test drills through three hundred to four hundred feet of ice into
the bedrock below the glacier, while a second mining company, Newmont
Exploration Ltd., buzzed the ice field with helicopters, landing here and
there to take surface samples. According to historian Theodore Catton,

> Analysis of the many core samples confirmed the existence of a large
> mineral deposit underlying the Brady Icefield. By 1963, the mining
> companies had filed twenty claims and invested $800,000 in mineral
> exploration. At the same time, an increase in prospecting was caus-
> ing the monument staff "grave concerns." A jump in gold and silver

prices attracted dozens of new companies into the field. During the summer of 1964, there were no fewer than five companies prospecting in the monument: two in Muir Inlet, one using a drill rig near Lake Seclusion, one using helicopters without a permit, and one that made a mess of an area on Lituya Bay. In a report titled "Information Required for Legislation to Redesignate Glacier Bay as a National Park," [Superintendent L. J.] Mitchell included photographs of the degradation caused by this last operation—of "slashed forests, heavy equipment abandoned to rust, and supplies left to rot."

Mitchell and his staff referred to it as the "legalized rape of Glacier Bay."

"Legalized" because the strongest opposition to the establishment of Glacier Bay National Monument had come from the pro-mining/prospecting community, including none other than the US Geological Survey's Alfred Brooks, an early explorer in Alaska (who had the world's northernmost mountain range named after him). Brooks wrote to Cooper, "I do not think it is possible or advisable to establish a park in Alaska from which the prospectors are shut out." Novelist Rex Beach wrote a feature article in *Cosmopolitan* magazine entitled, "The Place is Alaska—the Business is Mining." His point: What better way to put America back to work during the Great Depression than to open up Alaska in general, and Glacier Bay in particular, to mineral exploration.

In another article, a copy of which he reportedly sent to President Franklin Delano Roosevelt, Beach asserted that the greater portion of the Glacier Bay region

is absolutely barren and the only timber, such as there is, lies along the southern edge. It is not a good game refuge, nor are there any fishing streams or lakes in which salmon spawn. Presumably there are some sheep and goats in the St. Elias Range but it is the last place anybody would go for bear, moose or caribou. In fact the whole area is like a haunted house and I doubt if ten white men have visited it in the last ten years aside possibly from some surveying parties.

In a book published by the Sierra Club thirty years later, Dave Bohn would respond that Beach was "utterly wrong."

At the time, however, in the 1930s, with America down on its luck, Beach's appeal played well into Roosevelt's New Deal image of putting the country back to work.

William Cooper wrote to National Park Service Director Arno Cammerer, "If Congress passes the proposed bill . . . I cannot imagine a precedent more dangerous to each and every reservation under control of the Park Service."

It felt like the ghost of Hetch Hetchy. Was no place safe from enterprising, industrial man? Even glaciers could be mined.

The provision to allow mineral exploration in Glacier Bay passed into law in 1936, one year after Robert Marshall, Aldo Leopold, Olaus Murie, and other visionaries—fearful this kind of thing could happen again and again—founded The Wilderness Society.

HETCH HETCHY got started around then, the first water arriving into San Francisco ten years later than promised, twenty years after John Muir's passing. The dam ended up costing one hundred million dollars, more than twice the original estimate, all while the city of Oakland, across the bay, found a cheaper water source and began to use it. But of course Oakland's source provided no electric power, and that was always the point with Hetch Hetchy. Although the 1913 enabling legislation said power would be sold only by public utilities, the Pacific Gas and Electric Company, with so many politicians in their pockets, wrested control of the power partway between the mountains and the city and got what it wanted: huge profits.

The dam advocates had always said the flooded valley would be beautiful and provide wonderful recreational opportunities, with a new lake for boating and good fun. Historian Stephen Fox observed,

> In the reservoir itself, as the water level rose and fell with the changing seasons the shoreline was marred by slimy mud and decaying vegetation. Nothing could grow at the edge of the artificial lake.

Under moonlight, with tree trunks scattered around like so many bodies, it resembled a battlefield one day after the fight: a wasteland bearing stark testimony to man's befuddled ingenuity.

Had it been left pristine, the valley could have provided joy and wonder for tens of millions of visitors. It could have been a life-changer, a place of inspiration like her more famous sister, Yosemite Valley, what John Muir called "God's garden." Now nobody went there. It was a dead place, drowned by shortsightedness. Fox concluded that from the perspective of many years later, the dam "seems a comprehensive mistake."

HOW THEN to save Alaska? *Let it be*, said the many disciples of John Muir, a growing legion of young, environmentally aware Americans. Slow down. Go softly with an open heart. Stop calling it a frontier. The last frontier is not Alaska, outer space, the oceans, or the wonders of technology. It's open-mindedness. Honor the land and its first nation peoples, and their ability to acquire wisdom, sustenance, and happiness from the wild plants and animals around them. Learn through story. Sleep on the ground. *Listen*.

Travel by kayak and canoe.

In 1964, while mining companies ran around Glacier Bay staking claims and making noise with their helicopters and drills, Congress passed the Wilderness Act, an unprecedented piece of legislation designed to protect wild places from our worst impulses and leave them "untrammeled." Seven years later, in 1971, the Alaska Native Claims Settlement Act (ANCSA) bequeathed to Native Alaskans forty-four million acres (roughly 12 percent of Alaska) and nearly one billion dollars to invest in their future. There would be no Indian reservations in Alaska. Instead, ANCSA created thirteen regional corporations and more than two hundred village corporations for Native Americans to manage their resources and investments. Buried in section 17(d)(2) of ANCSA was a clause directing the secretary of the interior to withdraw up to eighty million acres for study and possible inclusion as new national parks, preserves, monuments, and wildlife refuges.

The very thing Tom Smith didn't like—government intervention—was the only thing that could save Glacier Bay and other parts of Alaska from becoming what he didn't want, a mine pit. A large and complicated bill, the Alaska National Interest Lands Conservation Act (ANILCA) would be nine years in the making, the first—and last—of its kind, filled with compromise and provisions for protecting wild areas and safeguarding indigenous ways of life.

"We had to get it right," said National Park Service historian William E. (Bill) Brown, a member of the NPS D2 task force that came north in the mid-1970s to select new parklands to be protected in perpetuity. "This was our chance to save America. Many of us had been too young to fight in World War II; that rankled us. Now was our time. This was our chance to do things right, and—by God—we did. We saved Alaska. We saved America."

It would have made William Cooper smile. And John Muir sing.

EPILOGUE: 2012–2014

blue ice and brown bears

NEARLY EVERY DAY of summer two large cruise ships slide into the cold nutrient-rich waters of Glacier Bay National Park. A small boat comes alongside, and park rangers climb a ladder to board each ship. One ranger heads to the bridge, another to a large lounge, where they spend the day explaining to passengers—often two thousand or more per ship—the natural and human histories of Glacier Bay: the behavior of glaciers, the feeding strategies of humpback whales, the arrival of sea otters that didn't exist in the bay twenty-some years ago and now number in the thousands, the power and intrigue of coastal brown bears, the homeland story of the Huna Tlingit, the complexities of primary plant succession, the ramifications of climate change. A journey that took John Muir and his companions weeks by canoe now takes days by cruise ship. Passengers feel no discomfort. Hardtack and seal meat appear on no menus. The buffets last for hours and offer a dozen confections of carved and ornamental chocolates. The linen is clean. The pillows are soft.

This is a special day, the one day on the weeklong itinerary that focuses on wild Alaska. By request of the National Park Service, the ships offer no casino gambling this day, no dance lessons, art auctions, comedy shows, or other activities that might conflict with the rangers' presentations and with the ostensible reason why everyone is there, the park itself: the whales, bears, mountains, and ice.

Yesterday the ships spent the day in Skagway; the day before that, Juneau. Tomorrow, Sitka. Jewelry stores and T-shirt shops. Rides on helicopters and trains. Today, however, the focus is blue ice and brown bears in a 3.3-million-acre national park—a park 50 percent larger than

Yellowstone—that's also an international biosphere reserve and a world heritage site. While a few people on board have no idea where they are, most are keenly aware they're in Glacier Bay and are up early to see it all. They've dreamed of this for years. They've read London's *Call of the Wild*, McPhee's *Coming into the Country*, and John Muir's *Travels in Alaska*.

JOHN MUIR has been gone for a century, yet he lives. Across America, schools, parks, and awards are named for him. Universities have his books as required reading. New biographies explore his thousand-mile walk to the Gulf of Mexico, his boyhood in Scotland and Wisconsin, his trip to South America and Africa in his sunset years, and his time in Alaska. Film, art, stage plays, and musical scores are inspired by his life and vision. When California had to choose a design for its commemorative quarter, hundreds of submissions—the iconic Hollywood sign, the 1849 Gold Rush, the Golden Gate Bridge—fell away until one remained: an image of John Muir. "Muir lit the torch of conservation in our state," said Governor Arnold Schwarzenegger. "He has inspired generations of Californians to preserve our natural beauty, and this is what makes him so special."

If caught in a storm halfway up a mountain, Muir would go up, Thoreau down. He was fearless, rapturous, infectious. Storms were his friends, mountains his sanctuaries.

How did he attain this passion for Nature?

"All through history," observes Thomas J. Lyon, a Muir scholar and professor of English and environmental studies, "we have searched for states of mind which could transcend the apparent alienation of communicable consciousness from the overall stream of life." The answer, he says, lies in poetry, religion, and mystical literature, and how they contribute to "the background urge of wilderness writing. John Muir had that urge; he felt keenly the difference between the language-mind and the wilderness-mind."

What he looked for, Lyon believes, and what he found in Alaska on a scale that inspired him for the rest of his life was a transcending metaphor—glaciers—that "arose naturally from what glaciers do: they *flow.* In their stately progress and again in their retreat, they break and grind rocks, move soil, make watercourses, create homes for plants and animals, affect the weather and much else. They are history, but their participation in the world is alive."

———

THE CRUISE SHIPS arrive at Margerie Glacier, in Tarr Inlet, the upper West Arm of Glacier Bay, seventy miles north of the bay's entrance, and spend an hour or so off the tidewater face, all while lunch is served buffet style. On sunny days passengers take their meal out on deck to eat and drink while they watch and listen to the glacier. Many find themselves slowing down to take it in, the ice face staring back at them. The glacier might calve many times or not at all. There's no telling.

The mood is festive, yet most people say little. They stare, transfixed by the power and beauty of an ice wall some 250 feet high and a mile wide, standing there in defiance of a warming world. The rangers rove. They've spoken over the loudspeaker earlier and given formal presentations inside a large auditorium. Now it's time to hit the outside decks and let the ice do the talking. One should never upstage a glacier.

A few people have questions.

"Why is the ice blue?"

"How old is the ice?"

"How long is this glacier?"

"Is the glacier advancing or retreating?"

"Is climate change a factor?"

———

KEVIN RICHARDS, a seasonal park ranger/naturalist in his nineteenth summer in Glacier Bay, explains that the science of glaciology has matured considerably since John Muir's time. We now have ice cores from Greenland and Antarctica that tell us the same thing: for the last 800,000 years, and probably longer, carbon dioxide (CO_2) in the earth's atmosphere has fluctuated between 180 and 280 parts per million (ppm).

In 2013, atmospheric CO_2—a greenhouse gas that traps solar radiation at the surface of the earth and warms the climate—reached 400ppm for the first time in perhaps three million years, and the level is rising about three parts per million per year. The last time atmospheric CO_2 was that high, sea level was roughly 65 feet higher than it is today. California, the most progressive state in the nation, has passed a law to *slow the rate of increase*. That is, California still pumps more CO_2 into the air each year than it did the year before, and it's more enlightened on this issue than any other state. In Oklahoma, people might wonder about the National Severe Storms Laboratory raising the Fujita Scale of tornado intensity from F6 to F8 while their senator, James Inhofe, stands by his claim that "global warming is the greatest hoax ever perpetrated on the American public."

Kevin says calmly and quietly that climate change is not only real, it's a global catastrophe-in-the-making due to our rising numbers, our rising levels of consumption (more gasoline-powered cars and bigger homes in the US and elsewhere), and our addiction to burning coal, oil, and other hydrocarbons that produce CO_2 and other greenhouse gases.

Why the concern? Storms, fires, and droughts will intensify and become more common. They already have. Sea level, today eight inches higher than it was in 1900, will continue to rise, likely at an accelerated rate, and be three to six feet higher by the close of the twenty-first century. "Even if we stopped burning all fossil fuels tomorrow," writes Tim Folger in *National Geographic Magazine,* "the existing greenhouse gases would continue to warm the Earth for centuries. We have irreversibly committed future generations to a hotter world and rising seas." Oceans will turn acidic as atmospheric CO_2 is absorbed by seawater and converted into carbonic acid.

The Earth will survive, top scientists say. Humanity will survive. But civilization will radically change as we face what novelist James Kunstler calls "The Long Emergency," a generations-long crisis in a post-growth world that we'll need to manage with focus and dignity. Adds Paul Gilding, the former head of Greenpeace International, this challenge "will require a major evolution in human values, politics and personal expectations." Say good-bye to shopping. Say good-bye to malls.

"SO THEN," a passenger asks Kevin, "you believe in climate change?"

"It's not a belief," Kevin says again, calmly, quietly. "Climate change is a fact supported by overwhelming scientific consensus." To debate it is to give credibility to an argument that shouldn't exist.

But it does exist. Despite the best science that documents human beings burning more and more fossil fuels, and pumping more and more carbon into the atmosphere, the debate goes on. As best-selling author Mary Pipher notes:

> Newscasters and talk show hosts often go to great lengths to present both "sides" of a story. But not all points of view are equally credible. Some are based on knowledge and careful study of a question. Others come from hired guns or ideologues . . . For an honest analysis of a situation, we need the media and the talking heads to distinguish between experts and propagandists and between objective analysis and public relations.

One passenger mentions Republican congressmen who say carbon dioxide in the atmosphere is not a problem because people are also made of carbon.

Laughter ripples through the crowd. Some passengers shake their heads.

Kevin samples the chocolate and says, "Watch the glaciers. Listen to the ice. The ice does not lie."

According to Pipher, a grandmother therapist who lives in Nebraska, "People avoid facing problems they have no idea how to solve." In *The Green Boat*, her book that focuses on how to revive our capsized culture, Pipher talks about moving from "trauma to transcendence." First comes awareness, followed by pain, acceptance, and then finally, action. The trick is to see insurmountable problems as golden opportunities, as chances to invent new sources of energy, new models of sustainable living, new ways to honor and preserve the beauty and diversity of the natural world.

Author Bill McKibben, one of America's leading environmentalists, knows about action. He's written extensively about climate change, marched on the White House and been arrested there for protesting the Keystone XL Pipeline. The pipeline would carry oil from the Alberta Tar Sands to refineries in Texas; he calls it "a 1,700-mile fuse to the biggest carbon bomb on the continent." Time is running out, he says. The climate crisis is deepening and may be inevitable before it's fully realized. We're sleepwalking into the future. He recommends that we find a suitable bad guy—the oil giants, the pushers in our addictions—and stop giving them taxpayer subsidies as they make the highest profits in history; that we stop letting them buy elections and corrupt our democracy. Instead, McKibben says, given their power and influence in remaking our world, we should name major hurricanes after them: Hurricane Exxon, Hurricane British Petroleum, Hurricane Shell.

If that seems severe, recall that John Muir and Teddy Roosevelt, leading environmentalists in their day, men of vision and action who righted many wrongs, called greedy capitalists "timber thieves" and "fools."

Saving the natural world and finding our rightful place in it can be a nasty business.

———

AND FULL OF IRONY.

Ice doesn't lie, but glaciers can deceive. Natural systems are complex, with tipping points, thresholds, oscillations, and feedback loops.

Kevin explains that while the world grows warmer, and glaciers everywhere retreat, one or two in Glacier Bay hold steady, and even threaten to advance. Why? Warmer sea surface temperatures in the Gulf of Alaska create more storms that slam into the highest coastal mountains in the world. Precipitation increases. At lower elevations, where it used to snow, it rains, which starves many glaciers of new ice. As such, they retreat. But here's the irony. At higher elevations, where it once snowed, it snows *more*. What few glaciers begin from those high catchment areas are well-fed, even robust.

One passenger mentions that in another thirty years Montana's Glacier National Park will probably be without glaciers. Another says that last summer was the worst fire summer in Colorado's history, and this summer is even worse. And then come the torrential rains, and floods. A voracious reader, Kevin mentions a column in *Orion* magazine where

Derrick Jensen writes, "October 2012 was the 323rd consecutive month for which the global temperature was above average. The odds of that happening randomly are literally astronomical." In his film *Chasing Ice*, environmental photographer James Balog documents glaciers disintegrating in Greenland, Iceland, Alaska, and Colorado. The largest glacier in Greenland retreated more in the last ten years than it did in the previous one hundred, he says. The surfaces of many Greenland glaciers are pockmarked by dark stains of dust, carbon soot, and algae that act as solar heat absorbers and accelerate melting.

What does all this mean? "Many of our culture's most cherished ideas are no longer viable," says writer Naomi Klein in her article "Capitalism vs. the Climate" in *Nation* magazine. Vigorous economic growth never existed in human history until we began to burn fossil fuels and pump CO_2 into the atmosphere, a trend that continues to go only one direction: up. The climate change crisis is therefore so vexing and fundamentally at odds with our good guy image of ourselves, and our mantra of Economic-Growth-Forever, that denial is easy.

"The bottom line," Klein writes,

is that an ecological crisis that has its roots in the overconsumption of natural resources must be addressed not just by improving the efficiency of our economies but by reducing the amount of material stuff we produce and consume. Yet that idea is anathema to the large corporations that dominate the global economy, which are controlled by footloose investors who demand ever greater profits year after year.

Klein concludes with an observation by University of Surrey economist Tim Jackson that "we are therefore caught in the untenable bind of . . . crash the system or trash the planet."

LITTLE WONDER we don't want to face it.

In 2010, when the Scottish government issued a press release titled "John Muir Legacy Lives On," Sierra Club Chairman Carl Pope said,

Through his visionary work preserving America's most pristine wilderness, John Muir bent the arc of history. We simply would not have wilderness to save if Muir had not fought to protect it. In an era of climate change, we are challenged, again, to bend the arc of history. The Sierra Club is honored to share John Muir's legacy with the John Muir Trust and the Scottish Government. Together, we can face the greatest global challenge of our generation.

———

KEVIN takes the opportunity to tell passengers good news about the great Alaska lands act of 1980. It built on Muir's vision, changed Glacier Bay from a national monument to a national park, and added many new national parks and wildlife refuges and other preserved lands—more than one hundred million acres total—to the maps of Alaska. Jimmy Carter, inspired by Teddy Roosevelt, who was inspired by Muir, signed the act into law in the final weeks of his presidency. He dared to take criticism from many don't-tread-on-me Alaskans who said the act "locked up" their state. Carter shrugged it off, saying you may not appreciate this now, but the next generation will.

———

AS THE CRUISE SHIP begins to leave Margerie Glacier, somebody spots a kayak halfway between the ship and the glacier, impossibly small and vulnerable from the ship's rail. Everybody watches the paddler boldly approach the ice wall, apparently undaunted by the size and danger of it all.

Is it madness? A death wish of some kind?

"What's he doing?" a passenger asks.

"He's having a big adventure in wild country," Kevin says. "That's what people do in their national parks."

———

THAT NIGHT in Bartlett Cove, at park headquarters, at the southern end of the bay, Kevin joins his fellow rangers for dinner and conversation.

There's no television, traffic, or malls, only the tides and forest and birds, the occasional bear and moose, the distant blow of a humpback whale. All during dinner the conversation spins around mountain goats and a recent kayaking/camping trip to Queen Inlet and Gloomy Knob. Kevin mentions that he's going to take next summer off and hike the entire 215-mile John Muir Trail, beginning in Yosemite and ending atop Mount Whitney, the highest point in the contiguous United States. It's something he has wanted to do for forty years. Last year Kevin ran the Boston Marathon and ranked thirty-ninth out of more than one thousand in his age group. He's in his mid-fifties, doesn't carry an extra ounce, lives on less than twenty thousand dollars a year, has a fine singing voice, and is content.

He and his fellow off-duty rangers pull out guitars and tell stories. Always stories. They talk about wildness and science, and new modifications to the Milankovitch Cycles, and theories on plant succession, why things are the way they are, out beyond what poet Mary Oliver calls "the machinery of our wits." They talk about the initiative that appears on California voting ballots every few years to tear down the Hetch Hetchy Dam. Can you imagine? The very idea creates its own electricity.

A few rangers live year-round in the nearby town of Gustavus, a friendly place, like Glacier Bay, reachable only by boat or plane, with a population of about 400 people; 300 moose; 200 dogs; 100 ukuleles, banjos, and guitars; 50 bald eagles; 10 horses; and 5 bears, most of them black bears, though a few brown bears show up now and then.

Bumper stickers say, What's your hurry? You're already here. Or, I'd rather live here than have a career.

Like John Muir, Kevin is himself something of a glacier, flowing through space and time. He reads Muir's books (all still in print) and talks about a Declaration of Interdependence to make us less self-involved and money crazy and more dedicated to the natural world and our own human community. His fellow rangers are his family; they sustain him with friendship; they work to make park visitors better understand the importance of the natural world. They're a tribe, of sorts, these rangers, with their own fire to share. They talk about traveling during the winter, but also about staying in Alaska, something John Muir never did, though he was tempted, no doubt, after that first epic canoe journey in 1879. A good woman awaited him in California, so he went south to a life of husbandry, fatherhood, farming, activism, sacrifice, and fame.

One ranger mentions that somebody recently went to Muir Point and found the old cabin that Muir built there with Harry Fielding Reid and Reid's geology students. Today, it's a pile of moss-covered chimney rocks about five feet high, deep in a spruce forest. Nothing more. The timbers have rotted into the ground. A silence falls over the conversation. Though the cabin site has been mapped with GPS waypoints of its exact location, rangers consider it bad form to use technology to find it. They like to find the cabin on their own, those few who give it a try. It's a grail, a holy place, no longer visited by steamships that toot their whistles and belch black smoke and off-load eager tourists in their Victorian dresses and feathered hats.

AND THERE JOHN MUIR greeted them, lean and spry, the ice-chief still, fifty-two going on twenty-five that magical summer of 1890, his namesake glacier rising behind him. He loved his time among the glaciers, the freshness of it making him feel "happily rich" and young again, far from what he called the "defrauding" duties of civilization.

Eleven years before, as he made his way north, he'd written to his fiancée Louie and her parents, "The world is all before me," paraphrasing Milton's Adam and Eve. This was Alaska, Muir's home away from home, his glacier garden, his wildest dream, a place of healing distances and open space.

As it remains today.

ACKNOWLEDGMENTS

I am indebted to many dedicated people: Melanie, my wife, sat by me for three weeks and chased down the most elusive sources as I compiled endnotes. My literary agent, Elizabeth Kaplan, embraced this book early on and found it a home. Jon Sternfeld, a razor-sharp editor and student of history, gave me many good ideas that improved the story. Thanks also to Kate Hertzog, who did a beautiful job of copyediting, and project editor Meredith Dias. Hank Lentfer and Nick Jans read an early draft of the prologue and made valuable comments. Tom Banks, Greg Streveler, Melinda Webster, and Dan Henry read the full manuscript and caught many small mistakes, and some big ones. If others remain, they're mine. For photo research, I thank Jim Simard and Sandy Johnston at the Alaska State Library (Juneau), Trish Richards at the Holt-Atherton Library (Stockton), Allaina Wallace at the National Snow and Ica Data Center (Boulder), and Artemis BonaDea with the National Park Service in Glacier Bay. Additional thanks to Kevin Richards and Brad Mason, park rangers in Glacier Bay, and John Baston and Lori Varsames, gracious friends in Alameda.

ENDNOTES

EPIGRAPH

"The Master Builder chose for a tool . . . seasons." Gifford, *John Muir: His Life and Letters and Other Writings*, 395.

"I learned from Muir . . . a boulder." Young, *Alaska Days with John Muir*, 105.

PROLOGUE

xii: *"the Range of Light."* Muir, *The Yosemite*, 5.

xiii: *"To seek knowledge."* Muir, *Travels in Alaska*, 178.

xiii: *"Gilded Age."* Worster, *A Passion for Nature: The Life of John Muir*, 305–6.

xiii–xiv: *"citified. . . which suggests . . . cynicisms."* Twain, *Autobiography of Mark Twain*, 111.

xiv: *"Nothing dollarable is safe."* Muir, Letter to the 1908 Governor's Conference on Conservation.

xvii: *"the invisible breath of the sky."* Cohen, *The Pathless Way: John Muir and American Wilderness*, 40.

xvii: *"gospel of glaciers."* Muir, Letter to Robert Underwood Johnson, 5/3/1895.

CHAPTER ONE

3: *"That wild Muir."* Wolfe, *Son of the Wilderness*, 204.

4: *"From cluster . . . goddesses."* Fox, *John Muir and His Legacy*, 65.

5: *"Hold fast . . . keep cool."* Young, *Alaska Days with John Muir*, 41.

5: *"The Blue Bells . . . How he did it . . . All that night . . . indomitable spirit."* Ibid., 44.

7: *"O Friend Beloved . . . land of mists . . ."* Fox, *John Muir and His Legacy*, 65.

7–8: *"sisters under the skin . . . Surely you would not . . . Farewell."* Wolfe, *Son of the Wilderness*, 208–9.

8: *"the world's prizes."* Ibid., 23.

8: *"Round-faced . . . unsmiling and uncomfortable."* Fox, *John Muir and His Legacy*, 62.

9: *"the doleful . . . lark."* Wolfe, *Son of the Wilderness*, 209.

9: *"So truly . . . the heaven he is in."* Ehrlich, *John Muir: Nature's Visionary*, 150.

9: *"chief of protocol for the party."* Bohn, *Glacier Bay: The Land and the Silence*, 43.

10: *"God has to . . . lessons."* Ehrlich, *John Muir: Nature's Visionary*, 58.

11: *"All drawbacks overcome . . . a tramp."* Ibid.

11: *"He appeared . . . a pair of shoes . . . "* Ibid.

11: *"Dutifully but resentfully, John paid."* Ibid.

11: *"the wildest, leafiest, least trodden way."* Ibid., 62.

11: *"John Muir, Earth-planet, Universe."* Ibid., 58.

12: *"compact solid mountains of ice."* Bohn, *Glacier Bay: The Land and the Silence*, 38.

13: *"compact solid mountains of ice."* Ibid.

14: *"a desolate, snow-covered . . . failed us altogether."* Muir, *Travels in Alaska*, 172.

14: *"Who are you?" "Friends . . . missionary."* Ibid., 173.

CHAPTER TWO

15: *"seal-hunters . . . meat and skins."* Muir, *Travels in Alaska*, 173.

18–19: *"Muir was a devout theist."* Young, *Alaska Days with John Muir*, 97.

20: *"John, do you remember . . . bread for lunch."* Wolfe, *Son of the Wilderness*, 43.

20: *"Old Man Muir . . . like cattle."* Wolfe, *Son of the Wilderness*, 45.

21: *"a barren empty shell."* Ibid., 43.

21: *"His inventive genius . . . for the world's beauty."* Ehrlich, *John Muir: Nature's Visionary*, 50.

21: *"Wisconsin bird-people."* Ibid., 37.

21: *"Too often . . . enslaved."* Ibid.

22: *"broken into an imposing array . . . just been discharged."* Muir, *Travels in Alaska*, 180.

23: *"lifting their white skirts . . . and sublime."* Ibid., 181–82.

24: *"boyish days . . . holier love."* Wordsworth, *Lyrical Ballads*, "Lines Composed a Few Miles above Tintern Abbey."

25: *"One impulse . . . sages can."* Young, *Alaska Days with John Muir*, 97.

25–26: *"Glacier Bay is . . . to my mind certain."* Muir, *Travels in Alaska*, 194–95.

26: *"The climax of . . . unscrupulous."* Gifford, *John Muir: His Life and Letters and Other Writings*, 643.

26: *"the most quarrelsome . . . Columbia River."* Young, *Alaska Days with John Muir*, 83.

27: *"sat on boulders . . . bright neckties."* Muir, *Travels in Alaska*, 204.

27: *"Oh yes . . . Chilcats."* Ibid.

27: *"Mr. Young . . . the noble Thlinkits."* Ibid.

27: *"as was our custom."* Young, *Alaska Days with John Muir*, 83.

27: *"Who are you? . . . far-reaching."* Muir, *Travels in Alaska*, 205.

27: *"A great preacher-chief . . . a good message."* Young, *Alaska Days with John Muir*, 85.

28: *"living telephone."* Muir, *Travels in Alaska*, 205.

28: *"too warm a reception . . . ut-ha . . . pull."* Young, *Alaska Days with John Muir*, 84.

CHAPTER THREE

29: *"as if . . . at his door."* Young, *Alaska Days with John Muir*, 86.

29: *"without . . . stolen glances."* Muir, *Travels in Alaska*, 206.

30: *"To Chief . . . Seward."* Henry, "Kaalaxch' and the Great Tyee," 19.

30: *"able to purchase . . . to be strong."* Ibid., 16.

30–31: *"The famed naturalist's . . . Tlingits."* Ibid.

31: *"the Indian . . . heart to heart."* Muir, *Travels in Alaska*, 210.

32: *"though the wind . . . it is not a sin to go home."* Ibid., 216.

34: *"mere sheepherder . . . ignoramus."* Wolfe, *Son of the Wilderness*, 133.

35: *"Man, man . . . . What a great death that would be."* Young, *Alaska Days with John Muir*, 117.

35: *"the beyond."* Muir, Letter to Jeanne Carr, 8/20/70.

36: *"Oh never fear . . . next summer."* Muir, *Travels in Alaska*, 235.

36: *"a blue, jagged ice-wall . . . as yet seen."* Ibid., 235.

36: *"there could be . . . about a town."* Muir, *Travels in Alaska*, 237.

36: *"they all behaved well . . . and even friends."* Ibid., 237.
36: *"You must be social . . . become impure."* Wolfe, *Son of the Wilderness,* 171.
37: *"I want you to meet my John Muir."* Ibid.
37: *"Write as often as you can . . ."* Letter from Jeanne Carr to John Muir, May 28, 1870.
37: *"a woman whose life . . . repeated discouragements."* Fox, *John Muir and His Legacy,* 47.
37: *"What she brought Muir . . . Father's love for us.'"* Ibid., 46.
38: *"free the science from Moses."* McPhee, *Annals of the Former World,* 98.
38: *"Darwin goes too far."* Ibid., 262.
38: *"Darwin has left us no escape . . . of our forefathers."* Fox, *John Muir and His Legacy,* 46.
39: *"You are . . . It will do you good."* Wolfe, *Son of the Wilderness,* 149.
39: *"My Men."* Ibid., 151.
39: *"O John, John . . . Thanksgiving."* Fox, *John Muir and His Legacy,* 65–66.
40: *"For his lonely fiancée . . . suggested the match."* Ibid., 66.

CHAPTER FOUR

41: *"When can you . . . let us be off."* Young, *Alaska Days with John Muir,* 126.
42: *"the noblest old Roman of them all."* Muir, *Travels in Alaska,* 248.
42: *"the darkest . . . were responsible."* Young, *Alaska Days with John Muir,* 129.
42: *"never under any . . . uttered anywhere."* Muir, *Travels in Alaska,* 248.
42: *"the work before them . . . island after island . . ."* Ibid., 253.
45: *"lords and possessors of nature."* Safina, *The View from Lazy Point,* 35.
45: *"without any injustice . . ."* Safina, *The View from Lazy Point,* 35.
45: *"the world . . . the world."* Ibid.
46: *"feeling for the other."* Ibid., 40.
46: *"what is"* . . . *"what ought to be."* Ibid.
46: *"Man is born . . . in chains."* Ibid.
46: *"There is grandeur . . . evolved."* Ibid., 41.
48: *"against the protest . . . and nothing to hunt."* Young, *Alaska Days with John Muir,* 138.
48: *"What a plucky . . . and laugh."* Ibid., 146.
48: *"[R]ight proud was I . . . grand larcenies."* Ibid., 147.
48: *"unmixed pleasure"* Ibid.

48: *"unfussy as a tree."* Wolfe, *Son of the Wilderness*, 217.

50: *"At the entrance . . . with ours."* Bohn, *Glacier Bay: The Land and the Silence*, 27.

50: *"Small and worthless . . . toy-dogs."* Fox, *John Muir and His Legacy*, 68.

50–51: *"showed neither caution nor curiosity . . . skipping muscle."* Ibid., 69.

51: *"At such times . . . knowledge."* Ibid.

51: *"Hush your fears . . . to save them."* Muir, *Stickeen: The Story of a Dog*, 57.

CHAPTER FIVE

55: *"In the ten years . . . his lifetime."* Wolfe, *Son of the Wilderness*, 231.

55: *"Through want of . . . like serfs."* Thoreau, *Walden*, 187.

58: *"Ah! My friend . . . have you not?"* Wolfe, *Son of the Wilderness*, 238.

58: *"To dine . . . sunbeams."* Muir, letter to His Sister Sarah, 1873.

58: *"Pray find a new genus . . . spicy wild perfume."* Letter from Asa Gray to John Muir, January 4, 1872.

59: *"This is a good place . . . not my home."* Fox, *John Muir and His Legacy*, 74.

59: *"I am degenerating into . . . making money."* Young, *Alaska Days with John Muir*, 204.

59: *"Condemned to penal . . . And for money."* Wolfe, *Son of the Wilderness*, 238.

59: *"Keep not standing . . . briskly roam."* Dudley, *Poetry and Philosophy of Goethe*, 37.

59–60: *"He flashed and darted . . . Saved!'"* Fox, *John Muir and His Legacy*, 69–70.

60: *"the many great things . . . the moon . . ."* Young, *Alaska Days with John Muir*, 179–80.

60: *"I wish you to pray . . . make the ice mountain stop."* Ibid., 180.

61: *"If God . . . to invent him."* Voltaire, Letter to the Anonymous Author of *The Three Impostors*, 1768.

61–63: *"Everything busy . . . are not shut out.'"* Fox, *John Muir and His Legacy*, 80.

64: *"The Alaska book . . . our children."* Wolfe, *Son of the Wilderness*, 244.

64: *"Johnson, Johnson . . . on occasion."* Fox, *John Muir and His Legacy*, 87.

65: *"Every cell . . . of the harmony."* Ibid., 82.

65: *"conceit and lofty importance."* Ibid., 85.

66: *"I fancy I could . . . fresh enthusiasm . . ."* Ibid., 98.

66: *"Tinkering the Yosemite waterworks . . . the Domes."* Ibid.

66: *"tears in his voice."* Wolfe, *Son of the Wilderness*, 245.

67: *"whether they was made, or only just happened."* Marx, *The Machine in the Garden*, 335.

67: *"If you go . . . with my life."* Wolfe, *Son of the Wilderness*, 246.

67: *"an interesting old salt . . . unbeliever."* Muir, *Travels in Alaska*, 330–31.

68: *"delightful even in the dullest weather."* Ibid., 331.

68: *"in the flesh."* Ibid., 334.

68: *"there are now . . . ten cents each."* Ibid., 336.

68: *"to see . . . San Francisco time."* Ibid.

CHAPTER SIX

71: *"The world is . . . his hand."* Agassiz, *Geological Sketches*, 11.

72: *"Precisely because he . . . professional scientist."* Gifford, *Reconnecting with John Muir: Essays in Post-Pastoral Practice*, 42.

73: *"They had come also . . . Camp Muir."* Bohn, *Glacier Bay: The Land and the Silence*, 62.

73: *"I am delighted . . . village."* Muir, *Travels in Alaska*, 345.

74: *"abounding in beginning lessons on landscape making."* Dennis C. Williams, *God's Wilds: John Muir's Vision of Nature*, 80.

74: *"What a show . . . poor hut."* Bohn, *Glacier Bay: The Land and the Silence*, 62.

74–76: *"To Mrs. Muir . . . Ever thine, J.M."* Ibid., 62–64.

76: *"made as light as possible."* Muir, *Travels in Alaska*, 355.

76: *"hideous and desolate wilderness."* Nash, *Wilderness and the American Mind*, 23–24.

76: *"a tradition of repugnance."* Ibid., 24.

77: *"Anticipations of a . . . wild country."* Ibid., 25–26.

77: *"There is a pleasure . . . but nature more."* Ibid., 50.

77: *"discovered the literary . . . of these novels . . ."* Ibid., 76.

77–78: *"holiness of . . . the woods!'"* Ibid.

78: *"Democratic nations . . . useful."* Tocqueville, *Democracy in America*, vol. 2, 531.

78: *"In wildness . . . the world."* Nash, *Wilderness and the American Mind*, 84.

78: *"For one . . . axe or rifle."* Ibid., 92.

79: *"be . . . the Lewis and Clark . . . higher latitudes."* Ibid., 89.

79: *"storm-bent . . . rolled and sifted."* Muir, *Travels in Alaska*, 373.

79: *"Nothing could be more striking . . . flower-enameled mosses."* Ibid., 356.

79: *"they had a mind . . . frontal attack."* Ibid., 358–59.

80: *"How often and by . . . gardens."* Ibid., 360.

81: *"It has been . . . soft evening light."* Ibid., 362.

81: *"Just as I got up . . . not yet!'"* Ibid., 363.

81: *"soft, tender light . . . icy scenery."* Ibid., 364–65.

81: *"a glorious and instructive day . . . nothing but good."* Ibid., 366.

81: *"Anything seems easy . . . jump crevasses . . ."* Ibid., 370.

82: *"my eyes . . . scarce see."* Ibid., 370.

82: *"Nearly blind . . . for work."* Ibid., 370–71.

82: *"sloppy heap."* Ibid., 374.

82: *"a miserable job . . . experiences."* Ibid., 374–75.

82: *"I had a good rest . . . and hungry I was."* Ibid., 376.

82–83: *"Prof. Muir . . . good deal of smoke."* Bohn, *Glacier Bay: The Land and the Silence*, 64.

83: *"And at odd moments . . . appetite."* Worster, *A Passion for Nature: The Life of John Muir*, 319.

84: *"[I]t was the first roped . . . for forty-one years."* Ibid., 66.

84: *"crystalline prairies."* Worster, *A Passion for Nature: The Life of John Muir*, 316.

84: *"the heat and smoke of politics."* Ibid.

84: *". . . the good Father . . . storms."* Ibid., 318.

84: *"Many good Californians . . . . manifold destroyers."* Worster, *A Passion for Nature: The Life of John Muir*, 320.

85: *"The preservation . . . to the people."* Ibid.

CHAPTER SEVEN

87: *"Truth is stranger . . . Truth isn't."* Twain, *Following the Equator; Maxims*.

87: *"a farce . . . and sincerity."* Worster, *A Passion for Nature: The Life of John Muir*, 305.

87: *"not made for any useful . . . regret to the Creator."* Twain, *Autobiography of Mark Twain*, vol. I, 312.

88: *"It's one of . . . and live."* Twain, *Mark Twain's Own Autobiography*, 26.

88: *"a kind of ecstatic holy man."* Burns, *The National Parks: America's Best Idea*.

88–89: *"My love . . . emotion of the past."* Holmes, *The Young John Muir*, 102.

89: *"[W]e valued . . . of the populace."* Emerson, *The Works of Ralph Waldo Emerson,* 600.

89–90: *"picked out . . . without graduating."* Holmes, *The Young John Muir,* 103.

90: *"In the devastated South . . . lost cause."* Von Drehle, *TIME* Magazine, 4/18/2011, 40–42.

91: *"to towns . . . from the frontier."* Census from the Superintendent of the Census 1890, www.census.gov.

91: *"get by/get rich . . . Dishonestly if we can . . . if we must."* Worster, *A Passion for Nature: The Lie of John Muir,* 305.

92: *"the invisible hand of the market."* Harrison, *Journal of the History of Ideas,* vol. 72, num. 1, Jan. 2011.

92: *"gobble, gobble school of economics."* Wolfe, *Son of the Wilderness,* 102.

92: *"Money is God . . . mighty and supreme."* Worster, *A Passion for Nature: The Life of John Muir,* 305–6.

92: *"Muir wanted to spend the remainder . . ."* Ibid., 306.

93: *"I had never seen . . . of a lifetime."* Fox, *John Muir and His Legacy,* 107.

93: *"this formal, legal . . . my line."* Ibid.

94: *"evaporating our coal mines into the air."* McKibben, *The End of Nature,* 9.

94: *"It is now half-past nine . . . continue to rain."* Reid, Field Journal, August 4, 1892.

95: *"irreconcilable . . . our visits."* Bohn, *Glacier Bay: The Land and the Silence,* 69.

95: *"For the years . . . in that year (1890)."* Ibid., 69.

96: *"badly smashed . . . to the glacier's surface . . ."* Catton, *Land Reborn,* 38.

97: *"[T]he Pacific Coast . . . with Muir Glacier."* Ibid., 39.

97: *"constantly regaled . . . . with icebergs . . ."* Bohn, *Glacier Bay: The Land and the Silence,* 57.

97: *"that large . . . confining fiords."* Catton, *Land Reborn,* 38.

97–104: *"The crashes of falling ice . . . and mystery."* Bohn, *Glacier Bay: The Land and the Silence,* 57.

104: *"descriptions of it . . . to what followed."* Ibid.

105: *"Dear Louie . . . with excitement . . ."* John Muir letter to Louie, 5/29/1893.

CHAPTER EIGHT

107: *"We are great, and rapidly . . . growing!"* Turner, "The Significance of the Frontier in American History," 1.

108: *"So long as . . . benefits."* Ibid., 6.

108: *"that practical, inventive turn of mind . . . energy . . . ?"* Ibid., 9.

108: *"I had no idea . . . have written."* Worster, *A Passion for Nature: The Life of John Muir*, 334.

109: *"I'd rather sit . . . on a velvet cushion."* Thoreau, *Walden*, 47.

110: *"The waves made . . . a boy again . . ."* Wolfe, *Son of the Wilderness*, 263.

110: *"maple, yew, pine . . . glacial gospel."* Ibid., 264.

110: *"sort of national . . . heart to enjoy."* Wordsworth, *A Guide through the Lakes in the North of England*, 88.

111: *"by some great protecting policy . . . nature's beauty."* Allin, *The Politics of Wilderness Preservation*, 14.

111: *"receive a thousand-fold . . . shall see God."* Fox, *John Muir and His Legacy*, 19.

111: *"The Tao that can be told . . . not the eternal name."* Lyon, "John Muir, the Physiology of the Brain, and the 'Wilderness Experience,'" 27.

111: *"Even the dogs . . . bon chien.'"* Wolfe, *Son of the Wilderness*, 265.

111: *"hemmed in by . . . hundreds . . . exquisite taste."* Ibid.

112: *"a synthetic wilderness . . . place behind."* Worster, *A Passion for Nature: The Life of John Muir*, 337.

112: *"A grand church . . . to write about."* Wolfe, *Son of the Wilderness*, 265.

112: *"snowflowers."* Muir, *The Mountains of California*, 16.

112: *"a current of ice derived from snow."* Muir, "Living Glaciers of California," 775.

113: *"The glaciers of Switzerland . . . diminishing . . ."* Muir, *The Mountains of California*, 20.

113: *"met with immediate . . . sore problem."* Wolfe, *Son of the Wilderness*, 268.

114: *"He will not listen . . . every thing."* Worster, *A Passion for Nature: The Life of John Muir*, 298.

114: *"broad Scotch . . . dear wanderer."* Ibid., 300.

114: *"Oh, John . . . terribly ill!"* Wolfe, *Son of the Wilderness*, 269.

115: *"There is but one man . . . John Muir."* Ibid., 273.

115: *"hoofed locusts . . . going on."* Ibid., 271.

115: *"in his late fifties . . . too much time."* Worster, *A Passion for Nature: The Life of John Muir,* 352.

116: *"[T]he lumber, stock . . . and impractical dreamers."* Wolfe, *Son of the Wilderness,* 272.

116: *"The American Forests . . . the globe."* Ehrlich, *John Muir: Nature's Visionary,* 190.

116: *"turned to elegy . . . essay."* Ibid.

116: *"Any fool can . . . bole backbones."* Ibid.

116: *"Those western corporations . . . fight must go on!"* Letter from John Muir to R. U. Johnson, 6/18/1897, in Wolfe, *Son of the Wilderness,* 273.

117: *"a wild, discouraging mess."* Ibid., 275.

117: *"Are you correctly quoted . . . of harm."* Ibid., 275–76.

118: *"A man is rich . . . alone."* Thoreau, *Walden,* 75–76.

118: *"Much is said . . . background."* Fox, *John Muir and His Legacy,* 113.

118: *"were concealing their . . . protection."* Ibid.

119: *"make their lives . . . by the woods."* Letter from John Muir to Theodore P. Lukens, 4/18/1897.

119: *"Gentlemen . . . never have again."* Limerick, *Something in the Soil,* 296.

120: *"the authentic voice . . . commercial propaganda."* Wolfe, *Son of the Wilderness,* 277.

120: *"Sabbath for the Land."* Lentfer and Servid, *Arctic Refuge: Circle of Testimony,* 101.

121: *"Think of the beautiful woods . . . destruction."* Wolfe, *Son of the Wilderness,* 278–79.

121: *"New Colossus of Roads."* Worster, *A Passion for Nature: The Life of John Muir,* 409.

CHAPTER NINE

125: *"the most velvety . . . ever saw."* Wolfe, *Son of the Wilderness,* 280.

125: *"To him I owe . . . of my life."* Gifford, *John Muir: His Life and Letters and Other Writings,* 861.

126: *"Only after Merriam . . . national figure."* Goetzmann and Sloan, *Looking Far North,* 10–11.

126: *"Ornithologist and Author . . . Author and Student of Glaciers."* Litwin, *The Harriman Alaska Expedition Retraced,* 260.

127: *"Cold Storage Muir . . . playground . . . on the subject."* Lord, *Green Alaska*, 15–17.

127: *"George W. Roller."* Goetzmann and Sloan, *Looking Far North*, 33.

127: *"floating university."* Lord, *Green Alaska*, xvi.

128: *"All along . . . a place of promise."* Ibid., xvi–xvii.

128: *"Big Four . . . Little Two . . . Admiral."* Wolfe, *Son of the Wilderness*, 281.

129: *". . . you naughty bad boy . . . anymore."* Worster, *A Passion for Nature: The Life of John Muir*, 303.

129: *"Kill as few . . . Nature's harmony."* Ibid., 363.

130: *"Whatever they are today . . . ought to do."* Grinnell, *Alaska 1899: Essays from the Harriman Expedition*, 154.

130–31: *"Well, are you . . . if I do."* Wolfe, *Son of the Wilderness*, 281.

131: *"You ought to . . . on the Hudson."* Ibid.

131: *"He is as modest . . . gifted."* Carr and Muir, *Kindred and Related Spirits*, 166.

131: *"an age of . . . of success."* Goetzmann and Sloan, *Looking Far North*, xi–xii.

131: *"A fearful smell . . . themselves canned."* Lord, *Green Alaska*, 77.

131: *"Seaweed Saunders."* Goetzmann and Sloan, *Looking Far North*, 45.

132: *"dirty, miserable."* Ibid., 46.

133: *"bicycle suits."* Ibid., 58.

133: *"a nest of ants . . . by a stick."* Ibid., 56.

133: *"ribs of the earth."* Ibid., 61.

134: *"Alaska's grandeur . . . will be enormous . . . . finest first."* Brinkley, *The Quiet World*, 47.

134: *"new kind of Niagara."* Catton, *Land Reborn*, 37.

135: *"Howling Valley."* Wolfe, *Son of the Wilderness*, 282.

138: *"all the howling."* Ibid.

138: *"The comforts of . . . his control."* Lord, *Green Alaska*, 136–37.

138: *"No bears, no bears . . . servants done?"* Ibid., 52.

139: *"wild to get on . . . from the steamer."* Goetzmann and Sloan, *Looking Far North*, 85.

139: *"every little fish pond."* Ibid., 110.

142: *"mother and child."* Wolfe, *Son of the Wilderness*, 284.

143: *"the most barren and . . . its size."* Goetzmann & Sloan, *Looking Far North*, 137.

143: *"I don't . . . scenery."* Lord, *Green Alaska,* 151.

143–44: *"I never cared . . . and happier."* Worster, *A Passion for Nature: The Life of John Muir,* 362.

144: *"did not accept . . . conservation movement."* Ibid., 362–63.

144: *"an entire success."* Goetzmann and Sloan, *Looking Far North,* 171.

145: *"Gilbert's work . . . and others."* Ibid., 206.

CHAPTER TEN

147: *"an assault on . . . order."* Morris, *Theodore Rex,* 4.

147: *"If it had . . . him first."* Ibid.

147: *"practicing fearlessness."* Ibid., 6.

147: *"Experiences had . . . fellows."* Ibid.

148: *"By then he was producing . . ."* Morris, *Theodore Rex,* 6.

148: *"freshness, spontaneity . . . from the false."* Brinkley, *The Wilderness Warrior,* 184–85.

148–49: *"Though chiefly . . . with him."* Ibid., 186.

149: *"This cannot last . . . of the victims."* Ibid., 187.

150: *"an extremely dangerous man."* Morris, *Theodore Rex,* 227.

150–51: *"Every man . . . of the laws."* Ibid., 221.

151: *"I don't know . . . who come after you."* Ibid., 225–26.

151: *"air of the ridiculous."* Ibid., 227.

151: *"There is nothing . . . Euphrates."* Ibid.

151: *"were the rightful . . . American people."* Brinkley, *The Wilderness Warrior,* 535.

152: *"I do not want . . . with you."* Ibid., 543.

152: *"It is only . . . get lost."* Fox, *John Muir and His Legacy,* 125.

152: *"Now . . . out of school."* Wolfe, *Son of the Wilderness,* 181.

153: *"ideal training . . . murder business."* Brinkley, *The Wilderness Warrior,* 544.

153: *"Mr. Roosevelt . . . you're right."* Nash, *Wilderness and the American Mind,* 139.

153: *"Muir had an . . . planet in peril."* Brinkley, *The Wilderness Warrior,* 337.

154: *"Disturbing as . . . society and nature."* Stoll, *The Great Delusion,* 5.

155: *"This is . . . anything."* Wolfe, *Son of the Wilderness,* 292.

155: *"We slept . . . I wanted."* Ibid., 293.

155: *"John Muir talked . . . without a tent."* Fox, *John Muir and His Legacy,* 126.

156: *"Goodbye, John . . . my life!"* Wolfe, *Son of the Wilderness*, 293.

156: *"I never before . . . love with him."* Fox, *John Muir and His Legacy*, 126.

156: *"I stuffed him . . . thieves."* Brinkley, *The Wilderness Warrior*, 543.

156: *"We are not . . . through the ages."* Wolfe, *Son of the Wilderness*, 294.

158: *"huge yellow . . . paintings."* Worster, *A Passion for Nature: The Life of John Muir*, 378.

158: *"I'm still alive . . . and all."* Wolfe, *Son of the Wilderness*, 296.

158: *"the tallest . . . have seen."* Worster, *A Passion for Nature: The Life of John Muir*, 379.

158: *"indomitable birch."* Wolfe, *Son of the Wilderness*, 296.

158: *"never seemed to think . . . bother him."* Worster, *A Passion for Nature: The Life of John Muir*, 380.

159: *"I feel alive . . . be free . . ."* Wolfe, *Son of the Wilderness*, 297.

159: *"There are . . . before I die."* Ibid.

159: *"had once befriended . . . with the public."* Worster, *A Passion for Nature: The Life of John Muir*, 346.

160: *"Would you . . . children?"* Ibid., 383.

163: *"Going around . . . been different."* Ibid., 385–86.

164: *"a noble . . . earthquake."* Muir, *The Yosemite*, 78.

165: *"She had learned . . . mountain joy."* Ehrlich, *John Muir: Nature's Visionary*, 204.

165: *"get out . . . woman can."* Worster, *A Passion for Nature: The Life of John Muir*, 393.

CHAPTER ELEVEN

169: *"Not in history . . . are all gone."* London in *Collier's* magazine, 5/5/1906.

170: *"The glory . . . out of my ears . . ."* Wolfe, *Son of the Wilderness*, 309.

170: *". . . after making about . . . even Yosemite."* Ibid.

170: *"Finding her . . . company."* Ibid., 309–10.

171: *"O dear . . . up a canon."* John Muir letter to daughters Helen and Wanda, 1/15/1906.

171: *"I hope sincerely . . . in my power."* Worster, *A Passion for Nature: The Life of John Muir*, 400.

171: *"They all . . . sound substantial irrefragable ignorance."* John Muir letter to T. Roosevelt, 9/9/1907.

171: *"nine tenths or more."* John Muir letter to T. Roosevelt, 9/9/1907.

171–72: *"and I have been . . . silver firs."* Fox, *John Muir and His Legacy*, 140.

172: *"promises to be the worst ever."* Ibid.

172: *"mischief-makers and robbers of every degree."* Ibid., 141.

172: *"John Muir loves the Sierras . . . quibbling."* Ibid.

173: *"made an ironic . . . work."* Ibid., 139.

173: *"In all forestry . . . Gifford Pinchot."* Nash, *Wilderness and the American Mind*, 163.

173: *"He could squeeze . . . heard of."* Wolfe, *Son of the Wilderness*, 310.

175: *"began his career . . . of God superior . . ."* Ibid., 316.

175: *"Never mind, dear Colby . . . to ourselves."* Ibid., 314.

175: *"A dam! . . . damning himself."* Ibid., 323.

175: *"attacks more violent than before."* Ibid., 325.

176: *"It is all . . . than the materialist."* New York Times, 12/5/1909.

176: *"Pinchot spoke for . . . public opinion."* Fox, *John Muir and His Legacy*, 121.

176: *"there has been . . . magazine articles."* Nash, *Wilderness and the American Mind*, 168.

176: *"hoggish and mushy esthetes."* Ibid., 169.

176: *"short-haired women and long-haired men."* Worster, *A Passion for Nature: The Life of John Muir*, 433.

177: *"I've . . . bondage . . ."* Wolfe, *Son of the Wilderness*, 319.

179: *"I wonder . . . falling."* Worster, *A Passion for Nature: The Life of John Muir*, 440.

179: *"vanish . . . other America."* Ibid., 441.

179: *"like the skin of an elephant."* Ibid., 445.

180: *"hot continents."* Ibid., 446.

180: *"the great thundering crystal world."* Muir, *Travels in Alaska*, 353.

181: *"No one of substantial fortune . . . to the other side."* Worster, *A Passion for Nature: The Life of John Muir*, 452.

181: *"Grand scenery . . . some of it."* Fox, *John Muir and His Legacy*, 144.

181: *"God invented . . . immense."* Nash, *Wilderness and the American Mind*, 179.

181: *"It is hard to bear."* John Muir letter to Vernon Kellogg, 12/27/1913.

181: *"desolation work."* Worster, *A Passion for Nature: The Life of John Muir*, 460.

182: *"cult of the self."* Hedges, *Death of the Liberal Class*, 7.

182: *"California and Alaska ... of things ..."* Worster, *A Passion for Nature: The Life of John Muir*, 458.

182: *"no trace of pessimism ... fatigue."* Wolfe, *Son of the Wilderness*, 345.

185: *"robbery."* Goetzmann and Sloan, *Looking Far North*, 165.

185: *"The long ... surely come."* John Muir New Year's letter to R. U. Johnson, 1/1/1914.

186: *"The most ... public protest ..."* Nash, *Wilderness and the American Mind*, 181.

CHAPTER TWELVE

189: *"forget everything ... over again."* Oreskes, *The Rejection of Continental Drift*, 313.

189: *"strongly reminiscent ..."* Catton, *Land Reborn*, 45.

189: *"Cooper studied ... in Glacier Bay."* Ibid., 45–46.

190: *"in three ... exceedingly modest."* Ibid.

191: *"In the first case ... to the idea."* Ibid., 50.

191–92: *"A MONSTROUS ... faddists ... ask him about."* Bohn, *Glacier Bay: The Land and the Silence*, 92–94.

192: *"I can show ... dust."* Eliot, *The Waste Land*, line 30.

193: *"Tell me ... life?"* Oliver, *New and Selected Poems*, 94.

193: *"Thousands of ... a necessity ..."* Muir, *Our National Parks*, 1.

193: *"I owe ... a mere gypsy."* Fox, *John Muir and His Legacy*, 121.

194: *"I got my money ... acknowledgment."* Ibid., 146.

194: *"Without parks ... our nation young."* Nash, *Wilderness and the American Mind*, 189.

194: *"Was there ever a time ... forsaken?"* Ibid.

194: *"many of the attributes ... civilization."* Meine, *Aldo Leopold: His Life and Work*, 244.

195: *"without giving so much ... keeping them alive?"* Nash, *Wilderness and the American Mind*, 188.

195: *"I am glad ... on the map?"* Ibid., 189.

196: *"And over and above ... But not always."* Bohn, *Glacier Bay: The Land and the Silence*, 85.

197: *"Dear Bill ... Tom Smith."* Ibid.

197–98: *"Analysis of the ... left to rot."* Catton, *Land Reborn*, 174.

198: *"legalized rape of Glacier Bay."* Ibid., 175.

198: *"I do not think . . . are shut out."* Ibid., 53.

198: *"The Place is Alaska—the Business is Mining."* Beach, *Cosmopolitan,* January 1936.

198: *"is absolutely barren . . . parties."* Bohn, *Glacier Bay: The Land and the Silence,* 94.

199: *"utterly wrong."* Ibid.

199: *"If Congress . . . Park Service."* Ibid., 95.

199–200: *"In the reservoir . . . ingenuity."* Fox, *John Muir and His Legacy,* 146.

200: *"seems a comprehensive mistake."* Ibid.

201: *"We had to get it right. . ."* William E Brown, in conversation with author Kim Heacox.

EPILOGUE

204: *"Muir lit the torch . . . so special."* Schwarzenegger, Arnold. MSNBC News Service Report: Feb. 1, 2005.

204–5: *"All through history . . . is alive."* Lyon, "John Muir, the Physiology of the Brain, and the 'Wilderness Experience,'" 27–30.

206: *"Even if we stopped . . . rising seas."* Folger, *National Geographic,* Sept. 2013, 40.

206: *"will require . . . and personal expectations."* Gilding, *The Great Disruption,* 97.

207: *"Newscasters . . . relations."* Pipher, *The Green Boat,* 62.

207: *"People avoid facing . . . solve."* Ibid., 3.

208: *"a 1,700-mile fuse . . . on the continent."* McKibben, "The Keystone Pipeline Revolt," 1.

209: *"October 2012 . . . astronomical."* Jensen, "The Victim Liked It," 11.

209: *"Many of our . . . we are . . . planet.'"* Klein, "Capitalism vs. the Climate," 6.

210: *"Through his visionary . . . our generation."* Pope, Scottish Government, April 9, 2010.

211: *"the machinery of our wits."* Oliver, "Of Power and Time," *Blue Pastures,* 1.

212: *"happily rich."* Engberg and Merrell, *Letters from Alaska,* 94.

212: *"defrauding."* Ibid.

BIBLIOGRAPHY

Agassiz, Louis. *Geological Sketches*. Boston: Fields, Osgood & Co. 1870.

Alley, Richard B. *The Two-Mile Time Machine. Ice Cores, Abrupt Climate Change, and Our Future*. Princeton: Princeton University Press, 2000.

Allin, Craig W. *The Politics of Wilderness Preservation*. Fairbanks: University of Alaska, 2008.

Berton, Pierre. *The Klondike Fever: The Life and Death of the Last Great Gold Rush*. New York: Knopf, 1958.

Bohn, Dave. *Glacier Bay: The Land and the Silence*. New York: Sierra Club Ballantine, 1967.

Branch, Michael P. (editor). *John Muir's Last Journey*. Washington, DC: Island Press, 2001.

Brinkley, Douglas. *The Quiet World: Saving Alaska's Wilderness Kingdom, 1879–1960*. New York: Harper, 2011.

———. *The Wilderness Warrior: Theodore Roosevelt and the Crusade for America*. New York: Harper, 2009.

Burns, Ken, and Dayton Duncan. *The National Parks: America's Best Idea* (film). Walpole: Florentine Films, 2009.

Carr, Jeanne, and John Muir. *Kindred and Related Spirits*. Salt Lake City: University of Utah Press, 2001.

Catton, Theodore. *Land Reborn: A History of Administration and Visitor Use in Glacier Bay National Park and Preserve*. Anchorage, US National Park Service, 1995.

Cohen, Michael P. *The Pathless Way: John Muir and American Wilderness*. Madison: University of Wisconsin Press, 1986.

Dudley, Marion Vienna Churchill. *Poetry and Philosophy of Goethe*. Chicago: S.C. Griggs & Co., 1887.

Ehrlich, Gretel. *John Muir: Nature's Visionary*. Washington, DC: National Geographic, 2000.

Eliot, T. S. *The Waste Land*. New York: Boni and Liveright, 1922.

Emerson, Ralph Waldo. *The Works of Ralph Waldo Emerson*. Boston: Houghton-Mifflin, 1887.

Engberg, Robert, and Bruce Merrell. *Letters from Alaska: John Muir*. Madison: University of Wisconsin Press, 1993.

Folger, Tim. "Rising Seas." Washington, DC: *National Geographic* Magazine, Sept. 2013.

Fox, Stephen. *John Muir and His Legacy: The American Conservation Movement*. Boston: Little Brown, 1981.

Gifford, Terry. *John Muir: His Life and Letters and Other Writings*. Seattle: Mountaineers Books, 1996.

Gilding, Paul. *The Great Disruption*. New York: Bloomsbury, 2011.

Goetzmann, William H., and Kay Sloan. *Looking Far North: The Harriman Expedition to Alaska, 1899*. New York: Viking, 1982.

Gore, Al. *Earth in the Balance: Ecology and the Human Spirit*. Boston: Houghton Mifflin, 1992.

Gosnell, Marianna. *Ice. The Nature, the History, and the Uses of an Astonishing Substance*. Chicago: University of Chicago, 2005.

Grinnell, George Bird. *Alaska 1899: Essays from the Harriman Expedition*. Seattle: University of Washington Press, 1995.

Hawken, Paul. *Blessed Unrest*. New York: Viking, 2007.

Heacox, Kim. *The Making of the National Parks*, Washington, DC: National Geographic, 2001.

Hedges, Chris. *Death of the Liberal Class*. New York: Nation Books, 2010.

Henry, Daniel Lee. "Kaalaxch' and the Great Tyee." Sitka: Address at Tlingit Clan Conference. March 29–April 1, 2012.

Highland, Chris (editor). *Meditations of John Muir: Nature's Temple*. Berkeley: Wilderness Press, 2001.

Holmes, Steven J. *The Young John Muir: An Environmental Biography*. Madison: University of Wisconsin Press, 1999.

Jensen, Derrick. "The Victim Liked It." Great Barrington: *Orion*, March/April 2013.

Klein, Naomi. "Capitalism vs. the Climate." New York: *Nation*, Nov. 28, 2011.

Kolbert, Elizabeth. *Field Notes from a Catastrophe: A Frontline Report on Climate Change*. New York: Bloomsbury, 2007.

Lacayo, Richard. "A Man in Full." New York: *TIME*, 11/22/2010, pp. 103–5.

Lacy, Susan, et al. "John Muir: In the New World." Kulture Films, 2011.

Lentfer, Hank, and Carolyn Servid. *Arctic Refuge: A Circle of Testimony.* Minneapolis: Milkweed, 2001.

Limerick, Patricia Nelson. *Something in the Soil.* New York: W.W. Norton & Co., 2001.

Litwin, Thomas (editor). *The Harriman Alaska Expedition Retraced: A Century of Change, 1899-2001.* New Brunswick: Rutgers University Press, 2004.

Lord, Nancy. *Green Alaska: Dreams from the Far Coast.* Washington: Counterpoint, 1999.

Lyon, Thomas J. "John Muir, the Physiology of the Brain, and the 'Wilderness Experience.'" *The Living Wilderness,* Summer 1974.

Marx, Leo. *The Machine in the Garden: Technology and the Pastoral Ideal in America.* London: Oxford University Press, 1964.

Mathez, Edmond A. *Earth: Inside and Out.* New York: New Press, 2000.

McKibben, Bill. *The End of Nature.* New York: Anchor Books, 1990.

———. "The Keystone Pipeline Revolt." *Rolling Stone,* Sept. 28, 2011.

McPhee, John. *Annals of the Former World.* New York: Farrar, Straus, Giroux, 1998.

Meine, Curt D. *Aldo Leopold: His Life and Work.* University of Wisconsin Press, 2010.

Morris, Edmund. *Theodore Rex.* New York: Random House, 2001.

Muir, John. "Living Glaciers of California." *Harper's,* Nov. 1875.

———. *The Mountains of California.* New York: Century Co., 1907.

———. *My First Summer in the Sierra, 1911.* New York, Penguin, 1997.

———. *Northwest Passages: From the Pen of John Muir.* Palo Alto: Tioga, 1988.

———. *Our National Parks.* Boston: Houghton-Mifflin, 1901.

———. *Stickeen: The Story of a Dog.* Boston: Houghton-Mifflin, 1909.

———. *The Story of My Boyhood and Youth, 1913.* San Francisco: Sierra Club, 1989.

———. *Travels in Alaska.* Boston: Houghton-Mifflin, 1915.

———. *The Yosemite.* 1912. San Francisco, Sierra Club, 1988.

Nash, Roderick. *Wilderness and the American Mind (Revised Edition)*. New Haven & London: Yale University Press, 1973.

Nelson, Richard. *The Island Within*. San Francisco: North Point, 1989.

Oliver, Mary. *New and Selected Poems*. Boston: Beacon Press, 1993.

Oreskes, Naomi. *The Rejection of Continental Drift*. Oxford: Oxford University Press, 1999.

Pipher, Mary. *The Green Boat: Reviving Ourselves in Our Capsized Culture*. New York: Riverhead, 2013.

Rawls, James J. "John Muir: Celtic Saint." California Environmental Conference, October 28, 2006.

Reid, Harry Fielding. "The Reid Papers: Field Journal." August 4, 1892. Boulder: National Snow and Ice Data Center.

Rowthorn, Anne (compiled by). *The Wisdom of John Muir: 100+ Selections from the Letters, Journals, and Essays of the Great Naturalist*. Birmingham: Wilderness Press, 2012.

Safina, Carl. *The View from Lazy Point*. New York: Henry Holt, 2011.

Stoll, Steven. *The Great Delusion: A Mad Inventor, Death in the Tropics, and the Utopian Origins of Economic Growth*. New York: Hill & Wang, 2008.

Thoreau, Henry David. *Walden*. Oxford: Oxford University Press, 1999.

Tocqueville, Alexis de. *Democracy in America, Volume II*. London: Saunders and Otley, 1840.

Turner, Frederick Jackson. "The Significance of the Frontier in American History." Chicago: Address to the American Historical Association at the World's Columbian Exposition, 1893.

Twain, Mark. *Autobiography of Mark Twain, Volume 1*. Berkeley: University of California Press, 2010.

———. *Following the Equator*. Hartford, CT: American Publishing Co., 1897.

———. *Mark Twain's Own Autobiography*. Madison: University of Wisconsin Press, 1924.

Von Drehle, David. "The Way We Weren't." New York: *TIME* Magazine, 04/18/2011, pp. 40–51.

Williams, Dennis C. *God's Wilds: John Muir's Vision of Nature*. College Station: Texas A&M University Press, 2002.

Wolfe, Linnie Marsh. *Son of the Wilderness: The Life of John Muir*. Madison: University of Wisconsin Press, 1978.

Wordsworth, William. *A Guide through the Lakes in the North of England*. London: Longman & Co, 1835.

———. "Lines Composed a Few Miles Above Tintern Abbey," *Lyrical Ballads*. New York: Penguin Classics, 2007.

Worster, Donald. *A Passion for Nature: The Life of John Muir*. Oxford: Oxford University Press, 2008.

Young, Samuel Hall. *Alaska Days with John Muir*. New York: Fleming H. Revell Co., 1915.

INDEX

ABOUT THE AUTHOR

Kim Heacox is the author of several books on history, biography, and conservation. His Alaska memoir, *The Only Kayak*, was a 2006 PEN USA Literary Award finalist in creative nonfiction. In 2009 he appeared on camera in the Ken Burns film *The National Parks: America's Best Idea*, and in 2012 he was the writer-in-residence in Denali National Park. He lives in Gustavus, Alaska, with his wife Melanie, two sea kayaks, two guitars, one piano, and an African drum. He often volunteers as a music teacher at the local school. Visit him at kimheacox.com.